Britain Colonized

Britain Colonized

Hollywood's Appropriation of British Literature

by Jennifer M. Jeffers

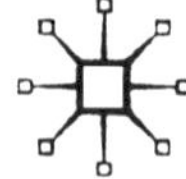

First published in 2006 by
PALGRAVE MACMILLAN™
175 Fifth Avenue, New York, N.Y. 10010 and
Houndmills, Basingstoke, Hampshire, England RG21 6XS
Companies and representatives throughout the world.

PALGRAVE MACMILLAN is the global academic imprint of the Palgrave Macmillan division of St. Martin's Press, LLC and of Palgrave Macmillan Ltd. Macmillan® is a registered trademark in the United States, United Kingdom and other countries. Palgrave is a registered trademark in the European Union and other countries.

ISBN-13: 978–1–4039–7276–7
ISBN-10: 1–4039–7276–1

Library of Congress Cataloging-in-Publication Data

Jeffers, Jennifer M.
Britain colonized : Hollywood's appropriation of British literature / Jennifer M. Jeffers.
p. cm.
Includes bibliographical references and index.
ISBN 1–4039–7276–1 (alk. paper)
1. Film adaptations. 2. British literature—Film and video adaptations. 3. Motion pictures—United States—History. I. Title

PN1997.85.J45 2006
791.43′6—dc22 2006042963

A catalogue record for this book is available from the British Library.

Design by Newgen Imaging Systems (P) Ltd., Chennai, India.

First edition: August 2006

10 9 8 7 6 5 4 3 2 1

Printed in the United States of America.

For
Beckett Rhiannon
and
Samuel Reid

Contents

List of Figures

Acknowledgments

I would like to thank several individuals at Cleveland State University for assisting me with completion of this book. I would like to cordially thank Earl Anderson and Louis Barbato for funding to obtain rights to reproduce illustrations. A special thanks to Jim Bandes, MultiMedia Design, Production, Cleveland State University, for kindly taking the time to isolate and make the film stills I needed from *Possession* for Chapter Three. I want to thank the Cleveland State University's OhioLink staff, especially Dominic Tortelli. As always, I appreciate Anne Barnett's and Rita Hammond's help and good humor.

I wish to thank several individuals with the British Tourist Authority: Paul Chibeba, Seren Welch, Tim Stubbings, and a special warm thanks to Nadine Docherty and Marcia Oliver. I want to thank Helen Trompeteler, Picture Librarian, National Portrait Gallery, London, for obtaining permission for me to reprint *Charles Dickens* by Daniel Maclise. A particular thanks to Roni Lubliner at Universal Studios for assisting me with securing the rights to reproduce four stills from *Possession*. Special thanks to The Tate Gallery, London and Art Resource, New York for permission to reproduce Simeon Solomon's *Sappho and Erinna in a Garden at Mytilene*, Dante Gabriel Rossetti's *The Beloved (The "Bride")*, and Edward Burne-Jones' *Clara von Bork 1560*. I wish to thank the *Journal of Narrative Theory* for permission to reprint part of my article, "Rhizome National Identity: 'Scatlin's Psychic Defense' in *Trainspotting*," 35.1 (Winter 2005): 87–110.

I would like to thank Farideh Koohi-Komali Senior Editor at Palgrave Macmillan for supporting this book and expediting its publication. I wish to express my gratitude to Todd May the original Palgrave Macmillan reviewer whose helpful suggestions, I can only hope, I successfully incorporated into the final text.

I owe special thanks to Michael Sepesy who proofread the entire manuscript and compiled the final bibliography and index. I also want to give Stacey Duwe a special thanks for last minute proofreading, and checks and double checks on the citations.

Mary Jeffers, it has just been announced, has won "Twins Grandmother of the Year" for her tireless devotion to her grandchildren while their mommy was at "work." I owe her my deepest thanks and love. Lastly, as ever, Gene Blocker always gets the lion's share of the proofreading tasks and unintelligible previews of my raw and half-baked ideas. Inevitably my texts are better because of the personal "intertextuality" we have shared for so long.

Introduction

VANHATTEN. The prodigal, sir, has returned to his father's house. Not poor, not hungry, not ragged, as of old. Oh no. This time he returns bringing with him the riches of the earth to the ancestral home.

MAGNUS, *starting from his chair.* You don't mean to say——

VANHATTEN, *rising also, blandly triumphant.* I do, sir. The Declaration of Independence is cancelled. The treaties which endorsed it are torn up. We have decided to rejoin the British Empire. We shall of course enjoy Dominion Home Rule under the Presidency of Mr. Bossfield. I shall revisit you here shortly, not as the Ambassador of a foreign power, but as High Commissioner for the greatest of your dominions, and your very loyal and devoted subject, sir.

The Apple Cart (1930)

In George Bernard Shaw's 1930 play, *The Apple Cart*, the American diplomat Vanhattan proposes to Magnus and the Queen what he views as a fait accompli: the "amalgamation of the British Commonwealth with United States." While *The Apple Cart* is a futuristic and fantastic view of Britain's political future, it presents a striking analogy to what the American film industry, "Hollywood," has done with its appropriation of British literature, especially in the last couple of decades. Vanhatten sums up this appropriation very succinctly when he addresses the Queen of England, "The United States, ma'am, have absorbed all the great national traditions, and blended them with their own glorious tradition of Freedom into something that is unique and universal."[1] In the course of this book, I interpret the movement to the universal as a controlling act of appropriation; and so, the claim that to Americanize is to *universalize* is one that we consider over and over again.[2]

By the time Shaw wrote *The Apple Cart*, British anxiety that America was taking over the English-speaking and English-controlled world had been decades in the making. For instance, in 1902, British journalist William T. Stead published *The Americanisation of the*

World; or, the Trend of the Twentieth Century, in which he, like Shaw, fantasized that the "United States of the English Speaking Peoples" was a natural union because "the creation of the Americans is the greatest achievement of our race" and reassured his readership, "there is no reason to resent the part the Americans are playing in refashioning the world in their image, which, after all, is substantially the image of ourselves."[3] Another 1902 British publication, *The American Invasion*, by Sir Christopher Furness, discusses the economic might of America and the implicit threat to Britain, British territories, and Europe: "almost simultaneously with the appearance of the United States as a conquering and colonising power, Europe has been appalled by the sight of America bursting her bonds and stepping armed cap-a-pie into the arena as an industrial giant of almost irresistible power, with the openly proclaimed determination to conquer the world's markets and gain universal commercial superiority."[4] Turn-of-the-century British perspectives often viewed the United States as a "prodigal" or a suddenly too-big-for-his-britches child. Many contemporary American readers will chafe at Stead's biblical analogy: "For there is too much reason to fear that many Americans regard the English with the same unfilial ingratitude that many Christians regard the Jew. It is useless to remind them that the men of the *Mayflower* were English, as it is to remind anti-Semites that Christ and His apostles were Jews. Yet it was through the Christian Church, too often unmindful of Jewish parentage, that the ethical ideals of the Jew permeated and civilised the world."[5] Although Stead's jingoistic view that England should bask in its founding of such a great country as America seems anachronistic to us today, many of his basic points cannot be denied at the beginning of the twenty-first century. America does share a common history with Britain, particularly colonial and twentieth-century, which includes the English language and a system of representation with a two-house chamber modeled on the English parliament. The way in which Americans might characterize these commonalities in the contemporary period would most likely be very unsettling to Stead. In any case, the important point is that Stead and Furness are among the many who foretold the rise of the United States. In fact, eighty years before Shaw's play, the eminent French historian Alexis de Tocqueville envisioned the rise of both America and Russia in the twentieth-century.

What we can see with Stead, and moreso with Furness—as with the popular British magazine *Punch*'s cartoons, British journalists, politicians, and even with advertisements defending English products over comparable American ones—is that there is a role reversal evolving in the relationship between the would-be mother country, England, and her well-heeled progeny, the United States, which begins in the nineteenth century.[6] We can see then that the invention of an "English America" by English writers is as fabricated as the contemporary Hollywood Americanization of British literature. The American film industry's invention of a tradition of British literature for the American viewing public may be compared to all-American Vanhatten's attitude that the United States blends other traditions with its "own glorious tradition of Freedom" so that it is not so much unique, or especially universal, as conventionally *American.*

This book aggregates the most popular, and hence the most enduring, forms of Hollywood's invention of Britain by adapting its literature. The colonization of Britain occurs when iterative traditions evolve into bodies of normalized citation. For instance, British literature is frequently appropriated by stereotypical popular Hollywood genre films (the Western, the buddy movie). Instead of dismissing this trend, this book analyzes the iterative power of these appropriations. As leading genre critic Stuart M. Kaminsky argues, "Genre study in film is based on the realization that certain popular narrative forms have both cultural and universal roots—that, for example, the Western of today is related both to folk tales of the past two hundred years in the United States and to the archetypes of myth."[7] Even if we grant that the Western film genre of the twentieth century is related to timeless archetypes, we still must recognize that the American Western depicts a very specific era and situation in American history as interpreted overwhelmingly by white Americans. Being able to understand the economic, cultural, and historical reasons for production, as well as the intended audience, tells a good deal about why the genre, or any genre, is successful in connecting to members of our society: "A major value in examining particular genres of film is in discovering what the elements are to which we are responding in the form—what makes it popular, makes it survive, relates it to forms that have existed before it, and informs us about what there is in film to which we respond."[8] As Kaminsky asserts, too often we search for the "high art" meaning in film and miss the importance of popular film; I argue that this is especially the case with the British literary adaptation. As film-genre critics have shown, social, political, and historical issues, the question of moral value, life and death, are all played out in popular genre film. In the same way, this book is concerned with deciphering the formulas involved in adapting British literary texts for film, and the reasons for citationality of certain enduring stereotypes and patterns of representations of Britishness in the American popular imagination.

Perhaps unsettling is the idea that Hollywood's production of British literary texts often involves satisfying an American-desired nostalgia for racial and national superiority. While it may be argued that America never could—or should—have claimed racial and national homogeneity, England did. White America's sense of heritage might or might not trace back to England, but given common historical and cultural experiences in the twentieth century, and a common language in a world flooded by various immigrant citizens and migrant workers, the American film industry can appropriate what it *needs* from the hefty cultural capital of British literature to *construct* an "England," a British Empire and its history, in such a way as to find an elitist, even racial, comfort from its self-made "Britain."

The modern English-language need for popular narratives to bind a diverse nation of people goes back to the nineteenth century with Matthew Arnold in England. The late twentieth and early twenty-first centuries do not rely on literature for this "cultural glue"; rather they depend on popular media, arts, and sports. According to John G. Cawelti, "homogeneous cultures" rely on "religious ritual" to articulate and reaffirm a culture's uniqueness. In America, homogeneity is not possible in terms of religion or ethnicity, but masses of people do watch media spectator-sports events (e.g., the Superbowl and the World Series draw millions of viewers together worldwide) and popular narratives such as "blockbuster" films and television programs. While Cawelti emphasizes the importance of games in cultures, he acknowledges that "Artistic formulas also fulfill this function in that they constitute entertainments with rules known to everyone. Thus, a very wide audience can follow a Western, appreciate the fine points and vicariously participate in its pattern of suspense and resolution."[9] This book shows that British literature narratives are often appropriated to fit into recognizable American narrative formulae so that complex and "foreign" narrative content can be repackaged into a "high concept" narrative "which is very straightforward, easily communicated, and easily comprehended."[10]

Due to the potentially enormous nature of this project, I have elected to focus on certain strands of citations most often repeated and most influential in the last few decades. Each chapter in this book considers a cluster of citations in film from the 1990s to the present. The clusters of citations might also be thought of as formulae, or, in some instances, distinct genres; my groupings will be familiar to everyone: heritage, American Western, British colonialism, Cool Britannia, American masculinity, and the myth of Shakespeare. Yet, with each chapter and each group of citations, one thing is clear: the

American film has colonized and plundered the British literary text in order to make the film appeal to mainstream audiences.

In chapter 1, I lay out a critical strategy that allows me to interpret the various ways in which contemporary British novels are adapted to fit into prescribed formulae. The connection between desire and capitalism's need to produce commercially viable products manifests itself in the "Hollywoodization" of British literary texts. Utilizing Jacques Derrida's *Margins of Philosophy*, various texts by Gilles Deleuze, and Deleuze's work with Felix Guattari, I uncover new dimensions to the Hollywood colonization of British literature and culture. Discussing *Margins of Philosophy*, I argue that contemporary American film adaptations of British literary texts simultaneously enact both sides of the John Searle and Derrida debate: the filmmaker radically reiterates the literary text at all levels—narrative, plot, circumstances—into a different context of meaning, while at the same time repeating familiar citations, which reconstitute the film into a *recognizable* and predictable product (in order to satisfy a mass-market audience).

From Gilles Deleuze and Felix Guattari's perspective, when the filmmaker radically reiterates the literary text, the text is deterritorialized; the other side of this maneuver, however, is the reterritorialization that occurs when the film is reconstituted into a recognizable product. However, capitalism deterritorializes with one hand as it reterritorializes with the other. Despite its creative possibilities, capitalist deterritorialization is not a process of decoding (or coding) that is qualitative. Deleuze and Guattari assert that money is the principle by which the system functions. Capitalism does not create moral and ethical values; rather, capitalism creates axioms that are designed to create more capital: money only functions to create *more* money, or surplus-value. Hollywood's appropriation is thus predictably centered squarely on profit, potential surplus-value; yet, values are disseminated, though only as secondary concerns, to cater to those who will *buy* a product because it displays certain values. I argue throughout this book that British literature is colonized to cater to American values and Hollywood tastes in order to be marketed to a mainstream audience.

I begin my analysis of contemporary British literature with Kazuo Ishiguro's Booker Prize–winning novel, *The Remains of the Day* (1988), in which an English butler in the 1950s narrates the events he was witness to at Darlington Hall in its prewar prime, including events that lead up to the Second World War. In chapter 2, I argue that, for Americans in particular, the heritage or nostalgia aspect of the film is not triggered by British heritage sentiment. Rather, the film

The Remains of the Day (1993) creates an analogy between the filmic postwar Britain and the 1990s American audience: each country is past the pinnacle of its power in what remains of each country's "day." Perhaps American viewers are primarily unconscious of this analogy, but this chapter shows that Americans enjoy the English heritage "nostalgic" experience of *The Remains of the Day* as a catharsis of emotional nostalgia concerning America's great postwar empire of global capitalist hegemonic control. From a British perspective the film mourns the loss of empire and dwells upon all those quintessential British heritage things: the English countryside, manor houses, servant quarters, lovingly shot details of the furniture, paintings and costumes. Yet, from an American point of view, the film celebrates the ascendancy of America as a world power from the Second World War on, and at the same time creates nostalgia for that lost era of emerging greatness and dominance. According to Spencer Golub, American audiences were primed for feature-length film adaptations by decades of literary classic adaptations, and from the "Masterpiece Theatre" fare that piqued the appetite for manor-house dramas with the January 1982 airing of the eleven-part dramatization of Evelyn Waugh's 1945 novel, *Brideshead Revisited.* Golub theorizes that Americans take voyeuristic pleasure from watching the English upper classes struggle with their pure white, upper-class problems in the fantasy time-capsule of the English past: "It permits an American audience to indulge its own racist and classist fantasies, along with its liberal conscience, defined in its break-up with the offending empire."[11]

Chapter 3 examines an exemplary case of the paradox of Hollywood's appropriation of a British literary text. The adaptation of A.S. Byatt's Booker Prize–winning novel, *Possession*, is lavishly and seemingly lovingly rendered by American film maker Neil LaBute in the 2002 film of the same title. Yet, the lavish scenery and loving dedication to the text masks the reterritorialized structure of the narrative: the citationality of "Englishness"—evident in everything from attitudes to cars to landscape—is repackaged into a Western-genre frame via the transformation of Roland Mitchell from lower-middle-class Englishman to mysterious American loner abroad. However, enfolded in the American Western structural frame of the film is the Victorian love story minus the novel's extensive view of Victorian life. The Victorians function as time-frozen heritage tableaux waiting to be uncovered by the contemporary eye of the camera. The Victorian tableau is consistently revealed inside of an actual written Victorian text that the contemporaries *unfold*: a text unfolds and we see Randolph Henry Ash walking in the country, and, as it refolds, we are returned to the present in Sotheby's; or when the LaMotte–Ash correspondence is initially discovered, as the words unfold, we glimpse the Victorians. The capitalist axiomatic of the heritage film depends on getting the "look" of the historical period; LaBute imitates heritage-style dress, manner of gesture, attitude, and period details for the Victorian scenes.

Chapter 4 interprets the film *The English Patient* (Anthony Minghella, 1996), adapted from Michael Ondaatje's 1992 novel, and updates the imperial adventure with a war-drama love story. Commercially successful, winner of nine Academy Awards, including Best Picture, the film was directed and its screenplay written by Anthony Mingella, who utilizes two stable (sub)generic formulae that provide the context for audience empathy and participation. In the first, the filmic Almasy undergoes a leading man make-over transforming him into an adventurer hero; second, Almasy as desert-map maker is a recognizable European colonial figure as he participates in the colonial enterprise of the "anticonquest" hero along the lines of Richard Burton (*Mountains of the Moon*, 1990) or T. E. Lawrence (*Lawrence of Arabia*, 1962). These two subgenres are part of the same Hollywood tradition that goes back to the black-and-white swashbuckler and Robin Hood films starring Errol Flynn and forward to films such as *Raiders of the Lost Ark*, starring Harrison Ford. The third convention that *The English Patient* seemingly exploits is the romance; but, as the book reveals, I believe this hyped aspect of the film actually belongs to the genre of the colonial adventure, and thus, is only *marketed* as a romantic drama to increase ticket sales.

Chapter 5 interprets two films that embody the spirit of 1990s Cool Britannia in different ways, both equally seductive. The phrase "Cool Britannia" appeared in the British press near the end of 1996, shortly after *Newsweek* declared London to be the coolest city on the planet.[12] Earlier that year film-director Danny Boyle vaulted Scotsman Irvine Welsh's debut novel *Trainspotting* (1993) into global fame and trendiness with the Miramax Films release. The film is reterritorialized into, according to Andrew Macdonald, a "buddy movie," which explains its narrow focus on the exploits of Mark Renton and his small group of friends.[13] Less subversive, but equally "cool," the London-based exploits of Bridget Jones in the film version (2001) of Helen Fielding's novel *Bridget Jones's Diary* (1996) show us that modernism has failed and in its place has arisen the postmodern "return of the repressed"—the longing for a premodern way of life—a desire to "return to a non-alienated condition, understood as something we have left behind us in the past."

Chapter 6 studies the appropriation of a British novel for an American film audience and asserts that American cultural citations are *universal* and *male*. The male panic elicited by these texts is the central commonality they share. With *Waterland*, middle-aged Tom Crick's narrative struggles with the memory of his teenage girlfriend, now his middle-aged wife, who after becoming pregnant aborts the child, which results in her inability to bear children. In seemingly attitudinal and stylistic contrast, *High Fidelity* is another male-centered narrative that deals with an abortion, break-ups, and insecurity of the postfeminist kind. Perhaps more lucidly than in previous chapters, the novels' content is not important to the films; the films are driven by a set of Hollywood conventions. The Derridian paradox is alive and well. It is even more alive with *High Fidelity*; in this film the British content is simply obliterated: the radical reiteration of the literary text occurs at all levels—narrative, plot, circumstances—into an *Amercian* context, while at the same time repeating familiar *Amercian* citations, which reconstitute the film into a *recognizable* and predictable *American* cultural product.

Chapter 7 focuses on the persistent popularity of William Shakespeare's texts, his person, and his image as the greatest English-language poet. *Shakespeare in Love* (John Madden, 1998) provides an Elizabethan "Cool Britannia" because it takes a writer whose personal life is obscure (and who has been dead for four-hundred years) and creates a life filled with "sex, intrigue, raw physicality and violence": a near-perfect formula for the commercial film in the United States.[14] Yet, there is a deeper level of reterritorialization with the signature of Shakespeare in *Shakespeare in Love*. There is no "original" text for this film; but also there is no "text" of Shakespeare. "Shakespeare" is the twenty-first century's ultimate floating signifier because the signifier, Shakespeare, never connects to the signified, a material Shakespeare. Of course, hundreds of years and thousands of pages of signifiers have tried to make Shakespeare a transcendent signifier. The film is framed in script; the marketing of the film in the form of a book of Shakespeare's poems features this script (as well as the internationally famous actors from the film); and a scene in the film is devoted to "Will" signing his name—but it is counterfeit as the author of the new play about "Ethel" is not yet "Shakespeare." Although not based on a single literary text, *Shakespeare in Love* deterritorializes the centuries-old discourses about Shakespeare, and reterritorializes the Bard into the role of a contemporary Hollywood screenwriter. The stodgey middle-aged, balding guy we knew in high school is reterritorialized as sexy, dynamic, plain-old "Will."

In conclusion, the significance of *Britain Colonized: Hollywood's Appropriation of British Literature* is cultural, literary, racial, and patriotic. As discussed above, popular media-and-arts-narratives bind a culture together. The power of American film to invent and reterritorialize an English-language tradition is very real, especially in an age when American schools choose not to force-feed their students British plays and novels, and rather choose to "show the movie" instead. This practice in U.S. schools thus begins a lifelong association with Britain—perhaps for some individuals their *only* connection with British culture and history. It is now apparent that there are dire consequences for literary texts, especially novels and plays, that are not adapted for film. A literary text's canonical status rests on its adaptability to film. Therefore, the "original" must have a "copy" in order to be valued as an "original."

Lastly, an invented tradition is also more triumphant when the "rapid transformation of society weakens or destroys the social patterns for which 'old' traditions had been designed,"[15] which undoubtedly describes our own digital age. The logical outcome will be that citations of heritage England or Shakespeare in "hose-and-doublet" will be the circulating images of the future. Although the terms "patriotic" or "patriotism" are generally associated with conservative forces in any given country, a patriotic or nationalistic zeal coupled with racism best exemplifies reterritorialized iterations in American-produced film. These films exhibit developments in cultural appropriation that need to be recognized, discussed, and analyzed. The films discussed in this book are evidence of the way one nation remakes another, often in the image of itself or what it needs the Other to be (as the British Empire once did). Reterritorialization also manifests American cultural and capitalist hegemony over the English-speaking world. While there may be no halt to the production of American-appropriated Englishness, this text identifies the phenomena portending the future of British and Anglophone literary and cultural studies as a group of citations appropriated for American ends.

CHAPTER 1

Context and Desire in the Colonization of British Literature

Par rapport aux cineastes americans, je crois que nous sommes tous des intellectuels.

Francois Truffaut[1]

How could the masses be made to desire their own repression?

Wilhelm Reich

In this chapter I map out an interpretive strategy that will allow us in the following chapters to come to an enriched understanding of American Hollywood film adaptations of contemporary British literature in the last decades of the twentieth century and the early twenty-first century. These films, constructed from commercially successful British texts, are made to fill a certain space in contemporary culture. While most of these films, excluding the Bond films based on Ian Fleming's popular fiction, cannot vie for the blockbuster status of certain homegrown narratives such as the action-packed *Terminator* series or the romantic *Titanic*, some are commercially successful, such as Anthony Minghella's *The English Patient* (1996) or Danny Boyle's *Trainspotting* (1996), mapping out a terrain in contemporary American film culture. The star power, huge budgets, and formulaic devices and narrative patterns of films like *The English Patient* add up to predictable box-office commercial success. American audiences, and audiences worldwide, desire the ever bigger and better Hollywood blockbuster. The connection between desire and capitalism's need to produce commercially viable products manifests itself in the "Hollywoodization" of British literary texts. In this manifestation we have the colonization of another culture, its literature, and its use of language. What we will uncover in this chapter is that the desire for "more of the Same" is the very foundation of American cultural narrative, and it is this narrative which fuels the global capitalist machine.

Let us first contemplate America's media and cultural hegemony. While I am explicitly interested in Hollywood's cultural recoding of British literary texts, we must also consider Hollywood's, and hence America's, global position in terms of politics, military power, and economics in order to understand the potentially insidious nature of this kind of cultural reterritorialization. As the Introduction discussed, America's economic and industrial supremacy began in the late nineteenth century. American filmmaking begins to assert global influence between 1910 and 1920; and when European, especially French, film industries were slow to recover from WWI, it assumed complete dominance: "by 1911–1912, the export of American films—mostly to Europe—surpassed the flow of European films into America. It was at this time that relocation of much of the American film industry to Hollywood began in earnest. What remained of the European competition collapsed during the First World War."[2] Hollywood's dominance continues in the twentieth century but also draws from international sources, especially in the latter quarter of the century.

Another way to view contemporary America's stake in world affairs is to situate it historically. A nation which engages in international trade must keep its borders porous and solid at the same time. An economist discussing global trade, Colin Flint, theorizes that a "world-systems" approach "contends that the tensions between global flows and domestic politics are not unique to the contemporary period of globalization, but have been in existence since the establishment of the capitalist world-economy approximately 500 years ago.[3] Therefore, America in the twenty-first century follows a historical pattern of not only implementing commerce with other nations, but also attempting to influence American "domestic politics" in regard to commercial trade with other nations. Domestic policy (territory) almost always has its sights on international policy (extraterritorial). Also, because America has decided that it will remain a presence in world affairs and policies, it needs to continue to exert influence over other nations and their "domestic politics." Military might and trade sanctions are "hard power" options for a nation, though a less expensive and less overtly controversial way to exert control is through "soft power."[4] Successfully executing soft power involves projecting moral values, economic prosperity, judicial accountability, and integrity—qualities that are cross-culturally desirable. More than any other method, procedure or technique, Hollywood is a global phenomenon creating the desire to emulate, to fantasize and to *be*. One might even conjecture that Hollywood has been America's number one soft power work horse. Yet, the universalizing narrative and American directed forms of desire could be construed as constrictive.

According to Flint, America sets its "soft power" agenda through political and cultural volition: "From the Marshall Plan and the imposition of a political constitution in postwar Japan to the powerful cultural influence of Hollywood, the United States has exerted its influence into other sovereign spaces, sometimes as a matter of conscious political acts and in other instances as a result of entrepreneurial agency."[5] The expense of "blockbuster" film making necessitates what Paul Willemen calls a "cultural cross-border raid" which occurs in the film industry because of the need for larger international investment:

> The capital-intensive nature of film production, and of its necessary industrial, administrative and technological infrastructures, requires a fairly large market in which to amortise production costs, not to mention the generation of surplus for investment or profit. This means that a film industry—any film industry—must address either an international market or a very large domestic one. If the latter is unavailable, then cinema requires large potential audience groups, with the inevitable homogenising effects.[6]

"Homogenising effects" are created when Hollywood, which relies on a large domestic market, models its films on the American public's viewing tastes, regardless of the "original" source material. Therefore, catering to a large domestic audience and hoping to sell to an international audience as well as "to amortise production costs," American filmmakers use normative citations to replace cultural "foreignness" with American citations so that not only is America fed more of "the Same" but so is the rest of the world. Willemen asserts that this is essentially a nationalist discourse that is the other side of imperialism. Hollywood's move to Americanize a literary text for film while keeping the text's title and publicity creates a nationalist discourse. As Willemen theorizes, "the construction [of] national specificity . . . encompasses and governs the articulation of both national identity and nationalist discourse. Nationalist discourses forever try to colonise and extend themselves to cover, by repressively homogenising, a complex but nationally specific formation."[7] The entire world sees British characters, for example, reduced to clichés or even replaced by an "American" in order to eradicate "the unknown."

American film's appropriation of British literature over time creates its own tradition. For example, the Robin Hood myth is easily recognized in the figure of Errol Flynn that was created out of a British text, by a handsome Australian/British actor who could embody the myth in a glamorous and dynamic manner; Robin Hood became an American adventure film commodity invention. In fact, most Americans probably would have difficulty separating the textual or historic figure from the legend created in film. According to Eric Hobsbawm in *The Invention of Tradition*, "Inventing traditions . . . is essentially a process of formalization and ritualization, characterized by reference to the past, if only by imposing repetition."[8] The fact that Hollywood invented a tradition of citations does not abrogate the very real effect that these stories, myths, and images have on our imagination. As Michael Ryan and Douglas Kellner assert in *Camera Politica: The Politics and Ideology of Contemporary Hollywood Film*, images in film have power at both the representational level, such as subject matter, and the formal level, such as narrative closure, to indoctrinate the audience into acceptance of a film's "basic premises of the social order, and to ignore their irrationality and injustice."[9] The citations not only circulate in the films and texts, but encompass the cultural exchange between the United States and Britain, and their ongoing interpretation of each other.

A less-extreme view of American dominance would simply state that filmmakers who Americanize novels are showing that these stories are "universal." For example, a male thirty-something record store owner in the throes of a life crisis can be made "universal" by transporting him from London to Chicago. One could claim that the narrative structure of *High Fidelity* is basically identical from the novel version to the film adaptation, and thus the "story" is "universal." Yet, if we reposition ourselves slightly, we could also claim that this appropriation of an English novel for an American film audience is actually asserting that American cultural citations are not culturally relative, but universal. In the discussion that follows, I flesh out a theoretical strategy for understanding these American claims of universality and wholesale cultural appropriation as restricted contexts for utterances and worldwide reterritorialization.

Copy to Original

The very subject of film adaptation poses the problem of copy to the original instead of original to copy. The counterfeit is primary. One needs to be careful that in delineating the ways in which American films reterritorialize desire one does not promote a fetishizing of the "original." Fetishizing the original is known in adaptation criticism as "fidelity." After a century of critique concerning the relationship between literature and film, criticism often comes back to the issue of the film's fidelity to the original text. In the first part of this chapter, I want to pry open film and literature criticism in order to expose the impossible binary prison of such criticism.

Hollywood's relationship to literary texts is nearly a century old. Morris Beja's *Film and Literature* records that in terms of Academy Awards "more than three-fourths of the awards for 'best picture' have gone to adaptations . . . the all-time box-office successes favour novels even more" since the late 1920s.[10] These figures indicate that popular films are often literature adaptations, though most people are not aware of the "original" literary source. It is only when the adaptation is an adaptation of a well-known novel, perhaps deliberately advertised as such, that a viewer is aware of the literary precursor. More recently, the 1980s phenomenon of "fastseller" contemporary novels hastily made into feature-length or made-for-television films has changed the landscape of literature: how a text is produced, marketed, consumed. Many critics have noted that the Booker Prize competition for the best British novel creates a carnivalesque atmosphere as publishers vie to get their titles noticed by the Booker (now Man Booker) Prize committee. In *Consuming Fictions: The Booker Prize and Fiction in Britain Today*, Richard Todd lists the changes that have impacted the literary market place:

> These include the development of the Booker Prize *and its shortlist*; how other literary prizes have reacted to the Booker; how both agents and publisher have responded to the commercial possibilities of the serious literary blockbuster that can achieve both "fastseller" as well as "bestseller" status (this includes the controversial issue of authors' advances); how the serious literary fiction title and/or author can enter the canon through a (sometimes fortuitous) combination of skillful commercial promotion, publicity and review coverage in the various media (including radio and TV), and even be taken up into academic discussion; how booksellers co-operate with novelists to promote contemporary fiction; how adaptation for film and/or TV can affect a given title.[11]

Accordingly, even in Britain the "image" or "spin" of a book or of an author has replaced an old-fashioned, "time will tell" perspective of literature that impacts not only contemporary sales, but the entire literary milieu. The literary environment is affected because of the chain of events that follows a film adaptation; typically, the literary text will be reissued and featured on large displays at the leading bookstores, from Waterstones to Barnes and Noble, with tie-in images from the film; from the reissue, and the potential media hype (e.g., *Trainspotting*, *Bridget Jones's Diary*) the book will be read, interpreted, and perhaps canonically situated so as to displace another text. For example, although a flop at the box office, how would, hypothetically speaking, the 2004 adaptation of Thackeray's *Vanity Fair* affect the canonical position of, say, Charles Dickens, E.M. Forester, or even Virginia Woolf? It seems that any time a new adaptation is released it has (potentially) a reverberating affect among the other authors and texts traditionally positioned alongside or near the adaptation's "original" text.

Early American film pioneer D. W. Griffith, Sergei Eisenstein contends, was influenced by Charles Dickens's novelistic technique, which led to the film devices of parallel action, montage, framing, and close-up. According to Eisenstein, Griffith's genius for invention has less to do with technology than with the fictional and epistemological heritage of Dickens and Western culture: "Let Dickens and the whole ancestral array, going back as far as the Greeks and Shakespeare, be superfluous reminders that both Griffith and our cinema prove our origins to be not solely as of Edison and his fellow inventors, but as based on an enormous cultured past."[12] The other early connection routinely made by scholars in the field of literary adaptation is Joseph Conrad's wish for his readers to "see" images produced by his text, "My task which I am trying to achieve is, by the powers of the written word, to make you hear, to make you feel—it is, before all, to make you see."[13] Both Dickens's influence and Conrad's intention in his prose, however, do not directly address the central issue in adaptation, which concerns transforming one medium into another. Ironically, while Modernist novelists such as Conrad and Henry James were moving away from the omniscient narrator, film, by its very nature, moved toward it.

Therefore it seems that the cultural investment in Modernism is not one of technique for film, but one of cultural value and meaning that leads us directly to the issue of *narration*. The field of narratology crosses film and literature studies, and is too enormous to attempt a reasonable account here of either field. The primary epistemological legacy of literary Modernism is to show parallel as well as competing and intersecting points of view. The film through montage, for example, is easily able to execute parallel action, although the point of view issue is technically more difficult to render. First-person narration or a subjective perspective is difficult to achieve; typically, voice-overs or numerous shots supposedly from the main character's or characters' perspective are tricks used to emulate first person narrative. Overall, as we will see in subsequent chapters, the voice-over or oral narration is used to fill in background or necessary psychological detail so that the "action" will make sense for the viewer. Essentially, the voice-over is an economically suitable device for adaptation because pages of description and psychological investigation can be condensed into a few minutes of oral narration.

Contrary to a popular belief that the film can show more than a written text, one of the most important literary experimentalists of the Modern period, Virginia Woolf, indicates that in terms of film adaptation's "transferring" words into images, film is *less* able to "show" us a full meaning of an image: "Even the simplest image: 'My love's like a red, red rose, that's newly sprung in June' presents us with impressions of moisture and warmth and the flow of crimson and the softness of petals inextricably mixed and strung upon the lift of a rhythm which is itself the voice of the passion and the hesitation of the love. All this, which is accessible to words, and to words alone, the cinema must avoid."[14] One aspect of language that Woolf skirts is that language is highly subjective; and so, another person's interpretation of the rose sprung in June might not have anything to do with moisture or warmth or crimson, but might focus on the green of the leaves and thorns, the fertile soil, or the capriciousness of nature that produced it. However erratic interpretation of words might be, two constants in the adaptation of British novels are the stability of the images or types of citations, and the predictability of action and plot.

Predictability is put forward, unwittingly, in Raymond Williams's 1974 *Television: Technology and Cultural Form*, in which he establishes an early theory of television's transformation from "programming" to "flow." Although Williams is commenting on watching the flow of television broadcasting, his analysis of American television sequencing provides insight into the American viewing audience's expectation as media consumers. As Williams recounts, having just arrived in Miami (on his way to Stanford where he, in fact, wrote *Television*) he begins to watch a film on television. Accustomed to British television with predictable program breaks for commercials, Williams is unfamiliar with American broadcast of the film not only because of the more frequent commercial breaks, but also interlaced "trailers" of upcoming programs that are mixed into the sequence. In the following passage Williams does more than contrast the American "flow" with conventional British programming, he also points to the fundamental condition of American audiences' entertainment and expectation:

> I began watching a film and at first had some difficulty in adjusting to a much greater frequency of commercial "breaks." Yet this was a minor problem compared to what eventually happened. Two other films, which were due to be shown on the same channel on other nights, began to be inserted as trailers. A crime in San Francisco (the subject of the original film) began to operate in an extraordinary counterpart not only with the deodorant and cereal commercials but with a romance in Paris and the eruption of a prehistoric monster who laid waste New York. Moreover, this was a sequence in a new sense. Even in commercial British television there is a visual signal—the residual sign of an interval—before and after the commercial sequences, and "programme" trailers only occur between "programmes." Here was something quite different, since the transitions from film to commercial and from film A to films B and C were in effect unmarked. There is in any case enough similarity between certain kinds of films, and between several kinds of film and the "situation" commercials which often consciously imitate them, to make a sequence of this kind a very difficult experience to interpret. I can still not be sure what I took from the whole flow. I believe I registered some incidents as happening in the wrong film, and some characters in the commercials as involved in the film episodes, in what came to seem—for all the occasional bizarre disparities—a single irresponsible flow of images and feelings.[15]

What is notable about Williams's account is his lack of the American register of audience expectation and convention. The capitalist American broadcasting system is not only more overtly commercial, but also, and more significantly, has "trained" its audience to make connections among jumbled strands of narrative and even type (between advertisements, "trailers," and the film or show). What is telling in Willliams's "flow" is that American film audiences, "trained" in most cases by daily television viewing, easily adapt to various types (and quantity and quality) of sensory stimuli. The question that remains, however, even thirty years after Williams's book, is what do American viewers take away from their viewing experience? Do short sequences with commercial and network advertisement (trailer) interludes signal a short attention span? Or does the disjointed flow evidence a sophisticated viewing public? The technological advances from the infamous remote control to the internet to digital television in the intervening decades have intensified and made more complex the idea of "flow."

In contrast with Williams's view, I do not believe that the films contain "enough similarity between" them and the commercials, which in turn imitate them to make interpretation difficult; rather, the audience has been conditioned to expect that the plot of film A can be intertwined with films B and C. The audience recognizes and *desires* basically one set of plot devices; when a film or show deviates, I would wager, the remote control engages the next channel. Thus, Williams may be confused by American programming, but Americans are not. Therefore, however "irresponsible," the catalogue of recognizable citations for standard American audiences "raised" on television is predictable and conventional. Films or programs that deviate from the normalized fare generally will not be as commercially successful, which for television means that they will be "canceled" or broadcast on a minor cable channel. For film, of course, it means initially little investment, low working budget (no big stars, no fantastic pyrotechnics), smaller distribution market, less profit, and obscurity.

The fact that a mass viewer market has been normalized by predictable narrative devices, images, plot outlines, and even actor/character clichés, complicates the task of making a film authentic to the spirit of the novel. Scholars typically dismiss the fidelity issue as too simplistic, and yet repeatedly return to "fidelity to the original." Christopher Orr declares, "The concern with the fidelity of the adapted film in letter and spirit to its literary source has unquestionably dominated the discourse on adaptation."[16] William Luhr and Peter Lehman observe, "Criticism of films using novels as a source will frequently centre on the 'fidelity' to the events of the novel, not on their artistic integrity. References are constantly made to what is 'left out' or 'changed,' instead of what is there."[17]

Dudley Andrew's analysis tabulates three types of adaptation: "Borrowing, Intersecting and Transforming."[18] According to Andrew, borrowing is the "most frequent mode of adaptation . . . the adaptation hopes to win an audience by the prestige of its borrowed title or subject. But at the same time it seeks to gain a certain respectability, if not aesthetic value, as a dividend in the transaction."[19] Intersecting for Andrew is the "opposite" of from borrowing; he contends that "the uniqueness of the original text is preserved to such an extent that it is intentionally left unassimilated in adaptation."[20] Andrew's attitude toward the fidelity issue is clearly presented when he claims, "Unquestionably the most frequent and most tiresome discussion of adaptation (and of film and literature relations as well) concerns fidelity and transformation. Here it is assumed that the task of adaptation is the reproduction in cinema of something essential about an original text. Here we have a clear-cut case of film trying to measure up to a literary work, or of an audience expecting to make such a comparison."[21] Andrew then begins to cite several critics from Christian Metz to E.H. Gombrich and Nelson Goodman concerning what basically amounts to correspondence theory between (or among) the arts. Andrew cites Keith Cohen from *Film and Fiction: The Dynamics of Exchange* because Cohen clearly puts forward the semiotic relationship between film and fiction. For us, the valuable conclusion that Andrew arrives at is that narrative codes can be compared—though achieved in separate systems—but that the study of film adaptation will not ultimately lead us to the original literary text; rather, it will lead us, rightly so, to film styles, citations, and norms, and away from original and copy:

> The analysis of adaptation then must point to the achievement of equivalent narrative units in the absolutely different semiotic systems of film and language. Narrative itself is a semiotic system available to both. If a novel's story is judged in some way comparable to its filmic adaptation, then the strictly separate but equivalent processes of implication which produced the narrative units of that story through words and audio-visual signs, respectively, must be studied. Here semiotics coincides with Gombrich's intuition: such a study is not comparative between the arts but is instead intensive within each art. And since the implicative power of literary language and of cinematic signs is a function of its use as well as of its system, adaptation analysis ultimately leads to an investigation of film styles and periods in relation to literary styles of different periods.[22]

Concurring with Andrew and Gombrich, then, one can see that the impetus is already established in adaptation and correspondence theories, which leads me to the deterritorialization and reterritorialization of Hollywood's appropriation of British Literature. Following his discussion of adaptation, Andrew indicates that "[i]t is time for adaptation studies to take a sociological turn. How does adaptation serve the cinema? What conditions exist in film style and film culture to demand the use of literary prototypes?"[23] In the context of Hollywood adaptation of British literature, I address Andrew's queries in terms of film style and film culture and viewing audiences' normalization to these conventions.

Dealing directly with the English novel in *The English Novel and the Movies*, Michael Klein and Gillian Parker also echo the three-part classification with a first category listed as "faithful, that is, literal, translation"; a second level "retains the core of the structure of narrative while significantly reinterpreting, or in some cases de-constructing the source text"; the third level "regards the source merely as raw material, as simply the occasion for an original work."[24] In addition to reiterating the basic three levels of fidelity, Michael Klein's introduction for the co-edited text notes the cultural determinants at work when a novel from one culture is adapted by another. Klein considers that the English novel written from the eighteenth century to the early twentieth century is "filmed in accordance with the Hollywood codes and conventions familiar to the modern American market."[25] Although not all of the essays contained in Klein and Parker's volume address American-made films, familiar patterns of cultural iteration are acknowledged by Klein:

> Certain cultural distortions may occur when the English work is Americanized, even if the director intends to make a relatively literal adaptation, and then perhaps even more so as the disparities can be especially jarring. Thus if the children in the film of *Wuthering Heights* come across as types of American farm kids, and if the women in the film of *Pride and Prejudice* tend to be conventional midwestern small-town daughters and matrons, we think of Hollywood first and Bronte or Austen second, the clash of styles being even more evident where, as in these cases, the lead performers are English and the dress of the characters is relatively authentic.[26]

Unfortunately, Klein and Parker's collection does not stay focused on the issue of American citations appearing in British films. The essays included in the Klein and Parker volume discuss films made up to 1979 (Francis Coppola's *Apocalypse Now*, based on Joseph Conrad's *Heart of Darkness*); and while not all are concerned with American films, it is in this period that the colonizing or "inauthentic" pattern of iterations first appears, and which they persuasively identify in the above passage.

Indeed, the contemporary era of Americanized British literary adaptations mimics an earlier period in the twentieth century when Hollywood's big film studios found mass-market success reproducing standard, formulaic British characters ("I say," "by George," "dash it all") with the enduringly popular themes of imperial history and class-barrier distinctions. It is in this period that American film begins its invention of Britain. From 1930 to the end of the second world war, Hollywood produced over 150 "British" films. According to H. Mark Glancy in *When Hollywood Loved Britain: The Hollywood 'British' Film 1939–45*, there is a distinction between a "British" film which is "essentially American," and "actual British films."[27] Glancy notes that while five "British" films won Academy Awards during this fifteen-year period, including a three-in-a-row sweep, from 1940–1942, there were several other films made that did not win Academy Awards but which became "classics."[28]

According to Glancy there were four features of the 1930s and 1940s Hollywood version of Britain that delineate them as Hollywood "British"; these features still function, more or less, in the contemporary period. First, the films were made at Denham Studios in Britain, though others, such as *How Green Was My Valley*, which won the Academy Award for best picture in 1941, were shot entirely in California. Second, postwar films were based on British source material, such as *David Copperfield*, or British history, including British imperial involvement. Glancy thirdly points out that the films from the 1930s and 1940s had a "significant number of British personnel among the credits"; and while Hollywood had a "large British community" of "British producers, directors, writers, stars and character actors . . . an American perspective was maintained at the same time. The films often have American stars or an American director, and screenplays were often written in tandem by American and British writers."[29] As Glancy indicates, after the war, the studio system broke down and films became less centralized and more international, especially in terms of financial backing. From the 1980s especially there has been a greater global circulation of film personnel including stars—the most visible personnel of any production—whose national identity is often betrayed due to their on-screen roles.[30] Perhaps the strongest connection between the films of the 1930s and our present era is the fourth feature—the "tourist's view of the country"—as depicted by Hollywood:

> The characters tend to be aged and venerable aristocrats, young officers and gentlemen, and their comical cockney servants. The settings are often grand manor houses, idyllic villages that have not been touched by the modern age, and a London marked by Big Ben, St Paul's Cathedral, Tower Bridge, and heavy and constant fog. In many instances, and particularly in the historical films and the literary adaptations, this is further compounded by a pronounced sense of patriotism. "British" films often seem to be populated almost exclusively by the grandest historical figures, who are seen to be living lives of great national significance.[31]

Glancy notes that Anglophilia cannot explain why Hollywood pursued "British" subject matter; rather, as an industry run for profit, it simply catered to "a time when Americans remained fascinated by the British."[32] Yet, translating Anglophilia into capitalist profit is exactly what contemporary films based on British literature successfully do; so much so that the industry has created new capitalist axiomatics for global capitalism.

Context and Desire

I approach the contemporary Hollywoodization of British literature at two levels. For want of better terms, let me call them the micro level and the macro level. The micro level I discuss first; this level involves the actual theoretical strategy of the transfiguration from novel to film. The text must be turned into another medium—how is this done, to what end? I use the Derrida/Searle debate to elaborate this process. Next, the macro level discusses the products of these transformations through Deleuze and Guattari's philosophical theories concerning deterritorialization, reterritorialization, and capitalist axiomatics.

To begin, my interpretation of the films considered makes an analogy between Austin's closed system of language and the circular system of citations manufactured by Americanized film versions of British literature. The authority of a British text for an American audience is most often not gained through the reading of the text (even if the text is read); rather, the authority is granted through a process of recognizable citations in which what stands for "Englishness" is assembled. Because a text's iterability, the ability to repeat, allows infinite contexts to stage innumerable discourses, theoretically the film adaptation can "do what it likes" without heed to "fidelity." In reality, however, this is never the case. The iterability of the text is always controlled by a well-established context with a precise set of citations. Indeed, it is actually the series of citations that we typically take for Englishness or Britishness, not the literary text and certainly not factual or historical reality. A Hollywoodized film performance is authenticated by a repetition of citations which are formulaic and sometimes clichéd British, and often explicitly un-American: subject matter (e.g., monarchial succession); gestures; costumes; accent; and, in recent decades, landscape and the interior *mise-en-scene* (e.g., manor houses, ball rooms, servants' quarters). Without the continual repetition and re-enactment of these citations, these films cannot sustain meaning. In a circular fashion, it is the repetition of the citation that gradually hardens into something recognizable as meaningful, perhaps even important, culturally speaking.

In order to arrive at my working theory, let me recapitulate the relevant aspects of the Searle and Derrida dispute. As an Anglo-American analytic language philosopher, Austin wished to clarify what he deemed the confused and fallacious assumptions made by his peers. In *How to Do Things with Words*, Austin claims "it was for too long the assumption of philosophers that the business of a 'statement' can only be to 'describe' some state of affairs, or to 'state some fact,' which it must do either truly or falsely."[33] Austin relegates statements that can be "true" or "false" to the realm of *constative* utterances, and it is this sphere of language that we most often inhabit. For example, everyday statements such as "it is raining," "Vera dyed her hair red," or "my brother is coming to the party," are statements that describe various states of affairs, that can be empirically verified (it is raining, her hair is red, he is at the party; or it is not raining, her hair is not red, he is not at the party). The other category of language, Austin theorizes, is the *performative*, in which the words perform the deed. The most famous example of the performative is the statement made by the bride and groom during their wedding: "I do" legally binds them to each other. The "I do" is a response, of course, to the judge or minister who asks, "Will you do this thing?" to whom the bride or groom state the performative. The locutionary is the actual statement; but the illocutionary is the context (to legally bind in marriage) that gives the statement meaning. Hence, the illocutionary provides the conditions for this statement to be recognized as performative. However, problems arise for Austin when we ask what happens to the statement when two men or two women perform the marriage ceremony (in a state that has not yet ratified same-sex marriage), or when we see it on the stage or in a film or television show?

In reply, Austin makes lucid early in *How to Do Things with Words* that the performative utterances must be stated "seriously": "Surely the words must be spoken 'seriously' and so as to be taken 'seriously' ? This is, though vague, true enough in general—it is an important commonplace in discussing the purport of any utterance whatsoever. I must not be joking, for example, nor writing a poem."[34] "Writing a poem", like a joke, is a fiction, and Austin calls this a "hollow" utterance, one, we assume, that has no "legal" hold on the speaker:

> a performative utterance will, for example, be *in a particular way* hollow or void if said by an actor on the stage, or if introduced in a poem, or spoken in soliloquy. This applies in a similar manner to any and every utterance—a sea-change in special circumstances. Language in such circumstances is in special ways—intelligibly—used not seriously, but in ways *parasitic* upon its normal use—ways which fall under the doctrine of the *etiolations* of language. All this we are *excluding* from consideration. Our performative utterances, felicitous or not, are to be understood as issued in ordinary circumstances. (italics in original)[35]

"Ordinary circumstances," then, are circumstances *recognized* as valid or authorized; the real work of philosophy, then, occurs in this "serious" realm of language which has to be authenticated by the philosophical community (colleagues, reviewers, publishers). If we return to the example of the two men or two women performing a marriage ceremony, we can further understand that the weight of Austin's argument concerning "performatives" falls most heavily on the context for understanding the performatives, not the utterance itself. When two women, for example, stand before the justice of the peace in Massachusetts (where currently same-sex marriage is legal) and state their performative "I do," it is recognized as legally binding. Even if a witness to the ceremony has never seen two women state the "I do" of the marriage transaction, this witness knows that the illocutionary meaning makes their statements authoritative and binding.

But what if two women stand before the justice of the peace in Texas (where currently same-sex marriage is not legal) and state their performative "I do"? What is the illocutionary meaning of their statements? Is it mere performance and not performative? Is it authoritative and binding? The idea of hollow iteration in an illegal or, more euphemistically, nonrecognized marriage ceremony, is not linguistically possible—the witness at the Texas ceremony understands the "I do" the same way the witness in the Massachusetts ceremony does. The iteration itself is free of the contamination of the legal system, the ceremony still validates the words; it is the context which lacks authoritative meaning. Each witness recognizes "I do" as part of the proper marriage ceremony. Derrida posits that the statement "I do" is iterative; an iteration can be cited ad infinitum. With each citation ("I do") we have a singular context; and yet, the citation is only recognizable because it has become normalized in this particular kind of context. As Derrida indicates in "Signature Event Context," it is the repetition of the performative which sustains meaning:

> Could a performative statement succeed if its formulation did not repeat a "coded" or iterable statement, in other words if the expressions I use to open a meeting, launch a ship or a marriage were not identifiable as *conforming* to an iterable model, and therefore if they were not identifiable in a way as "citation"? Not that citationality here is of the same type as in a play, a philosophical reference, or the recitation of a poem. This is why there is a relative specificity, as Austin says, a "relative purity" of performatives. But this relative purity is not constructed *against* citationality or iterability, but against other kinds of iteration within a general iterability which is the effraction into the allegedly rigorous purity of every event of discourse or speech act. (italics in original)[36]

Although the citationality is a basis for meaning, and in ceremonies or common practices this basis is fairly straightforward, Derrida nonetheless suggests, contradictorily to Austin, that the iterative potential of statements exceeds our ability to control meaning. This is the crux of the Austin/Searle and Derrida philosophical debate. Searle, in defense of Austin, wishes to control the iterative potential of statements, which at that point ghettoizes his philosophy; less comprehensive, it is less useful. By omitting fictional, nonserious iterations, Austin's theory neglects an essential component for its own meaning-making, which is comprehending the differences between authoritative and nonauthoritative, between parasitic and "valid," and between fictional and nonfictional.

Another drawback of Austin's philosophy is that the intentionality of the illucutionary field must be held as infallible. The words must perform the deed no matter what the conditions or context. Thus, if we return once more to our same-sex marriage ceremony in Texas, we witness the ceremony performed flawlessly by all participants because their *intention* is sincere, and, hence, their performative utterances they *intend* to be binding. If we reverse the circumstances of intention, then we can understand the impaired nature of Austin's argument. If instead of two people fully sincere in their intention to utter performatives we have the clichéd Texas "shot-gun" ceremony, then we can see that the groom's intention (he does not wish to marry) is contrary to his speech act. Because Texas recognizes the union between a man and woman, when the groom says "I do" during the ceremony, though under threat and duress, it is still legally binding. Thus, it is not the individual speaker's words or his conscious intention that give meaning to the words; rather the *context* makes his "I do" meaningful, authoritative, and binding. The groom's statement under duress is a performance—not a performative. He is performing for the bride's father and others; he does not wish to be part of the performative.

Derrida problematizes Austin's position in regard to conscious intention, and contends that Austin's theory tries to control language so that no "remainder" of meaning escapes his system; in order to do that he has to limit what he permits to enter his system:

> I must take as known and granted that Austin's analysis permanently demands a value of *context*, and even of an exhaustively determinable context, whether *de jure* or teleologically; and the long list of "infelicities" of variable type which might affect the event of the performative always returns to an element of what Austin calls the total context. One of these essential elements—and not one among others—classically

> remains consciousness, the conscious presence of the intention of the speaking subject for the totality of his locutory act. Thereby, performative communication once more becomes the communication of an intentional meaning, even if this meaning has no referent in the form of a prior or exterior thing or state of things. This conscious presence of the speakers or receivers who participate in the effecting of a performative, their conscious and intentional presence in the totality of the operation, implies teleologically that no *remainder* escapes the present totalization. No remainder, whether in the definition of the requisite conventions, or the internal and linguistic context, or the grammatical form or semantic determination of the words used; no irreducible polysemia, that is no "dissemination" escaping the horizon of the unity of meaning. (italics in original)[37]

A remainder in our above examples would mean that the same-sex couple's commitment and love is binding, if not legal, and escapes the heterosexualization of sex and devotion; with the shot-gun example, the words are indeed "hollow" and "void," although legally binding. The context is repeatable with difference although the citation remains the same. The fissure of difference, then, does not occur at the level of the performative or locutionary, but at the level of context or illocutionary.

With this debate Derrida established a lasting impact in literary studies. Derrida's work brought to the fore the issue that while the language of a text may not change, the circumstances for its reception—temporal, cultural, theoretical—do change. Historically, New Criticism's primary interpretative strategy of fetishizing the text coincides with Austin's position concerning language. Quarrelsome and polemical, the debate concerning the context for a "right" reading of any particular text need not be rehearsed here at length. Perhaps the most famous example of this debate for Anglo-American literature studies is contained in Stanley Fish's *Is There a Text in This Class?* Fish demonstrates that his title when posed (to him by a student) opens up at least two contexts for understanding what is being asked. When the student asks, "Is there a text in the class?" the most probable illocutionary context suggests: "Is there textbook to buy at the book store?" The second illocutionary field is available to the student who has had Fish as teacher before in class, and the same words are interpreted as: "Are the texts we read in class determinable?" A third context is easily available if we imagine a student putting her head into classroom in session and inquiring: "Is there a (lost) text in the class?" We need to understand the context for the question before we can answer the question. In this way, Austin relies on a rather naive view that language is transparent. Language is not transparent because the framework or context from which we make meaning is always already singular and contingent.

What is relevant from these discourses for my interpretation is the curious—and paradoxical—manner in which contemporary American film adaptations of British literary texts simultaneously enact both sides of the Searle/Derrida debate: the filmmaker radically reiterates the literary text at all levels—narrative, plot, circumstances—into a different context of meaning (in order to satisfy a mass-market audience), while at the same time repeating familiar citations that reconstitute the film into a *recognizable* and predictable product (in order to satisfy a mass-market audience). From Gilles Deleuze and Felix Guattari's perspective, when the filmmaker radically reiterates the literary text, the text is deterritorialized; the other side of this maneuver, however, is the reterritorialization that occurs when the film is reconstituted into a recognizable product. Therefore, filmmakers reflect the larger social force:

> Civilized modern societies are defined by processes of decoding and deterritorialization. But *what they deterritorialize with one hand, they reterritorialize with the other.* (italics in original)[38]

The appropriation of the British text by American filmmakers is an overt attempt to appeal to an American mass consumer base. Another way to think about Willemen's assertion that "nationalist discourses forever" try to "colonise and extend themselves" is through the concept of reterritorialization that exposes the insidious nature of the Americanization of British literature.

By considering Deleuze and Guattari's concepts, we can see how deterritorialization, reterritorialization, and desire come together to form the basic tenets of American culture. We have discussed iterability in terms of its multiplicity. To iterate is to "express" or, like the word *trope*, to "turn." Gilles Deleuze and Felix Guattari develop the concept of territory, which they define as refrain (*ritournelle*).[39] The refrain for Deleuze and Guattari can be either a space or duration which makes a connection or connections. The refrain expresses the connection or connections, and in this movement marks a territory. A bird that sings is expressing itself, but it is also marking a territory. Before the bird sings, it sits on a tree branch in the woods and this is its milieu. When the bird sings, its refrain marks the milieu as its territory.[40] The bird's refrain "territorializes" the milieu: "The territory is in fact an act that affects milieus and rhythms, that 'territorializes' them. The territory is the product of a territorialization of milieus and rhythms."[41] Practically speaking, we create refrains and territorialize everyday when we walk to work, fantasize in our mind during a meeting, write, draw, hum. By way of extension, the novelist or filmmaker, too, marks a territory in language or film. Deleuze and Guattari hypothesize that the expressive nature of territorializing is art: "The artist: the first person to set out a boundary stone, or to make a mark."[42] The territory shares with iteration the need for reiteration, for repetition.

To understand territory is fundamental to understanding how reiteration and repetition affect what we know or what might be possible to know. Western philosophy since Plato is built upon knowledge as recollection. A simple way to think about recollection is to recall the *Ion* example in which Plato creates a hierarchy of "beds": the Form of the bed exists in "ultimate reality" (unattainable) and is the pure Form of "bed"; descending to the next level of bed is the carpenter's bed built for sleeping (the carpenter, according to Plato, builds his bed based on the Ideal or Form in ultimate reality of the bed); the lowest level is the artistic representation of the bed (a copy of the carpenter's bed). Plato's view is that the artistic representation of the bed is twice removed from the authority of the original and thus at least one level away from aspiring to the Ideal of the bed. Plato privileges a completely abstract, yet fully original, hence truthful, philosophy of knowledge. The closer one is to the abstract Form the closer one is to truth. Western Platonic "recollection" develops into what Deleuze and Guattari call "State philosophy"—also variously labeled "identity," "categorical thought," "representation," "recognition," "repetition of the Same," and "reterritorialization." In our tradition these terms are synonymous with logical thinking and what we typically call sense (*doxa*). When we speak of common sense (recognition and representation, for instance), we are always already speaking about something that has been determined.

Hypothetically, however, sense or making sense might be thought of as a territory. The philosophical tradition takes over sense—reterritorializes it—thereby defining and dictating how to participate in sense. To be recognized as enacting good sense, one must affirm the system's definition of good sense. In response to the Platonic tradition of good sense Deleuze argues in *The Logic of Sense* that sense is difficult to control because there is always already too much sense: "From the point of view of the structure, on the contrary, there is always too much sense."[43] This idea is strikingly similar to Derrida's objection to Austin's theory of language: the iterative potential of statements exceeds our ability to control meaning. There is something almost paranoid in the Platonic tradition concerning the safe-guarding of sense production, or for us, what we would call interpretation or meaning. What worries Plato, according to Deleuze, is that if he cannot control sense or meaning then his whole philosophical system—much like Austin's—will collapse. The solution for the Western Platonic tradition, buttressed by the "State philosophy," is to reterritorialize sense, suppress difference, thereby ensuring that reiteration and repetition is that of the Same. "State philosophy" would be a "soft power" option—perhaps in the form of an educational system or government, and perhaps promoted by local newspapers, television news, and reaffirmed in film, television programing, and music from the dominant culture.

The importance of understanding reiteration and repetition is paramount because of its current epistemological, ontological, and cultural ramifications. A nineteenth-century non-Platonist gives us a chillingly accurate twenty-first century example of repetition with this little tale:

> When the queen had finished telling a story at a court function and all the court officials, including a deaf minister, laughed at it, the latter stood up, asked to be granted the favor of also being allowed to tell a story, and then told the same story. Question: What was his view of the meaning of repetition? When a school teacher says:For the second time I repeat that Jespersen is to sit quietly—and the same Jespersen gets a mark for repeated disturbance, then the meaning of repetition is the very opposite.[44]

In the queen's-story example, the fact that the minister did not hear the first telling of the story—he laughs when others do because it is a good way to retain his head—makes the telling of his story independent from the queen's. So, despite the deaf minister telling the same story as the queen, he produces a repetition with *difference*. Difference is produced in a couple of ways. First, the deaf minister's story opens up the possibility of an ironic reading of the queen's story; irony, in this instance, functions similarly to parody, which could be a second way of reading the space opened by the deaf minister's story. A third manner of interpreting the deaf minister's story is blatantly political. By repeating the authoritative story, he violates the Same. The deaf minister produces difference. Jespersen's mark, on the other hand, although achieved through a repetition of disturbance, is a repetition of the Same. Jespersen's behavior earns him a second mark that verifies the original mark for the first disturbance. The second mark lends credibility to the first and to the authority of the system which records marks and punishes individuals. Jespersen may cause a thousand disturbances; but they would all be the Same in a system that has always already molded the action to fit the "mark," and thus, are absorbed by repetition of the Same.

It is not coincidental that this example of recollection and repetition with difference from Kierkegaard pertains to the preservation and violation of power. To preserve the system in place one reterritorializes; and to violate the system one deterritorializes. Now we can understand that although territory is hypothetically "neutral," there is very little territory in the world that is not quickly devoured by reterritorialization. Therefore, to produce American citations of British literature is first to deterritorialize; but the first movement is of service to the second, that of reterritorializing dominant images in order to control, regulate, and normalize in the image of commercial success.

Although Deleuze and Guattari privilege deterritorialization, when we invert their theory we can understand how the Americanization of British literature enacts "worldwide reterritorialization." In their book on Franz Kafka, Deleuze and Guattari discuss Kafka as well as writers such as Samuel Beckett who deterritorialize the major language tradition. To deterritorialize is to break up sense and the ability to make sense in traditional epistemological language use. A writer who deterritorializes and creates a minor tradition inside the major tradition is the writer who pushes sense into new spaces and creates something truly different. The major writer writes inside the dominant tradition, perhaps extending the tradition, but basically writing more of the Same. Kafka was a minor writer because of his texts, but also because the conditions or circumstances in which he produces his texts are unique: Kafka was a rural Czech Jew who chose to write in the major language—German. Deleuze and Guattari speculate that Kafka deliberately wrote to escape familial entrapment; the only way to defect from the father was to deterritorialize in language: "Because the father, as a Jew who leaves the country to settle in the city, is undoubtedly caught in a process of real deterritorialization; but he never stops reterritorializing, in his family, in his business, in the system of submissions and of his authorities."[45] Though the "father" could also be interpreted as the law of the father, as well as the "father land" (Germany), to undermine the "father" is to infiltrate his language and pervert sense.

Dominant Hollywood images produce a "major" normalized film tradition. To compare the minor and the major, a lucid example from

Kafka discusses Beckett and James Joyce because each writer grew up in or near Dublin; and although both were English speakers, Ireland was historically a Gaelic speaking island.[46] In discussing the major language tradition in relation to a minor writer who deterritorializes the tradition, Deleuze and Guattari position Joyce and Beckett accordingly:

> For these two possible paths, couldn't we find the same alternatives, under other conditions, in Joyce and Beckett? As Irishmen, both of them live within the genial conditions of a minor literature. That is the glory of this sort of minor literature—to be the revolutionary force for all literature.The utilization of English and of every language in Joyce.The utilization of English and French in Beckett. But the former never stops operating by exhilaration and over-determination and brings about all sorts of worldwide reterritorializations. The other proceeds by dryness and sobriety, a willed poverty, pushing deterritorialization to such an extreme that nothing remains but intensities.[47]

The Americanizaiton or "Hollywoodization" of British literature operates squarely in the major film tradition; and, like Joyce, it "never stops operating by exhilaration and overdetermination and brings about all sorts of worldwide reterritorializations." To understand the process that brings about these worldwide reterritorializations, we need to understand the minor tradition and deterritorialization. Minor literature, according to Deleuze and Guattari, has three characteristics: "the deterritorialization of language, the connection of the individual to a political immediacy, and the collective assemblage of enunciation."[48] The minor film tradition—if there exists such a designation—would have these three characteristics in analogous form. First, although not dubbed part of the minor tradition, independent films certainly correspond to a deterritorialization of the many "languages" of film: the films have political immediacy which is perhaps why they are ignored by the major film tradition; and the filmmakers speak for a group of people who might otherwise not have a voice (the fact that the film was even made is a political statement).

The films discussed in this book are decidedly not of the minor tradition. Rather, we can see that the films attempt to operate in the blockbuster, major film market through the process of reterritorialization. Instead of a deterritorialization of language, the American reterritorialization of film "language" happens at various formal, generic, stylistic, and even, of course, actual linguistic levels, either by standardizing expressions into American English or putting clichéd language into the mouths of British characters. Second, in opposition to "political immediacy," the political or potentially controversial (from the American standpoint) are removed or given "equivalents." Third, there is a "collective assemblage," but it is not deterritorializing; rather, it reterritorializes in line with the major cultural tradition of American film. Whatever might have been subversive in the territory of the British literature text is again translated, given an equivalent, or simply omitted.

The philosophical implication of this system is that it produces identity thinking that only *recognizes* what it already knows: a totalized system. According to Gilles Deleuze in *Difference and Repetition*, "The form of recognition has never sanctioned anything but the recognizable and recognized; form will never inspire anything but conformities."[49] Recognition functions in the philosophical "logic of identity," and that means we never have to *think* since thought has always already been subsumed under something recognizable. In terms of film, we are conditioned to recognize familiar patterns, from the narrative to casting to sequencing, and even as we enjoy what appears to be a new technique or some other kind of variation, we categorize, classify, and compare the new to films we already know. The political implication of this system is that it can convey an ideology that is accepted without question. According to Ryan and Kellner in *Camera Politica*, the film industry promotes certain "American" institutions and values, including capitalism, patriarchy, and racism.[50] From a formal perspective, according to Ryan and Kellner, "Films make rhetorical arguments through the selection and combination of representational elements that project rather than reflect a world. In so doing, they impose on the audience a certain position or point of view, and formal conventions occlude this positioning by erasing the signs of cinematic artificiality."[51] In terms of thematic conventions, the political implications are perhaps more obvious as "heroic male adventure, romantic quest, female melodrama, redemptive violence, racial and criminal stereotyping . . . promote ideology by linking the effect of reality to social values and institutions in such a way that they come to seem natural or self-evident attributes of an unchanging world."[52] Needless to say, millions of American film-goers desire to see and enjoy a film *because* they recognize the formal and thematic conventions that, it could be argued, "make sense" of the world by providing an illusion of "an unchanging world" in a world that is ever-changing.

As Deleuze and Guattari would argue, the American film industry has set a standard for the production of *desire*. According to Deleuze and Guattari, the political ramifications for the "desiring-machine" are the reterritorialization of desire in capitalist society through the primary function of the Oedipus complex which psychoanalysis enforces and perpetuates. Capitalism reduces all interpersonal relationships to a means of exchange or commodity. Through this commodification of social relations, capitalism gains control, deterritorializes desire by subverting productive, territorial desire and then reterritorializes desire by channeling all production toward the equivalence standard of exchange and commodity. The Oedipal triangle is a primary means of directing desire in order to control the masses in the capitalist society: all desire is concentrated, spent and bound in the configuration of the nuclear family. In the United States, the reterritorialization begins early with such corporations as Disney that target children and initiate them into capitalism and nuclear family; and, more importantly, Disney trains the child to desire to emulate their characters (e.g., little girls desire to be a "Princess"), and their various products (e.g., everything from films and cartoons to clothing, books, and toys based on Disney characters to vacations at Disneyland).[53] A quandary results when it becomes impossible to separate the individual from the culture that reterroritializes because, as Deleuze and Guattari stress, "desire can never be deceived":

> Interests can be deceived, unrecognized, or betrayed, but not desire. Whence Reich's cry: no, the masses were not deceived, they desired fascism, and that is what has to be explained. It happens that one desires against one's own interests: capitalism profits from this, but so does socialism, the party, and the party leadership.[54]

Capitalism, however, is incapable of creating values or even of creating desire *except* the desire to perpetuate itself. This point is essential to our understanding of Hollywood's—and even perhaps America's—hold on global capitialism and desire. Capitalism only has the capacitiy to create the axioms by which it keeps its system running; it cannot "code" values. Early in *Anti-Oedipus* Deleuze and Guattari state that: "unlike previous social machines, the capitalist machine is incapable of providing a code that will apply to the whole of the social field. By substituting money for the very notion of a code, it has created an axiomatic of abstract quantities that keeps moving further and further in the direction of the deterritorialization of the socius," and that in terms of desire, "Capitalism tends toward a threshold of decoding that will destroy the socius in order to make it a body without organs and unleash the flows of desire on this body as a deterritorialized field."[55] From this passage we understand that Deleuze and Guattari demarcate a line between previous economic state systems that had the ability to "code" values into the system. Feudalism, for example, bound the workers to the land (territorialized) and encoded them with a certain set of values. Capitalism frees the workers—deterritorializes them—from the "lord" and the land, but only temporarily, as Eugene W. Holland remarks, "This process of deterritorialization—detaching labor-power from means of production so that it becomes indeterminate 'labor-power in general'—is accompanied by a process of reterritorialization, which reattaches former peasants to new means of production: the looms of the nascent textile industry."[56]

It might, therefore, seem odd that capitalism deterritorializes with one hand as it reterritorializes with the other. Deleuze and Guattari see the *potential* of "world-wide deterritorializations," but critique the actualization of capitalist reterritorialization. Despite the creative possibilities of capitalist deterritorialization, deterritorialization is not a process of decoding (or coding) which is qualitative. When Deleuze and Guattari state that "by substituting money for the very notion of a code, it has created an axiomatic of abstract quantities that keeps moving further and further in the direction of the deterritorialization of the socius," they mean that money is the principle by which the system functions; and money only knows *more* money or surplus-value. Deterritorialization is quantitative not qualitative. Qualities or values might arise from capitalism, but they are by-products of the axiomatic that keeps the system intact. Therefore capitalism does not posit *value* in any society or system. If values are posited—and we often hear about "American family values," for instance—they are, according to Delueze and Guattari, a product of the axiomatics of capitalism. Capitialism creates axioms to keep itself functioning and needs to continually create new axioms, such as technological advances or outsourcing labor, to exist; but these axioms only concern the need to find surplus-value. Surplus-value guarantees investment capital which ensures capitalist investment in a new project (that seeks surplus-value); and so, the system perpetuates itself. Axiomatics are revised and invented all the time, but, as Holland theorizes:

> Whatever temporary local meanings capitalism does provide through recoding are strictly derivative of the axioms that happen to be in place: job-training and retraining, for instance, provide certain local meanings associated with manual labor; research projects in academic or corporate labs provide other meanings for intellectual work; taste-management through advertising provides still others for consumption, and so on. But they never "add up" to a stable global code or system of meanings[57]

This is essentially Willemen's argument that the expense of "blockbuster" film making necessitates the need for larger international investment, "[t]he capital-intensive nature of film production, and of its necessary industrial, administrative and technological infrastructures, requires a fairly large market in which to amortise production costs, not to mention the generation of surplus for investment or profit."[58] Thus, the reality of "new Hollywood" that is reliant on the "blockbuster" phenomenon is a near perfect analogy to the axiomatics of capitalism. Thomas Schatz discusses the fact that with the demise of the old, pre–Second World War system of Hollywood filmmaking, the "death of Hollywood" seemed imminent. Yet, as Schatz states, "the key to Hollywood's survival and the abiding aspect of its post-war transformation has been the steady rise of the movie blockbuster."[59] In "The New Hollywood" Schatz's cites the 1975 mega-hit *Jaws* as industry-changing "as a social, industrial and economic phenomenon of the first order, a cinematic idea and cultural commodity whose time had come."[60] In this way, the *Jaws* "phenomenon" created a new axiomatic: a new way to expand capitalism. Not only was the "summer blockerbuster" born in the mid-seventies, but film's recent discovery of television advertising, the emergence of pay-cable, and of the Betamax videotape recorder, which started the home-video revolution (1975), and its subsequent competition with VHS (1977), further shifted the industry away from pre-1970s expectations.[61] While pay-cable and home-video also created new axioms for Hollywood, Schatz also points out that blockbusters in the United States were exported to sell as well or even better overseas. According to Schatz, in the 1980s Hollywood continued to create new axioms:

> Another crucial secondary market for Hollywood has been the box office overseas, particularly in Europe. While the overseas pay-TV and home-video markets are still taking shape, European theatrical began surging in 1985 and reached record levels in 1990, when a number of top hits—including *Pretty Woman*, *Total Recall*, *The Little Mermaid* and *Dances with Wolves*—actually did better box office in Europe than in the US. The *Forbes* magazine has estimated that the European theatrical market will double by 1995, as multiplexing picks up in Western Europe and as new markets open in Eastern Europe.[62]

Hence, while it appears that Hollywood has a diabolical master plan for Americanizing the world, it actually has an axiomatic master plan for capitalizing the world. The difference between Americanizing and capitalizing the world may be neligible, since America itself only creates values as a by-product of capitalist axiomatics.

When American capitalism can sell a product at home or overseas, it sells it. The product reterritorializes, but the question is: does it recode potentially or in actuality? As noted above, Willemen posits that the high cost of making films "means that a film industry—any film industry—must address either an international market or a very large domestic one"; and therefore, he concludes, "If the latter is available, then cinema requires large potential audience groups, with the inevitable homogenising effects."[63] The question, however, is still: are the effects from a diabolical master plan to encode "American values," or an axiomatic capitalist plan to produce surplus-value? According to Deleuze and Guattari, the answer is the latter. Again, Holland is lucid on this matter: "Quantified flows under capitalism get conjoined solely on the estimation that this or that conjunction will produce surplus-value; such estimation involves economic calculation rather than belief; symbolic meaning has nothing to do with it."[64] Symbolic meaning is provided by the code and, in terms of film, it is theme or meaning we derive from watching it. "And the conjunction," Holland continues, "is direct, completely unmediated by codes; indeed, the qualities attributable to axiomatized flows *arise from* the conjunction itself, rather than pre-existing it."[65] As we will see in subsequent chapters, the qualities that arise from a product, even "quality" itself (e.g., in form of the heritage film in chapter 2), mean nothing to capitalist axiomatics.

Yet, reterritorialization *does* occur, and it, too, occurs at the two levels: axiomatic and symbolic (recoding). At the axiomatic level reterritorialization ensures that surplus-value is reinvested or reterritorialized for the ongoing expansion of capitalism. From the above example of the workers released (deterritorialized) from belonging to the land and to a master, we see that they are pulled back into the system (reterritorialized) by the need to earn a livelihood. That need literally reterritorializes them to cities and factory towns. The master evolves into the factory owner; the farmer or serf is transformed into the laborer in the factory. Perhaps reterritorialization is the most "diabolical" aspect of axiomatization because it "actualizes the power component of capitalism, the retrograde force that hinders development of new productive forces and, more importantly, prevents expenditure of surplus for purposes other than reinvestment in further surplus-production."[66] In terms of Hollywood ("new" and old Hollywood), the goal is to invest in known quantities, formulaic "blockbusters"; and this, as we will see, is how Hollywood appropriates British literature into its capitalist axiomatic machine. In this way, reterritorialization is a form of encoding or recoding, but it is "blind" symbolic coding.

Again, axioms carry no qualitative value. Reterritorialization occurs to preserve and perpetuate capitalism.

Thus, there is very little space devoted to "value" decoding or recoding in Deleuze and Guattari's analysis of capitalism. In fact, for Deleuze and Guattari the very terms decoding and especially recoding are increasingly useless as they move from *Anti-Oedipus* to *A Thousand Plateaus.* The reason is that capitalism's axiomatics reduce all interpersonal relationships to a means of exchange or commodity. Our discussion has come full circle, and we are faced with Reich's question: "How could the masses be made to desire their own repression?" Near the end of *Anti-Oedipus*, Deleuze and Guattari posit:

> Everyone in his class and his person receives something from this power, or is excluded from it, insofar as the great flow is converted into incomes, incomes of wages or of enterprises . . . But the investment of the flow itself and its axiomatic, which to be sure requires no precise knowledge of political economy, is the business of the unconsicous libido, inasmuch as it is presupposed by aims. We see the most disadvantaged, the most excluded members of society invest with passion the system that oppresses them, and where they always *find* an interest, since it is here that they search for and measure it. (italics in original)[67]

In the next volume of *Anti-Oedipus*, *A Thousand Plateaus* (1980, English translation, 1987), the capitalist axiomatic is characterized as singular in its ability to control (the Oedipal dimension of Deleuze and Guattari's theory is no longer necessary): "The four principle flows that torment the representatives of the world economy, or the axiomatic. . . . The situation seems inextricable because the axiomatic never ceases to create all of these problems, while at the same time its axioms, even multiplied, deny it the means of resolving them (e.g., the circulation and distribution that would make it possible to feed the world)."[68] Thus, the deterritorializations that make the circulation and distribution of all goods available worldwide are frustrated by the reterritorializations built into the system's axiomatics. Why should mid-West farmers sell food for little or no profit to feed people? Capitalist axiomatics dictates through supply-and-demand or through government subvention that to do so would be to deterritorialize out of the control of surplus-value axiomatic. Reterritorialization insures that the axiomatic for profit remains intact. Therefore, we can see that desire, too, is controlled and contained by the capitalist axiomatic.

An immediate response to Deleuze and Guattari's theory might be that America is the home of original thinking and "freedom of speech," but this is just so much reterritorialization in what sociologists call "dramaturgical" society. A dramaturgical society is "one in which technologies of social science, mass communication, theater and the arts are used to manage attitudes, behaviors, and feelings of the population in modern mass society."[69] According to this view, the technologies such as mass media and art promote notions of democracy, equality, individuality, creativity, and magnanimity that we wish to associate with a liberal democratic society, but all the while the few who control these technologies advance an elitist agenda. Contemporary American society conforms to Mary Jo Deegan's characterization of the structure of the dramaturgical society: "The structure of everyday life in a dramaturgical society is manipulated by elites who control symbols and images of the self and community that are incorporated into ritual events and products."[70] Deegan's research investigates two types of rituals: first, participatory rituals such as community events—dances, dinners, and amateur sports—in which individuals perform; and second, media-constructed rituals that are: "(1) constructed by professions who work in the mass media industry; (2) products that are present to an audience; and (3) organized by a set of rules portraying ritual action."[71] Media-constructed rituals function as leisure pursuits in our society; yet, as rituals we rarely examine why they are in place and if we even like them. Deegan argues that "fun" is coded into these leisure products so that we come to desire our own reterritorialization. "Fun" provides the illusion of escape from work, boredom, and the serious concerns of life. Instead of play, we get fun:

> American fun, nonetheless, provides its consumers with ritual experiences that are simultaneously attractive and alienating. This double-edged feature characterizes most media-constructed rituals in the U.S.A. Fun-producing rituals result when the "core codes," or pervasive and significant rules organizing everyday life in America . . . are imported into ritual events that could otherwise generate "play," community renewal, and culturally significant releases from the oppressive and repressive dimensions of our society.[72]

Accordingly, we can see that the media-constructed concept of fun is the reterritorialization of desire, whereas play deterritorializes. Yet, as Deleuze and Guattari point out, "difference in regime is greatest in the capitalist order of representation," because it needs to continually expand its axiomatics, which in terms of film, means that every film must appear "bigger, and better," appealing to the consumer's wish for something "new," when in fact, the consumer only recognizes "difference" inside of a philosophy and culture of identity.[73] Instead of difference and play, we get a new variation on "noodles, cars, or 'thingumajigs.' "[74]

America is still fascinated by the British, or as Glancy would term it the "British," the invented citational index of English and British iterations that Hollywood has reterritorialized. The American film industry keeps it simple for us: standard normalized images in familiar contexts, but nothing that would force us to think outside of identity—preprogramed "fun" for everyone. Of course, fun for Americans manifests itself in different ways. By the end of this book, the Americanization of British literature will have reterritorialized the Bard himself, and invented an English literary history that will soon be the official canonized version for college students all across the United States. The Oedipalized, castrated, insipid "Will" Shakespeare deterritorializes nicely from the stiff, unreadable, Elizabethan poet we encountered in school, to a reterritorialized hip, cool, all-around average film guy, Will.

CHAPTER 2

Heritage and Nostalgia: What Remains of *The Remains of the Day*

In Merchant-Ivoryesque films, then, class conflict takes the form of tension over relative levels of gentility. Once the less-genteel figures are vindicated, as by the film's end they inevitably are, we can all breathe a sigh of satisfaction, forgetting how limited the scope of inter-class tension has been. In many ways, these historical films function to efface the very social history they purport to portray; they provide North American viewers with a kind of sanitized, guilt-free nostalgia. It is, after all, the historical landscape of our trans-Atlantic cousins there on the screen, and while we are aware of empire and class injustices hovering somewhere beyond the movies' immediate social landscape, they trouble us not, as they do not signify any dirty historical laundry of our own.

Martin A. Hipsky[1]

Americanized British literary film adaptations are, generally speaking, wedded to notions of Britain's past that "mark" the work as nationalist, or as representing the nation. All the novels that I discuss are written by contemporary authors who, in 2006, are alive and still writing; yet, most of the novels' narratives take place in the past, concern the past, or interact with the past. Chapter 7, which focuses on Shakespeare, does not discuss at length any of the film adaptations of the plays, but rather looks at the Bard's postmodern "cult of personality," evidenced most sharply in *Shakespeare in Love* (screenplay by contemporaries John Madden and Tom Stoppard), set in late 1500s London. Like many of the films I discuss, *Shakespeare in Love* is considered a "costume drama."[2] The few novels and films discussed in the following chapters that have *contemporary* settings (roughly 1980s–2000s), rely on one of three strategies in order to "pass," or rather pass through, as nationalistically "British" novels and films: one, intertextuality with not only earlier British texts, but with an entire catalog of British historical and cultural citations (e.g., *Bridget Jones's Diary* with *Pride and Prejudice*); two, the contemporary period characters continually narrate the past (in the novel), which invariably gets translated into film as the "flashback" (e.g., *Waterland*); three, ironically, the novel that simply cannot "pass" as British because there is no American contemporary "translation" available or desirable (hence, marketable) becomes completely reterritorialized into an "American" film (e.g., *High Fidelity*). Therefore, although Hollywood does concentrate on the contemporary novel, the novels are often set in or dwell on the past. The cultural, economic, and social reasons for many novels, and in turn films, principally focused on the past are often attributed to the 1980s and early 1990s conservativism hallmarked by a postmodern nostalgia for values of an earlier era.

In "Nostalgia Isn't Nasty: The Postmodernising of Parliamentary Democracy," Wendy Wheeler argues that "nostalgia is not simply individual," but is a composite of "images" "fixed in our imaginations in the first place because they crystallize events and meanings which are already a part of our shared cultural symbolizations."[3] This nostalgia, Wheeler argues, should be viewed as more than "regressive sentimentalism" or the loss of historicity; rather "it is perhaps more useful to view it as an intense cultural expression of the desire for social forms capable of representing what is 'lost' in the experience of Enlightenment modernity."[4] Kantian Enlightenment modernity means that each citizen is not only responsible for abiding by the law, paying taxes, and performing routine civic duties, but also has the responsibility of debating issues and exercising critical thinking. This freedom of thought, of course, comes at the price of excluding all that does not fit this new model of thinking and "adult" expectation. Reason's other must be dispelled.[5] According to Wheeler, repression of all that does not fit into modernity's formula "re-emerges as a sense of uncanny (*unheimlich*), unhomely, self-estrangement and alienation."[6] Modernism has failed, and in its place is postmodernism's "return of the repressed"—the yearning for a pre-modern way of life—for desire to "return to a non-alienated condition, understood as something we have left behind us in the past."[7] In this chapter, and to some extent in all the chapters of this book, the contemporary novel seems to be looking for something left behind in Britain's past, *or* overtly attempting to move away from the legacy of colonialism or modernity (*Trainspotting* and *High Fidelity*, respectively).

Contemporary critics often discuss the specifics of the postmodern situation that allows nostalgia to take hold. Christopher Shaw and

Malcolm Chase demarcate three conditions that enable our era to yearn for an earlier period: "a secular and linear sense of time, an apprehension of the failings of the present, and the availability of evidences of the past."[8] With the first condition, we understand that our era is unique because not all periods or societies differentiate the past from the present; the last two conditions, are especially evident in the political rhetoric of the late 1970s and 1980s. The term *heritage* gained popular currency when the Thatcher administration pushed through the National Heritage Acts in 1980 and 1983. Robert Hewison analyzes the reality of this emerging growth sector in 1980s Thatcherite Britain: "Instead of manufacturing goods, we are manufacturing *heritage*, a commodity which nobody seems able to define, but which everybody is eager to sell."[9] *Heritage* is a diffusive word, and, as Hewison points out in his "Introduction," is defined by different people for different reasons. Yet, *heritage* in the British context means referencing certain eras, and certain versions of the national past. Everything from fashion to wine to local tourism to, of course, film indices citations from Britain's "glory days," such as pre-twentieth-century ruralism, colonial expansion, and monarchial history. Heritage, Hewison argues, is not history, and it celebrates a "heritage" that never really existed: "the heritage industry only draws a screen between ourselves and our true past. I criticise the heritage industry not simply because so many of its products are fantasies of a world that never was; not simply because at a deeper level it involves the preservation, indeed reassertion, of social values that the democratic progress of the twentieth century seems to be doing away with, but because, far from ameliorating the climate of decline, it is actually worsening it."[10] The climate of decline, loss of international power along with the growth of an increasingly multicultural and multiracial society (post–Second World War), has led many to speculate that British nostalgia functions "in the context of present fears, discontents, anxieties, or uncertainties."[11]

The fact that the heritage phenomenon has been a driving economic force since the 1980s, and that the heritage film, in particular, has acted as an ongoing mega-media advertisement for the heritage industry, means that it functions as a new axiom for capitalism. Undoubtedly, Hewison sees this new capitalist axiom as a weak one: How long can a society sell a fabricated past? How many new heritage museums to support local tourism can be opened and visited? In fact, it could be argued that the heritage film encodes symbolic value for other heritage enterprises such as the National Trust or English Heritage. Thus, if heritage seems to have limits—and remember capitalism must have expansion—it can rely on the heritage film to create desire for its products (not only the visiting and supporting of heritage sites, but also the buying of the huge range of heritage products marketed by the National Trust and English Heritage). Eugene Holland notes that "when extraction of surplus-value reduces buying-power to the point of threatening a crisis of over-production, axioms of marketing and advertising are added to bolster or fabricate consumer demand."[12] Thus, from the "local" British-heritage-industry perspective, heritage films may be considered part of the heritage industry, but function better axiomatically as "marketing and advertising" since the majority of heritage films are international in scope and, therefore, profit does not go directly into the local economy (like the basket-weaver's goods sold at the local English Heritage castle shop and tea room).

From the British economic perspective, heritage films could be considered extremely long, successful commercials for the British tourist industry. In fact, the "official travel guide to Britain," "VisitBritain's" website not only features recent and forthcoming "British" films, but also the filming locations and their tourist attractions. Thus, the citations utilized in the films very often create a desire to "see the real thing" in Great Britain. According to Amy Sargeant, the "touristic tie-in" has become big business for certain regions, and this activity is not restricted to the heritage film. There are now such tourist sites as the "dole office in *The Full Monty*" or the tie-in for "the making of" location guides that are now being successfully marketed to tourists:

> Current touristic tie-ins are not unique to historical drama. The East Midlands Film Commission's publication "On Location" (available free from all good information centres in the area) gives the locations for *Pride and Prejudice* and also for *Peak Practice*, and characters from this production are in turn used to advertise the Peak National Park . . . . Popular interest shifted last year from *the* lake that Darcy swam through to *that* dole office in *The Full Monty* (Peter Cattaneo, 1998). What interests me here is that the fact of filming at a particular location seems to attract public interest rather more than what was actually filmed. Perhaps location tourism owes as much to the perceived glamour and glory of the activity of making and selling cinema as to any particular film's subject matter. The activity of filming historic reconstruction is further celebrated in such Penguin tie-ins as *The Making of Pride and Prejudice* and *The Making of Jane Austen's Emma*, and coverage by the magazine *Homes and Antiques* of the making of *Vanity Fair*, authenticated by the involvement of production crew.[13]

The reality of the heritage industry, and, to some extent, any television or film project, is that any "authentically British" product (filmed on location) reinforces and renews this new capitalist axiomatic. In terms of heritage, a genre formula emanated from such 1980s films as *Chariots of Fire* (1981), *Another Country* (1984), *A Passage to India* (1985), *A Room with a View* (1986), *A Handful of Dust* (1987), and *Maurice* (1987). Three of these six films are Ismail Merchant (Indian) and James Ivory (American) productions—dubbed the "Laura Ashley school of filmmaking," and the biggest production team of heritage films.[14] The concept that heritage has come of age as a genre has been given much critical attention, even as the genre mutates and evolves.

As Claire Monk has recently noted, the term *heritage* was originally used by Charles Barr "with reference not to the 1980s films but to certain patriotic British films of the 1940s which had drawn upon aspects of the 'national heritage,' from *This England* (David MacDonald, 1941) to *Henry V* (Laurence Olivier, 1944) to *A Canterbury Tale* (Michael Powell, and Emeric Pressburger, 1944)."[15] These films were made to whip-up support for Britain's Second World War effort by presenting "England," or Britain, as having a long and unified history and moral purpose. There is a curious parallel to the dire needs of 1940s blitzed Britain and the 1980s nostalgic Thatcher years. In any case, the fact that Britain had a national cinema genre that concentrated on patriotic and historical aspects of the British heritage has deep roots. What happens in the 1980s to the heritage film is that while its subject matter is British or English history, the film is usually "British" in the way that Mark Glancy discusses the Hollywood "British" films of the prewar era. As Monk states, " 'British' period film successes are repeatedly made by non-British personnel with non-British money, and measured in terms of their reception and commercial performance abroad. Indeed, a case could be made that they have *characteristically* been products of international funding, migrancy or collaboration" (italics in original), and this is most clearly evidenced in "the highly international self-styled 'wandering company' Merchant Ivory Productions and the list of the 1990s 'British' period film hits backed by Miramax and other US studios."[16] The British heritage film has been colonized by Hollywood not only in terms of financial backing and talent, but in terms of the way in which it has affected the evolution of the genre into a commodity that can be sold to mainstream America. One only has to measure the distance between *Chariots of Fire* (1981) and *Shakespeare in Love* (1998) to fully appreciate the development, growth, and commercialization of the "quality" heritage film.

Therefore, when critics such as John Hill claim that "if the British heritage film is involved in the construction of a particular version of the national past and the national culture, it also does so in a way which distances itself from the mainstream conventions of Hollywood,"[17] it is clear that they have not been paying attention to the subtle blurring of technique or to the huge American consumer market that came of age in the pre-*Terminator* era. That demographic (baby boomers), along with younger middle-class, college-educated movie goers, buy into the cross-over film. Similar to the way the film industry adapted to the success of the summer release of *Jaws* in 1975, the industry has adapted to the success of the heritage film of the 1980s to create the blockbuster films of the 1990s such as *Howards End* (1992), *The Remains of the Day* (1993), and the various Austen and Shakespeare adaptations, including the marketed as such, but failed, "blockbuster" *Mansfield Park* (1999), the successful *Richard III* (1995), and the super-successful *Shakespeare in Love* (1998). The claims that heritage films are anticinematic, and that they are over-dependent upon material detail, and hence, "feminine," have been key critiques of the heritage film. Quoting Patrick Wright in an early seminal article on the heritage film, Andrew Higson asserts that the skewed perspective that the heritage film presents creates a certain kind of aesthetic: "In this version of history, a critical perspective is displaced by decoration and display, a fascination with surfaces, 'an obsessive accumulation of comfortably archival detail' in which a fascination with style displaces the material dimensions of historical context. The past is reproduced as flat, depthless pastiche, where the reference point is not the past itself, but other images, other texts."[18]

The heritage film's presentation of the "past" is actually a reflection of the anxiety of contemporary life. One significant issue in the 1980s was the emergence of "gay liberation," as well as moral and health issues in relation to homosexuality, brought to the fore by the AIDS epidemic. Films such as *Another Country* and *Maurice* dramatize sexual desire in the cloistered homosocial world of Edwardian England. Alison Light asserts that "the return to Edwardian England in the '80s is as much a rejection of Thatcherism and its ethics as a crude reflection of it . . . What the films have picked up on is the romantic longing within liberalism for making unions despite differences of nationality, sexuality, social class."[19] The fact that Merchant Ivory's *Maurice* features homosexual unions would naturally lead one to think that the latent homosexual desire Stevens displays in reference to Darlington in the novel *The Remains of the Day* would find its outlet in the eponymous film. But the Merchant Ivory production of *Maurice* has been criticized for *heterosexualizing* homosexuality. Thus, Stevens's closeted desire for Darlington is not "outted" in the film; rather, the unrequited heterosexual union between Stevens and Miss Kenton is the driving force of the film's narrative.

At the same time that the audience is enjoying the many attempts on the part of Miss Kenton to interest Stevens in a mutual game of heterosexual desire, it is also caught up in the film's heritage nostalgia. However, it is my argument that, for Americans in particular, the heritage or nostalgia aspect of the film is not triggered by British heritage sentiment. Rather, the film *The Remains of the Day* creates an analogy between the filmic postwar Britain and the 1990s American audience: each country is past the pinnacle of its power in what remains of each country's "day." Perhaps American viewers are primarily unconscious of this analogy, but this chapter shows that Americans enjoy the English heritage "nostalgic" experience of *The Remains of the Day* as a catharsis of emotional nostalgia concerning America's great postwar empire of global capitalist hegemonic control. As discussed in chapter 1, U.S. hegemony commenced at the beginning of the twentieth century, hit its zenith at the end of the Second World War, and, it could be argued, is in decline at the end of the twentieth century and beginning of the twenty-first. Flint reminds us that Britain followed a similar course:

> The establishment of the British Empire came toward an end of Britain's hegemonic reign; the need to exert territorial control through physical presence is a sign of hegemonic weakness rather than of strength (James, 1994; Kennedy 1987). In the past, great powers have entered a spiral of decline as they have become 'overstretched' in the need to police challenges to their power . . . contemporary U.S. military strength and political commitment do not seem strong enough at the moment to dismiss the possibility that we are seeing military adventurism that is the rearguard action of hegemonic decline, rather than the construction of a new period of hegemonic rule.[20]

The "first" Gulf War initiated by George H. W. Bush unfolded in 1991 and could be interpreted as the beginning of "military adventurism that is the rearguard action of hegemonic decline," and has been furthered by George W. Bush in Afghanistan and Iraq. The continuity of the analogy between British heritage and American nostalgia is established when we contemplate the fact that nostalgia is never a yearning for a personally lived or individual experience. From a British perspective, the film mourns the loss of empire and dwells upon all those quintessential British heritage places and objects: the English countryside, manor houses, servant quarters, lovingly shot details of the furniture, paintings, and costumes.

Yet from an American point of view, the film celebrates the ascendancy of America as a world power from the Second World War on, and at the same time creates nostalgia for that lost era of emerging greatness and dominance. Moreover, Britain had Thatcher; the United States had Reagan. In Britain, Thatcherism looked back to the 1930s as an era of "self-reliance," that "stiff dose of Victorian Values, transplanted from the very decade, the 1930s, when they had allegedly, last held sway. . . . Along with the rehabilitation of the Thirties as an age of robust self-reliance came the soft-focus discourse of 'heritage' which all but silenced the modernizing critiques of the Sixties: the past was now a good place to visit."[21] In the United States, the 1980s saw such Hollywood productions as the *Rambo* films (1982, 1985, and 1988) and the *Indiana Jones* trilogy—the latter described by Susan Aronstein as "Reaganite entertainment" that functions as a "part of Lucas and Spielberg's attempt to restore the individual citizen's faith in America as the 'promised land,' sanctioned to interfere in the affairs of its neighbors by its divine mission and moral superiority."[22]

In fact, American audiences can comfortably understand the film *The Remains of the Day* through the Lucas and Spielberg films because the action of the *Indiana Jones* films includes the same set of variables—a Nazi-infested world in the mid-to-late 1930s—and, in *The Temple of Doom*, "Indy" helps the British Empire win over evil, a formula uncannily similar to that of *The Remains of the Day*. The context for the filmic *The Remains* has near-perfect precursors: an evil (savages or Nazis), bumbling British aristocrats, loyal servants, and American heroes. In the film *The Remains of the Day*, Darlington is both a Nazi and a bumbling British aristocrat, while the American Lewis, who is put down by Darlington and his European cronies, after the war triumphantly conquers Darlington with his purchase of Darlington Hall. The problem, however, with the timing of the release of *The Remains* is that Reagan's "Teflon-man" appeal could only carry George W. H. Bush through one term, not to mention the first Gulf War. Perhaps ironically, the 1993 release of *The Remains* meant that for some a yearning for Reaganite confidence might be the object of the viewer's nostalgia. This nostalgia is triggered after the fall of Reaganite confidence and Reagan's ability to promote the state-supported American capitalist axiomatics in the late 1980s:

> Ronald Reagan's use of rhetoric allowed him, in the words of Robert Kolker, to "enact an extraordinary phenomenon. With the actor's

> talent for assuming a persona requisite to the situation at hand, and a national audience ready to become subject to a discourse of security, power, and self-righteousness, he was able to focus various ideological elements' into a new, conservative consensus. Reagan's ability to focus these elements waned, however, during the Iran-Contra scandal of 1986–1987, an event that, coupled with the increasing attention given by the press to the social problems of the homeless and the urban poor, led to the end of the conservative hegemony and the conservatives' loss of 'their ability to advertise specific interests of wealthy, white males as universal interests.' "[23]

The Reagan era itself, much like Thatcher's in Britain, nostalgically called for a return to values of a white (male) nationalistic past. Thus, for an American audience, *The Remains of the Day* is a nostalgic look at the U.S. glory days of the 1950s, as the film imitates Hollywood's 1980s and 1990s films featuring an American hero (Senator Lewis) who saves the British (everyone in Britain, including Stevens) from those nasty Nazis (Lord Darlington, Ribbontrop, Hitler's army).

The cross-over successes of *Howards End* and *The Remains of the Day* were due in large part to the Merchant Ivory Production Company's establishing a partnership with Sony Picture Classics. Although Merchant Ivory Productions next established a partnership with Disney, Columbia (a subsidiary of Sony) financed and released *The Remains of the Day.* In this chapter, I wish to show that the film *The Remains of the Day* utilizes three key elements of the novel in order to cash in on the heritage boom. First, the film captures the novel's quest to return to a lost England by simply displaying idyllic English landscape—from the grounds of the estate to the rustic countryside to quaint towns on Stevens's journey. The novel's narrative during this quest is parodic of the interwar era of "Little Englander" discourse which, of course, the film cannot replicate *except* by showing us in a highly effective way this fantasy England. The second and third elements involve the narrative structure of the film, which must be fairly straightforward and accessible. Thus, the film pulls from the novel its two most overt features: one, the "Nazi plot" which involves Darlington's participation in the "appeasement" of Germany in the 1930s; two, the would-be romance between Stevens (Anthony Hopkins) and Miss Kenton (Emma Thompson). The co-plot of the British aristocrat's appeasement of Nazi Germany in the late 1930s provides key heritage elements: the manor house, rich and powerful people, elegant dinner parties that showcase the servants as well as the aristocracy. As this chapter reveals, Ruth Prawer Jhabvala's screenplay heavily emphasizes the culpability of both Lord Darlington and Stevens during the 1930s.

The real dramatic action, then, is principally in the past; and the film's present-day action of the 1950s is de-emphasized from that in the novel. One reason for the film's emphasis on the past is that the medium cannot successfully produce narrative subjectively. Although narrative subjectivity is utilized at the beginning of the film with Miss Kenton's voice-over—which condenses scores of textual pages provided by Stevens (the sole narrative voice of the novel) concerning Lord Darlington, the period, Stevens's situation, as well as that of Miss Kenton—the film cannot sustain this view throughout the entire film. Another advantage in emphasizing the story in the past is that budding love between two young people is typically more marketable for a film than a romance between older individuals. An additional box-office bonus of Hopkins as Stevens and Thompson as Kenton is that they filled the starring roles of Merchant Ivory's *Howards End* the previous year. Casting the same "quality" actors, often associated with British theater (e.g., Judi Dench, Vanessa Redgrave), is a staple of the heritage genre. In E.M. Forster's novel the May–December relationship between Margaret Schegel (Emma Thompson) and Henry Wilcox (Anthony Hopkins) is consummated through marriage. *Howards End* contextualizes the romance of *The Remains of the Day*. Thus, the expectation is that Stevens will be able to communicate—finally—his love to Kenton.

The first-person narration by Stevens in the novel poses several interpretative problems in terms of memory, culpability, and sexual orientation. When Stevens narrates the past, we have only his version of events; when Stevens distances himself from Lord Darlington's pro-Nazi views thereby exonerating himself, we know only what he tells us; when Stevens longs for the return of Miss Kenton and remembers events leading up to her departure, the reader typically interprets this longing as repressed romantic and sexual desire. Since the film cannot capture the subtlety of the narrative—nor would it be particularly marketable to do so—it captures the broad strokes of the book's narrative: the relationship between Stevens and Kenton, and the ever-popular Hollywood "Nazi plot." In the novel, the relationship between Stevens and Kenton, however, could be interpreted as unrequited love on the part of Miss Kenton. Stevens's utter devotion to Lord Darlington and his repulsion to female intimacy is easily translated into homosexual desire that can be seen as "closeted." Stevens deliberately leads the reader to believe that he not only regrets his "service" to Lord Darlington, but that he also regrets losing Miss Kenton through his failure to express his love for her. Yet, this reading is only the most obvious because we live in a normatively heterosexual society. Stevens's narrative is *so conventionally formal* that irony and, hence, duplicity is blatant. Stevens's public self will not allow him to act "out"; therefore, he must play the scrupulous butler to the maximum in order to undermine his very narrative.

In fact, the novel's sophisticated presentation of Stevens's closeted public self may be viewed as an enactment of postmodern humor that is one step beyond irony. Irony is typically easy to detect because it follows the rules of representation and operates in the realm of "good sense." Humor, however, is that which plays on the surface of signification before, or at the point of, sense or meaning. Deleuze theorizes that we have passed beyond the order that privileges representation and the individual: subjectivity is a precondition for both tragedy and irony. Irony gives way to humor—which does not rely on representation and privileges neither subjectivity nor objectivity—for this new "sense" does not prioritize on a model of hierarchy: "The tragic and the ironic give way to a new value, that of humor. . . . Humor is the art of the surfaces and the doubles, of nomad singularities and of the always displaced aleatory point."[24] I argue that we are beyond irony in this text, as evidenced by the nuanced manner in which Stevens's narrative portrays his relationship with Miss Kenton and Darlington. The enactment of humor presents a subtle and surreptitious repetition of the category of representation; it makes the gesture of resemblance in the very act of discrediting and dismantling the heterosexual representational order. Stevens is not naïve, and we should keep in mind that there is an "element of contempt in the submission" to representation that the text's "apparent obedience conceals a criticism and a provocation."[25] Indeed, Stevens appears to be obedient in all things—except his own closeted desire for Lord Darlington.

Stevens is outwardly a heterosexual English butler overtly loyal to his English "master" and all that he represents. Yet, the double narrative calls into question England's place in the world in the postwar era, the empire legacy, and social conventions that maintain the heterosexual norm. For the film version, Stevens *should* question Lord Darlington's judgment as part of the "Nazi plot," which allows the American hero, Senator Lewis, to perform his Indiana Jones role. In terms of sexual duplicity, by the 1993 release the heritage film was turning into the "post-heritage" film and Stevens's duplicity could have easily been adapted to make the film more complex. Ability to sell to mainstream U.S. markets might have prohibited Merchant Ivory to deviate from the 1992 success of *Howards End*. Certainly, critics such as Claire Monk noted that mainstream Hollywood liked sex, but not nonheterosexual sex:

> What most unites the post-heritage films is undoubtedly an overt concern with sexuality and gender, particularly non-dominant gender and sexual identities: feminine, non-masculine, mutable, androgynous, ambiguous. In an increasingly international production context, in which the label "British film" becomes ever more meaningless, the insistence on filming left-field sexual narratives can simply be seen as a strategy of product differentiation—from other European cinemas, even other European heritage cinemas, as much as from Hollywood. But nonetheless the transgressive sexual politics of the post-heritage film places it in genuine opposition to a 1990s Hollywood-defined mainstream. From *Orlando's* transportation of its hero/ine through two genders and four centuries, the preoccupations of the post-heritage films would be found unthinkably deviant, both sexually and commercially, by the Hollywood of *Basic Instinct* and *Disclosure*, the Hollywood of predatory and punitive sexual politics, of Sadeian women and pro-family messages.[26]

For whatever reason, the novel's sexual duplicity is avoided by the filmmakers. One has to assume that the primary reason for the "straight" role of Stevens is the obvious marketing advantage of the romantic liaison between the tested coupling of Hopkins and Thompson the year before.

Territory: "Deep England"

The heritage film is devoted to presenting the upper classes or aristocrats, the country, and, in particular, the country house on a sculpted estate property, where the location is typically that of the Home Counties. In *The Pleasures of the Past*, David Cannadine caustically describes the actual "heritage" that the heritage film presents as one that belonged to a very select few in the past, but adds that, with the advent of heritage film, "national" history becomes inclusive: "the very idea of a 'national' heritage . . . is often little more than a means of preserving the artifacts of an essentially elite culture, by claiming—in most cases quite implausibly—that it is really everybody's."[27] Everybody is not of course *everybody*, as Patrick Wright's description of the emergence of the notion of "Deep England" testifies. Wright is critical of the interwar-period English jingoism propagated by such writers as Stanley Baldwin or J. B. Priestly. Wright quotes Baldwin's text to show that there is barely anything that clearly demarcates what this "Deep England" constitutes:

> The sounds of England, the tinkle of the hammer on the anvil in the country smithy, the corncrake on a dewy morning, the sound of the

> scythe against the whetstone, and the sight of a plough team coming over the brow of a hill, the sight that has been seen in England since England was a land, and may be seen in England long after the Empire has perished and every works in England has ceased to function for centuries the one eternal sight of England.[28]

Wright criticizes the nostalgia of these writers who construct this vague "Deep England" during the interwar era as a way to preserve an indigenous "heritage" against the imminent tides of change. The novel *The Remains of the Day* could be described as a pastiche of the interwar period of English-heritage celebration of the land (as we discuss below). Visually, what the book does not actually provide, James Ivory can certainly fill in. An example of this visualization of "Deep England" is presented, un-self-consciously in John Pym's coffee-table book *Merchant Ivory's English Landscape: Rooms, Views and Anglo-Saxon Attitudes*, which describes the scene (created for the film) of the English fox hunt:

> The scene is a pure picture of Old England: ladies and gentlemen, clad in scarlet and navy blue, seated with assurance on handsome horses, greeting one another as old friends, confident of who they are and where they've come from. The staff pass among the horses with stirrup cups; Lord Darlington emerges from his house and, strolling among his guests, greets the Master of Foxhounds. Then, suddenly, amid the generalized bustle, the scene is given dramatic focus: Stevens, the invisible, ever-present servant, is observed impassively holding up a cup that an unseen rider never troubles to take. The hunt then rides away, majestically, and the scene ends.[29]

Stevens is one of Hipsky's "less-genteel" figures and is definitely not the focus of the film at this point. In fact, up to now the audience has only been privy to the auction of the art and furniture from Darlington Hall and shots of the grounds with a voice-over from Miss Kenton. Though this scene does not appear in the book, we can easily imagine it *could have*—and it is for this reason that the novel is a perfect candidate for a Merchant Ivory production.

While there are several articles on the novel and national identity, such as "Refiguring National Character: The Remains of the British Estate Novel" by John J. Su, criticism of the novel has yet to fully investigate the curious historical parallels between 1956 and Ishiguro's having written the novel in the 1980s, namely in its relation to the 1982 Falklands crisis, and the growing discord between the white English and "colored" immigrants from Britain's former colonial empire. Su focuses on novels that feature the English country estate: "I will argue that nostalgia is essential to the effort in both *Brideshead Revisited* and *The Remains of the Day* to reenvision what constitutes 'genuine' Englishness."[30] Unquestionably, Darlington's estate is the place of focus for many of Stevens's memories; yet it is the landscape of England that is always before him as he "motors" away on his quest from Darlington Hall toward Little Compton, where he goes to persuade Miss Kenton to return to the estate. The landscape he sees and the people he encounters often prompt the narrator's confessions, memories, and musings. Stevens's quest to recover "Deep England" on his journey is not a quest to restore the nation that has an empire, but the nation the greatness of which is *indigenous.*

The most overt interpretation of the territory of the novel *The Remains of the Day* is the interior dialogue of a man who is on a quest to reunite with his lost love, Miss Kenton, whom he allowed to leave Darlington Hall twenty years prior to the narrative. This perspective opens up a romantic reading of the novel, and ignores Stevens's ambiguous closeted narrative. This selective perspective also removes much of the political repercussions of July 1956 which, as many critics have discussed at length, is the very month of the Suez Canal crisis. The quest romance (*roman*) novel features a hero who develops through a series of trials in order to gain the quest object. Ironically, *The Remains of the Day* presents us with an antihero, a "real old English butler," who has recently been "sold" along with Darlington Hall lock, stock, and barrel to a rich American, Farraday, whose primary interest in his purchase is English authenticity.[31] Contrary to the quest, the narrative ends without Stevens winning Miss Kenton (now Mrs. Benn), as he rather pathetically, and certainly antiheroically, contemplates all that "remains of his day": mastering his ability to "banter" with his American employer who enjoys this un-English type of conversation. One interesting feature of the traditional quest romance is the fact that the person on the quest encounters landscapes that are manifestations of his/her psychological state. The physicality of place stands in for desires, ideas, and, in *The Remains of the Day*, an entire ideology that Stevens intimately attaches to his identity as a (former) top butler by metonymically linking Englishness to the landscape. Thus, Stevens perceives himself as quintessentially English; and this is manifested everywhere he looks on his journey—the landscape—conveyed to us through the narrative.

As Stevens moves through the countryside, his objective is to "find" Englishness (Deep England). He tries to forget the British Empire: all the connections, lands, and people who have sullied the purity of English landscape. The empire is represented by Darlington, and the prewar mistakes Darlington made. British imperial history is also silently represented by Darlington Hall, which was most assuredly "built" on colonial profits.[32] In terms of the empire, one unique feature of England is its weather, which is distinct from that of most of the colonial territories. The "English weather" has been theorized as an important identifying feature of nationalism by Homi K. Bhabha. Similar to Stevens's narrative, the Englishness of English weather evokes its opposite, the Other on the other side of the world, which can never be English:

> To end with the English weather is to invoke, at once, the most changeable and immanent signs of national difference. It encourages memories of the "deep" nation crafted in chalk and limestone; the quilted downs; the moors menaced by the wind; the quiet cathedral towns; that corner of a foreign field that is forever England. The English weather also revives memories of its daemonic double: the heat and dust of India; the dark emptiness of Africa; the tropical chaos that was deemed despotic and ungovernable and therefore worthy of the civilizing mission.[33]

As his journey progresses, Stevens attempts to "forget" the "daemonic double"—the English landscape has the power to exclude the empire and its colonial citizen.[34] Early in the novel, "Day One—Evening—Salisbury," it is clear that the English landscape is an index of nationality or national pride for Stevens. In this narrative he recounts his day's journey, from his anxiety in leaving Darlington Hall alone to his motoring out of Oxfordshire, his adventures and thoughts along the way, and now his setting down of these events in a guest house in the city of Salisbury. In the prologue, Stevens states that he has "spent many minutes examining the road atlas, and perusing also the relevant volumes of Mrs. Jane Symons's *The Wonder of England*":

> If you are not familiar with Mrs. Symons's books—a series running to seven volumes, each one concentrating on one region of the British Isles—I heartily recommend them. They were written during the thirties, but much of it would still be up to date—after all, I do not imagine German bombs have altered our countryside so significantly. Mrs. Symons was, as a matter of fact, a frequent visitor to this house before the war; indeed, she was among the most popular as far as the staff were concerned due to the kind appreciation she never shied from showing. . . . But this was, as I say, back in the thirties, when as I understand, Mrs. Symons's books were being admired in houses up and down the country. (11–12)

As a frequent visitor to Darlington Hall before the war, Mrs. Symons would have most assuredly been among Lord Darlington's friends and associates who sympathized with and supported German interests. Other "frequent visitors" to Darlington Hall before the war include the infamous Sir Oswald Mosley, who headed the English pro-Nazi "blackshirts" organization. The fact that Mrs. Symons frequented the house in the 1930s tells us a great deal about her English travel books. The traveler's reliance on travel literature to "see" for him/her, to guide him/her to the "kind of" places the traveler will "want" to go must have ideological motivations. We rely on these texts, as Edward Said argues, "when the uncertainties of travel in strange parts seem to threaten one's equanimity."[35] Because any place outside of the estate grounds of Darlington Hall is strange, Stevens relies on Mrs. Symons, not only for her advice in regard to his tour, but also to comfort him and reassure him of his own position in the world. Mrs. Symons stands in as a representative of Darlington Hall: the politics, the parties, the people, the well-polished silver.

It is difficult to underestimate the comfort that Stevens receives from Symons's *The Wonder of England*. He states in the first few paragraphs of "Day One—Evening—Salisbury" that the landscape seemed familiar until he approached the Berkshire border, when "the surroundings grew unrecognizable and I knew I had gone beyond all previous boundaries" (23–24). For a man well into his sixties who has lived his entire life in England, to state that crossing into the next county is going "beyond all previous boundaries" seems odd. The idea, too, that Stevens could not "recognize" his surroundings seems more cryptic than stating that one simply has not been to that particular place before. Symons's *The Wonder of England* has not prepared Stevens for what it would *feel* like to cross into unrecognizable territory, and Stevens elaborates on the "alarm" it produced in him:

> I have heard people describe the moment, when setting sail in a ship, when one finally loses sight of the land. I imagine the experience of unease mixed with exhilaration often described in connection with this moment is very similar to what I felt in the Ford as the surroundings grew strange around me. This occurred just after I took a turning and found myself on a curving around the edge of a hill. I could sense the steep drop to my left, though I could not see it due to the trees and thick foliage that line the roadside. The feeling swept over me that I had truly left Darlington Hall behind, and I must confess I did feel a slight sense of alarm—a sense aggravated by the feeling that I was perhaps not on the right road at all, but speeding off in totally the wrong direction into a wilderness. (23–24)

From this passage we understand that the landscape is a reflection of Stevens's psychological state. However frightening it may be to leave Darlington Hall—*albeit* with *The Wonder of England*—for the first time in decades to embark on a motoring trip, the idea, even in the 1950s, that anywhere in England could be a fearful "wilderness," especially while one is in a car and on a road, is absurd. Stevens is projecting onto the landscape his temporary fear of displacement and more tellingly a lack of total control over his environment (controlling every aspect of Darlington Hall has been Stevens's life work); to be thrust out into the "wilderness" of unrecognizable English landscape is almost too much for such a man out of time. The inability to recognize the landscape correlates to the way we see landscape painting; the fact that English landscape painting is a quintessential English icon also resonates within the text. Erwin Strauss theorizes that the landscape painting dissolves the actual landscape and renders something that is not in the landscape: "Landscape painting does not depict what we see, i.e., what we notice when looking at a place, but—the paradox is unavoidable—it makes visible the invisible, although it be as something far removed. . . . Landscape is invisible, because the more we absorb it, the more we lose ourselves in it."[36] This idea holds true of an image of landscape—a photograph, a memory, a description.

Knowing that Stevens is completely anachronistic in all things from cultural references to motoring "costumes," we will assume his map is from roughly the same period as the fictionalized *The Wonder of England*, which he reads for pleasure as well as information. It apparently never occurs to Stevens that roadways might have altered through new construction or land development; even if "German bombs" did not manage to "alter" the countryside, perhaps English engineers have altered the roads or routes since the 1930s. Consulting the 1937 *Baedeker's Great Britain*, we may note that Stevens begins his journey in Oxfordshire, travels southward to Salisbury, and west to Taunton. After meeting with Mrs. Benn in Little Compton, Cornwall, he drives east to Weymouth, and expects to leave Weymouth early the next morning in order to be back at Darlington Hall by tea time. It is a six-day journey with day five "lost"; presumably upset, Stevens drives to Weymouth. While there is no literal Little Compton, Cornwall, there is an actual place called Little Compton in Warwickshire near the western Oxfordshire boundary. Fidelity to verisimilitude is not important, but it is curious how in terms of place names Stevens could arrive at Little Compton on the very day he begins a six-day journey. This detail could give rise to the speculation that Stevens's narrative is so unreliable that he, in fact, never ventured away from Darlington Hall—that the entire narrative is a fantasy.

Stevens's quest is to separate what is English, and thus England, from what is British, and hence, foreign. The postwar time-frame features India's independence, the Suez Canal crisis, and then the independence of "little countries," beginning with Africa in 1958. In Ishiguro's time-frame we have the culmination of the postwar events augmented by such political figures as Sir Oswald Mosly, Enoch Powell, and Margaret Thatcher. The 1950s and 1980s are perceived as analogous to the 1930s in British history, as British historian Jeremy Black points out:

> Just as references to the appeasement of dictators in the 1930s were initially to be expressed when the Argentineans invaded the Falklands in 1982, and it was thought, misleadingly, that the Thatcher government would not respond, most prominently by the Labour Leader Michael Foot; so, in 1956, the Prime Minister, Anthony Eden, was determined to act. He had resigned as Foreign Secretary in 1938 ostensibly in protest at appeasement, and saw Nassar as another Fascist dictator.[37]

Egyptian leader Gamal Abdel Nassar not only nationalized the Suez Canal but also pursued Arab nationalism, which was threatening to both Britain and French interests in Algeria. The poorly planned British invasion to restore access to the Suez Canal was further frustrated by America's lack of support for Britain.[38] British Ambassador Sir Roger Makins portended the future when in January 1954 he declared that "the Americans are out to take our place in the Middle East."[39]

Stevens's England is withdrawing from the world stage. America is taking over not only Darlington Hall in the form of Farraday, but literally the world at the same time when Stevens is personally withdrawing from Lord Darlington and his past of service to him. Stevens is in a crisis state that mirrors the British Empire—and its remains—in 1956, *and* English national identity near the end of Thatcher's administration. The framing of the novel in terms of the English countryside begins even before the trip starts, but on Stevens's very first day of observations, while neatly ensconced in the city of Salisbury, he discusses the English countryside as evidence of the temperament of the nation:

> Now I am quite prepared to believe that other countries can offer more obviously spectacular scenery. Indeed, I have seen in encyclopedias and the *National Geographic Magazine* breathtaking photographs of sights from various corners of the globe; magnificent canyons and waterfalls, raggedly beautiful mountains. It has never, of course, been my privilege to have seen such things at first hand, but I will nevertheless hazard this

> with some confidence: the English landscape at its finest—such as I saw it this morning—possesses a quality that the landscapes of other nations, however more superficially dramatic, inevitably fail to possess. It is, I believe, a quality that will mark out the English landscape to any objective observer as the most deeply satisfying in the world, and this quality is probably best summed up by the term "greatness." (28)

Stevens frames his discourse in words that refer to political unities, "nations." The English landscape is not mere "scenery," it represents the authentic character and quality of the people; whereas other "nations" may be "dramatic," they are woefully "superficial." Stevens also singles out the word *greatness* by putting quotation marks around it. He then questions *greatness* and answers, somewhat insufficiently, what this *greatness* is:

> And yet what precisely is this "greatness"? Just where, or in what, does it lie? I am quite aware it would take a far wiser head than mine to answer such a question, but if I were forced to hazard a guess, I would say that it is the very *lack* of obvious drama or spectacle that sets the beauty of our land apart. What is pertinent is the calmness of that beauty, its sense of restraint. It is as though the land knows of its own beauty, of its own greatness, and feels no need to shout it. In comparison, the sorts of sights offered in such places as Africa and America, though undoubtedly very exciting, would, I am sure, strike the objective viewer as inferior on account of their unseemly demonstrativeness. (28–29)

England, the land of "greatness," cannot be "unseemly" demonstrative even though territory that was once British—Africa and America—can be. This constitutes Stevens's calculated framing of the difference between the *indigenous* English, and the territories and people living, or formerly living, under British imperialism. The most compelling perspective concerning "Great" Britain is Ishiguro's present time-frame. The rhetoric of Margaret Thatcher's 1978–1979 campaign promises to return the "Great" to "Great Britain" when she is elected.

The film cannot accommodate Stevens's discourse on the English landscape, but it does want us to *see* this landscape, and to *feel* the calm of the pastoral scene as Stevens drives through 1950s England. The only scenes outside of the confines of Darlington Hall in the prewar era are those of Miss Kenton's standard Thursday-night rendezvous with Mr. Benn at the village pub. Up to this point the audience has been sheltered in the womblike enclosure of Darlington Hall; and so when we follow Miss Kenton out at night to meet Mr. Benn we find only a cold, tawdry little village where the underprivileged meet to discuss their sad lives. Indeed, Mr. Benn is not refined like Stevens; and small heritage-film details such as wet pavement stones of the village are not as genteel as the paving stones at Darlington Hall. Every time we follow Miss Kenton outside of the estate we enter a slightly seedy, cheerless, even depressing, world. These feelings are echoed at the very end of the film when Stevens visits Mrs. Benn in the West Country, which loses all the charm of its designation when we see the boarding house in which she has been staying, the hotel tea room, and the boardwalk, all of which add up to a certain hopelessness. These scenes are contrary to the Merchant Ivory world of "Deep England," of the open countryside and estate houses, which the audience has been basking in and enjoying. The film intentionally creates a feeling of security in the recreation of Darlington Hall and its grounds in the 1930s. Likewise, the countryside of the 1950s is also presented as safe: when Stevens runs out of gas, there is nothing threatening in the darkness, and the Moscombe locals are only too eager to help him. The fact that Miss Kenton/Mrs. Benn in the outside world creates a picture of decay, seediness, and even hopelessness further binds Stevens to the image of "his England," and, in turn, to his closeted desire for Lord Darlington. Finally, the camera favors Darlington (and Darlington Hall), even when it is apparent that he is a Nazi sympathizer and has lost touch with reality, because the Merchant-Ivoryesque film, as Hipsky points out, adores "gentility," and gentility represents heritage England.

The Nazi Plot

Harold Pinter was the first person to draft a screenplay for *The Remains of the Day*; but when the Merchant Ivory team assumed the rights to the novel, they brought in their long-time collaborator Ruth Prawer Jhabvala. Harold Pinter was offered co-credit for the screenplay released by Columbia Pictures, but he declined.[40] The changes that Jhabvala made are more along the lines of emphasis rather than large-scale additions or deletions. In terms of the dating of the action, Pinter set the year as 1954; Jhabvala made it 1958. Pinter scholars typically find this change insignificant, but find other features of the screenplay that Jhabvala altered to be more significant. Two such issues are Stevens's awareness of his own failure to act as a moral individual in terms of the political extremism of Darlington and his associates, and, in the end, how much responsibility Stevens accepts for his failure to act. Edward T. Jones believes that Jhabvala collapses and reduces this aspect of Ishiguro's text: "Not withstanding Stevens's moral ignorance, Ishiguro does permit him as least a moment or so of intellectual discovery in the novel, which Pinter echoes, although in a more reduced way, and Jhabvala omits altogether."[41] This omission occurs at the end of the film, which we will turn to momentarily. The more substantial changes Jhabvala makes, which Jones does not discuss but which would further buttress his interpretation, is the considerable reworking of the "Nazi plot," especially Jhabvala's handling of the Jewish girl refugees.

The Nazi plot is easy to lift from the pages of the novel. The deeply encrusted aristocrats, who do not know that the era of grand houses and colonial dominance is about to end, arrive with their servants, eat, drink, play, and depart without ever contemplating their link in the food chain of life. These scenes in Ishiguro's novel capture the last gasp of Edwardian England, though it is the early 1920s, and the first breath of fascist Europe:

> The next morning brought more early arrivals; namely, the two ladies from Germany—who had travelled together despite what one would have imagined to have been the great contrasts in their backgrounds—bringing with them a large team of ladies-in-waiting and footmen, as well as a great many trunks. Then in the afternoon, an Italian gentleman arrived accompanied by a valet, a secretary, an 'expert' and two bodyguards. I cannot imagine what sort of place this gentleman imagined he was coming to in bringing the latter, but I must say it struck something of an odd note to see in Darlington Hall these large silent men staring suspiciously in all directions a few yards from wherever the Italian gentlemen happened to be. (87–88)

The 1920s conference ushers in a new age at Darlington Hall—an increasing number of "gentlemen" thugs bring their bodyguards with them to see Lord Darlington. Stevens understands that this sort of precaution is not only unnecessary but unbecoming; his lordship should not be associating with these kinds of people. Baxendale and Pawling point out that Darlington, though a fictional character, is a compound of the 1930s gentleman involved in "country house Fascism":

> [Darlington] is clearly a composite figure based on actual individuals, such as Edward VIII and various "right-wing Fellow Travellers" amongst the aristocracy of the thirties. Hence, anyone who is acquainted with Richard Griffith's book *Fellow Travellers of the Right* and Robert Benewick's *The Fascist Movement in Britain* will recognize the similarity between Darlington's statements on the "malaise" of

Britain and the views of figures who were associated with right-wing mouthpieces such as the *Saturday Review* or *Link* in the Thirties.[42]

While Ishiguro gives the reader a distinct sense that Stevens knows what is taking place, thereby granting him some moral integrity, Jhabvala strips Stevens of all rectitude. Her hardness toward this character is most clearly seen in her handling of the firing of the Jewish maids. Jhabvala makes Stevens morally weak by removing him from the responsibility of telling the girls that they must leave. Pinter's version puts Stevens squarely in the line of fire as he tells the girls that they must go, though he does not say why; he also informs them that he has attempted to secure them a new situation. The unused Pinter script reads:

Butler's Pantry Morning
Stevens at his table. Miss Kenton and the German girls come in.
STEVENS. Miss Kenton, you don't have to stay if you don't wish to.
MISS KENTON. I'll stay.
The girls stand, looking at Stevens.
STEVENS. I am very sorry to say that his lordship has decided to cut down on staff. I am afraid we shall have to let you both go. You have worked very well and we have given you excellent references. Here they are.
He taps the references on the table.
SOPHY, *in German.* But it is so lovely here.
STEVENS. What does she say?
ELSA. She says it's so lovely here.
Sophy begins to cry quietly.
STEVENS. But I have good news. I have spoken this morning to Mr. Wellington—the butler at Railton House in Surry. He thinks there is every possibility of placing you there. Here is the address and directions and here is the address of a hostel in London where you will stay tonight.
He points to two envelopes.
Here are your wages . . . and here——
He takes money from his wallet.
——is a little extra for you. I am very sorry to see you go.
ELSA. Thank you, Mr. Stevens.
SOPHY. Thank you, Mr. Stevens.
The girls pick up all the papers and Miss Kenton goes out with them.[43]

Pinter grants more moral integrity to Stevens than even Ishiguro in the novel. With the actions of giving them good references, a possible new situation, a place to go to in the meantime, and giving them *extra* money out of his *own* pocket, Stevens is established by Pinter as a truly moral person with the ability to express himself. In the novel Stevens summarizes the firing of "Ruth" and "Sarah" in much-more-reserved and less-generous terms:

> It was evident from the moment the two maids stepped into my pantry the following morning that Miss Kenton had already spoken to them, for they both came in sobbing. I explained the situation to them as briefly as possible, underlining that their work had been satisfactory and that they would, accordingly, receive good references. As I recall, neither of them said anything of note throughout the whole interview, which lasted perhaps three or four minutes, and they left sobbing just as they had arrived. (149–150)

Jhabvala's and Ivory's version of Stevens firing the girls is nonexistent. Instead, the film's presentation of the Jewish maids' firing by Lord Darlington exactly midway through the film provides a more-remarkable presentation of Darlington's, and hence Stevens's, culpability.

It is difficult not to read Jhabvala's own 1930s wartime experience into her adaptation. Jhabvala was born in Cologne, Germany in 1927, the daughter of Marcus Prawer, a Jewish solicitor, and Eleanora Cohn, from Berlin. Despite Polish and Russian roots, Prawer considered her family steadfastly German: "I was born into what seemed a very solidly based family who had identified strongly with the Germany around them—had been through the 1914–1918 War with them—had sung for the Kaiser and the fatherland."[44] The Prawers remained in Germany during the rise of Hitler; finally they fled Germany in April 1939. Coming to England, Ruth and her older brother Siegbert were initially housed in Coventry as part of the London children evacuation plan. After several months the siblings rejoined their parents in Hendon, a London suburb, where Jhabvala's father worked in the clothing business.[45] The dislocation, relegation to the working class, and grief over friends and relatives left behind for imminent death made an indelible impression on Jhabvala. After the war, Jhabvala's father committed suicide. " 'Suicide,' Jhabvala said, 'became almost an epidemic at that time.' "[46] It should be noted that Jhabvala's and Pinter's early years have much in common. Although born in Hackney, a working-class neighborhood in London's East End, Pinter was the son of a Jewish tailor. Born in 1930, Pinter was evacuated from London at the beginning of the war and returned to London in 1944.

Jhabvala's emphasis on the "Nazi plot" centers on Darlington and, in turn, Stevens, who always acts according to his "master's" wishes.

Stevens does not personally fire "Erma" and "Elsa." In fact, there is no dismissal scene at all in the film. When he is told the girls must be let go, Stevens meekly protests to Lord Darlington that the Jewish girls are intelligent, polite, and clean yet he does not disobey his "Lord's command":

DARLINGTON. Stevens.
STEVENS. Yes, my Lord.
DARLINGTON. We have some refugee girls on the staff at the moment, I believe.
STEVENS. We do, my Lord. Two house-maids, Elsa and Erma.
DARLINGTON. You'll have to let them go, I'm afraid.
STEVENS. Let them go, my Lord?
DARLINGTON. It's regrettable, Stevens, but we have no choice. You, you've got to see the whole thing in context. I have the well-being of my guests to consider.
STEVENS. My Lord, may I say, they work extremely well, they're intelligent, polite, and very clean.
DARLINGTON. I'm sorry, Stevens, but I've looked into this matter very carefully. There are larger issues at stake. I'm sorry, but there it is. They're Jews.
STEVENS. Yes, my Lord.
Stevens exits the room[47]

The matter that Lord Darlington has been looking into, the audience is led to believe is Adolf Hitler's *Mein Kampf*.[48] The voice-over scene with Darlington reading from a book Jhabvala *creates* so that the viewer fully understands the insidious nature of Darlington's fascist sympathy. The scene begins with Erma and Elsa on their knees cleaning the fireplace: Darlington enters, goes to his desk, sits, and turns to the appropriate page. A voice-over reading of *Mein Kampf* begins:

DARLINGTON, *reading to himself.* We certainly do the Jews no injustice when we say that the revelation of Christ is simply something incomprehensible and hateful to them; although it apparently sprang from their midst, it embodies nonetheless the negation of their whole nature—a matter in which the Jews are far more sensitive than we are. This clear demonstration of the deep cleft that separates us Europeans from the Jew is by no means given in order to let religious prejudice for this dangerous bias settle the matter, but because I think that the perception of two so fundamentally different natures should reveal the real gulf . . . *Erma and Elsa make a noise, which distracts Lord Darlington, who looks at them as they look at him and then leave the room.*

In the very next scene, Darlington informs Stevens that the maids must be fired. Jhabvala leaves no doubt in the viewer's mind that Darlington has been sucked into the German camp, however unwittingly, much farther than "old chaps" playing at diplomacy.

Americans respond well to "Nazi plots" and snooty British elitism. Americans "get" these ruses; therefore, both Darlington and his social set are seen to be foolish, anachronistic, and perhaps even a bit evil by American standards. Their blindness to Hitler's evil in the film allows Senator Lewis (former "Superman" Christopher Reeve), who knows well that Europe is headed for disaster at the hands of amateur politicians such as Darlington and Spencer, to step in and save the day. The film has collapsed two characters from the novel into one in the film. In the novel, Lewis is an overweight whiskey-drinking kind of guy, who makes his sole appearance during a 1920s "convention" at Darlington Hall. A second character, Farraday, buys Darlington Hall, its contents, and butler in 1956. For viewer convenience the film combines the two into "Lewis." The filmic Lewis conspires with the French ambassador at the 1930s summit at Darlington Hall, although by this late date in European interwar history Germany had already invaded the Rhineland, and so, Lewis's prophetic abilities are not so impressive. Lewis is betrayed by the Frenchmen in the film at the final dinner of the conference as he is in the book in the 1920s, but in the film Lewis is portrayed as heroically standing up to not only the amateur politicians but also Hitler's Germany. Christopher Reeve's handsome, trim Lewis is symbolic of the American forces that stepped in and "saved" Britain from Hitler's war machine. This scene makes it only too clear that Britain is anachronistic, even naïve, and needs U.S. guidance and support.

In this way, the film suppresses the novel's anti-American sentiment. After the war when Darlington Hall is sold, continuity is provided in the film by Lewis's "returning" to buy the estate. Americans want to feel the glow of the nation's war heroics and their post-war dominance; "Superman" Lewis fulfills both of these roles. In the novel Stevens resents American financial power. He betrays Farraday when his American friends the Wakefields come to visit Darlington Hall: "I would often catch various American exclamations of delight coming from whichever part of the house they had arrived at"; and Stevens will not "authenticate" anything for Mrs. Wakefield, as Farraday complains, "She kept asserting everything was 'mock' this and 'mock' that. She even thought that you were 'mock', Stevens" (123–124). Stevens has told Mrs. Wakefield that he was not butler to Darlington, not only to hide his association with him, but also to embarrass

Farraday in front of his compatriots. Stevens's self-confessed "white lies" (126) belie his ongoing devotion to Darlington, which seems excessively passionate, leading us to the discourse of desire.

Stevens's Closeted Discourse of Desire

Above I stated that one interpretation of the territory of the novel *The Remains of the Day* is the interior dialogue of a man who is on a quest to reunite with his lost love, Miss Kenton, whom he allowed to leave Darlington Hall twenty years prior to the narrative. The other side of this interpretation I would now like to consider is that the novel *The Remains of the Day* is the interior dialogue of a man who *wishes to convince the reader* that he is on a quest to reunite with his lost love, Miss Kenton, whom he allowed to leave Darlington Hall twenty years prior to the narrative. With this idea, that Stevens is attempting to convince us of his sincerity, goes also his discourse on "dignity," which is a code word in his world for "masculinity." The various stories that Stevens tells the reader throughout the text are arguments for his profession, and more personally, are utilized to defend his father. There is a strong father/fatherland/male-authority motif throughout the text. Either Stevens is trying to vindicate his father or he is trying to vindicate himself *to* his father—perhaps as a silent admission of his homosexual desire. In the film, Stevens's utter devotion to Lord Darlington and his psychological repression could be interpreted as a faithful presentation of an English butler to his "Lord." Because the film markets itself as a heterosexual romantic drama, this psychological repression interpretation is the one we are supposed to use. In our dime-store post-Freudian culture, audiences typically attempt to assess a character's adult psychological damage by discovering the childhood trauma that led to this neurosis. The film presents the key figure in Stevens's emotional repression in the form of the father, especially with the film's invented "death-bed" confession by Stevens Sr. concerning Stevens's mother.

Indeed, Stevens's issues with his father cannot be ignored. Past his prime as a head butler on an estate, Stevens Sr. is employed by his son as the under butler. The "Downstairs" contingency has its own elaborate hierarchy, which is most vividly presented when Miss Kenton calls Stevens Sr. by his first name, William. In the novel, Stevens's stories function to defend Stevens Sr.'s profession, masculinity, and Englishness. The conservative, imperialist attitude that Stevens embraces throughout most of his narrative, save possibly the very end, manifests itself not only in his duty to Lord Darlington, but also in his attitude toward the death of his brother (Leonard) in the "South African War" and the "great-butler" story his father tells, of a butler in service to a gentleman stationed in India. Concerning the former example, Stevens's father is forced to attend as personal valet to the general who, through his negligence as a commander in the Boer War, caused the death of Leonard:

> [T]he notion that his son gave his life gloriously for king and country—was sullied by the fact that my brother had perished in a particularly infamous manoeuvre. Not only was it alleged that the manouevre had been a most un-British attack on civilian Boer settlements, overwhelming evidence emerged that it had been irresponsibly commanded with several floutings of elementary military precautions, so that the men who had died—my brother among them—had died quite needlessly. (40)

Stevens relates this personal story in order to relay the psychological duress his father was able to overcome to succeed as a great butler. Stevens's father did not relinquish his duty to the infamous commander, nor did he say anything to the gentleman about his command and his own son's death. Stevens sees this as pure "triumph" on the part of his father as a great *English* butler. Stevens tells this story not so much to celebrate his father's triumph as a great butler, but to defend Stevens Sr. from looking completely emasculated because he meekly administered to the needs of the infamous commander. To turn the story away from the fact that Stevens Sr. submissively attended to the bodily needs of this most "un-British" of commanders is to turn the story away from the feminized prostitute-like role his father is requested to fill. The fact that he fulfills his role shows that he is feminized in the face of the British ruling class.

The film utilizes another of Stevens's stories from the novel but has Stevens Sr. tell it in dramatic fashion at the servants' dinner table. Despite the fact that all the other servants listen intently to Stevens Sr. retelling the story of the perfect butler in India, the telling is marred by one of the unseen aristocrats ringing to be served. One feature of this tale is that the perfect butler in India plays out a Jeeves-like role: decisive, masculine, and completely competent. Stevens Sr. echoes "no discernible traces" of the recent shooting of the tiger, Stevens thanks "Mr. Stevens" for the story, and the bell rings. Stevens Sr. must leave his dinner and attend to the guest of Darlington. The next scene shows Stevens Sr. using a dustpan on the landing of the staircase; the camera is looking down on him—this further emphasizes that he is subservient and unmanly. Out of breathe and apparently feeling ill,

Stevens Sr. exits through the camouflaged door, leaving his dustpan on the step and his broom astride the landing. Given Stevens Sr. own code of proper butler behavior, he is failing at his manly profession.

The bedroom scene in which Stevens Sr. asks Stevens if he has been a good father is invented for the film. The fact that Pinter makes his Stevens Sr. embittered toward Stevens's mother is significant and covertly signals to the audience that all was not right in the Stevens's household:

> FATHER. There's something I have to tell you.
> STEVENS. What?
> FATHER. I fell out of love with your mother. Your mother was a bitch. I loved her once but love went out of me when I found out what a bitch she was. Your mother was a bitch.
> *Silence.*
> STEVENS. I'm glad you're feeling better.
> *He leaves the room.*[49]

The Pinter scene with Stevens and his father does show an embittered Stevens Sr., yet Jhabvala decides to "spell it out" for the viewer. She drops the word "bitch" but makes the mother an adulteress:

> STEVENS SR. There's something I have to tell you.
> STEVENS, *sighs.* I have so much to do father. Why don't we talk in the morning?
> STEVENS SR. Jim, I fell out of love with your mother. I loved her once, but love went out of me when I found her carrying on. You're a good son. I'm proud of you. I hope I've been a good father to you. I've tried my best. You better get down there or heaven only knows what they'll be up to. Go on—go on.
> STEVENS. We'll talk in the morning.

Both screenwriters knew that we must have a childhood psychological trauma so that the audience can have its "aha" moment and blame Stevens's extreme emotional repression on his mother. The silent, we assume dead, mother is an easy target. Even Stevens Sr.'s cynicism we can blame on his former wife. It works for the heterosexual plot; and so, it *works.*

Keeping Stevens in the Closet

The film goes to great lengths to make Stevens's character appear to be afraid of emotion and emotional commitment. The film's emphasis on the heterosexual attraction between Stevens and Miss Kenton is fortified in small ways. First, in the film Jhabvala creates an attraction between Darlington and the blond baroness who attends the conference to display, we assume, the beauty of the German Ayarian race and to present her gift, a German song. The fact that the baroness appears menacing and manipulative plays into the "Nazi-plot" theme, but does not deter the audience from noticing the affectionate gestures and looks between the baroness and Darlington. The Nazi baroness performs her role as seductress in order to help Darlington pass as heterosexual and normal. In the film the only clue to Darlington's sexuality or sexual life occurs in these scenes. The novel presents Darlington as never having or having had a romantic interest, but we have to remember that Stevens narrates to the reader what it is he want us to know about Darlington. Curiously, in the film the baroness sings in the scene preceding the one in which Stevens Sr. dies. Under the surface of the heterosexual plot is Stevens's desire to please both his father and his master, but his master is more important in the end; Stevens does not even attend to his father when he dies in the middle of the last night of the conference. Stevens remains true to Darlington every minute of the conference.

On the face of it, the scenes that both Pinter and Jhabvala scripted for Stevens and Miss Kenton serve to show that their attraction to and need for one another is increasing as time goes on. One major change from the novel to the film is the temporal sequencing. In the novel, Kenton arrives before the early 1920s conference and departs in 1936. That is roughly fourteen years of service to Darlington and long-suffering, patient waiting for Stevens to "come around." The film's time-frame is much shorter and is closer to what a contemporary audience would expect. Stevens's manner is so "public" at all times that the heterosexually charged scenes with Miss Kenton "stick to" Stevens like Teflon (to borrow the 1980s metaphor); Miss Kenton's sexual allure does not entice him. If the audience is aware of a certain irony on Stevens's part, then we cannot help but read at least two interpretations from these scenes. Both Jhabvala and Pinter include a scene that is significant for its ambiguity in terms of Stevens's sexual desire.

MISS KENTON. Lizzie has started well. She hasn't made one mistake.
STEVENS. I take my hat off to you.
MISS KENTON. Look at that smile on your face. That tells an interesting story in itself. A very interesting story.
STEVENS. What story is that?
MISS KENTON. Well, she's a very pretty girl, don't you think?

STEVENS. Is she?

MISS KENTON. I've noticed you have a curious aversion to pretty girls being on your staff.

STEVENS. You know you're talking absolute nonsense.

MISS KENTON. You don't like pretty girls to be on the staff. I've noticed. Might it be that our Mr. Stevens fears distraction? Can it be that our Mr. Stevens is flesh and blood after all and cannot trust himself?

STEVENS. You know what I am doing, Miss Kenton? I'm placing my thoughts elsewhere while you chatter away.

MISS KENTON. But why is that guilty smile still on your face?

STEVENS. It's not a guilty smile at all. I'm simply amused by the nonsense you sometimes talk.

MISS KENTON. It is a guilty smile. You can hardly bear to look at her. That's why you didn't want to take her on. She was too pretty.

STEVENS. You must be right, Miss Kenton. You always are.

If we assume Kenton is correct, then Stevens is embarrassed by Kenton's accusation. If Stevens is so professional that he truly never notices the girls on the staff, then Kenton is, as he states, talking "nonsense." However, if Stevens's professionalism is a public cover for his private closeted homosexual desires, then we see that Kenton is indeed speaking "nonsense" because Stevens is not attracted to, hence never looks at nor is distracted by, females. The second and third interpretations intermingle with Stevens's all-consuming desire to serve Lord Darlington. Stevens can serve Darlington completely, fulfilling one aspect of his closeted desire, and retain his professionalism by serving him in the public domain.

The climatic, or perhaps anticlimatic, scene between Stevens and Miss Kenton comes when she boldly attempts to invade Stevens's personal lodgings while he is reading. The film has slowly built up expectation for the development of Stevens and Kenton's romance, and the audience is primed for a mutual show of affection. Therefore, when Kenton attempts to physically get close to Stevens, we eagerly await their first Hollywood consecrated kiss:

MISS KENTON. What are you reading?

STEVENS. A book.

MISS KENTON. Yes, but what sort of book?

She approaches him.

STEVENS. What are you doing?

MISS KENTON. What's the book? Are you shy about your book? Show it to me. Is it racy?

STEVENS. Racy?

MISS KENTON. Racy. Are you reading a racy book?

STEVENS. You don't think "racy" books are to be found on his lordship's shelves, do you?

MISS KENTON. How would I know? What is it? Let me see it? Let me see your book.

STEVENS. Miss Kenton, please leave me alone.

She moves closer to Stevens.

MISS KENTON. Why won't you show me your book?

STEVENS. This is my private time. You are encroaching upon it.

MISS KENTON. Oh, is that so? I am encroaching upon your private time, am I?

She moves closer.

What's in the book? Come on. Let me see. Or are you protecting me? Is that what you're doing? Would I be shocked? Would it ruin my character? Let me see it.

She peels his fingers off the book and flips through the pages.

MISS KENTON. Oh, dear, it's not scandalous at all. It's just a sentimental old love story.

STEVENS. I read these books—any books—to develop my command and knowledge of the English language. I read to further my education.

MISS KENTON. Ah, I see.

This scene shows that Stevens is vulnerable in his private world. The heterosexual interpretation of Miss Kenton penetrating Stevens's privacy hinges on two assumptions: one, Stevens is sentimental because he cannot express his love for Kenton, and so he reads sentimental love stories, perhaps to play out his desire for her; or, two, he is so psychologically damaged from his childhood that he has no intention of committing to Kenton or anyone else, and reads these novels to participate in the warmth he cannot have in reality. Either interpretation leads one to feel sympathy for Stevens. The homosexual interpretation, however, makes more "sense," though this kind of sense is not permissible in this film because we see that when Kenton penetrates the private world of Stevens, she in fact finds a feminized subject who, in the above scene, totally rejects her heterosexual advances. After this rejection, Kenton realizes that she has no future with Stevens and begins to spend her Thursdays with Benn, who eventually asks her to marry him. When Kenton tells Stevens of Benn's marriage proposal, she gives him one last chance to respond and express his desire for her. Stevens, in the middle of a visit from high-level German diplomats, cannot do anything more than to congratulate her on her engagement. This ends the potential romance between Kenton and Stevens. Nothing happens; the audience cheers on Kenton, but to no avail. Thus, Stevens's 1950s "quest" to win her back to Darlington Hall should not be read as his quest to rekindle a lost romance; rather,

Kenton is the last link to his past with Lord Darlington during the hey-day of Darlington's influence. To bring back Kenton/Mrs. Benn twenty years later is to rekindle his longing for Darlington.

If the viewer opens up the interpretation that sees Stevens as a closeted homosexual, then Stevens's unusual devotion to Darlington begins to make more "sense." In fact, several times in the novel, Stevens's statements seem to indicate that he has "vowed" himself or "betrothed" himself to Darlington after a period of courtship: "if a butler is to be of any worth to anything or anybody in life, there must surely come a time when he ceases his searching; a time when he must say to himself: 'This employer embodies all that I find noble and admirable. I will hereafter devote myself to serving him' " (200–201). These are private, self-indulgent confessions, ones meant only for the reader. In public, Stevens denies even knowing Darlington—not only to Mrs. Wakefield, Farraday's American friend, but several times during his journey.

The turning point in the film, in which the viewer sees how deeply Stevens is still living in the past, comes from the novel. This scene shows an out-of-touch Stevens who, when he is mistaken for a "gentleman," goes along with the charade. Perhaps Stevens is discombobulated after this uncharacteristic mismanagement of detail, literally letting the car run out of gas; this slip-up also makes evident Stevens's naiveté toward practical matters outside of Darlington Hall. The Taylors, who have lost their son in the war, take Stevens in for the night, and the locals take the opportunity to come out for a pint and to talk. It is Stevens's choice to continue the misunderstanding that he is in fact a gentleman, and not a gentleman's man-servant, that causes the querulous Harry Smith to repeatedly challenge Stevens to share his views on politics. In the film, Smith states that the war was fought for English freedom,

> SMITH. It's one of the privileges of being born English that no matter who you are, no matter if you're rich or poor, you're born free and you're born so that you can express your opinion freely, and vote in your member of parliament or vote him out. That's what dignity's really about, if you'll excuse me, sir.

The heterosexual interpretation sees Stevens wincing as his precious "Deep England" dignity is defined in terms utterly *foreign* to him—he failed to vocally stand up for his personal dignity in front of Darlington's cronies when Mr. Spencer humiliated him with questions concerning political affairs; he failed to support the Jewish refugee maids when Darlington fired them; and he even failed to respond to the love of Miss Kenton, a love that would have enabled him to achieve personal success, happiness, and dignity. The closeted-Stevens interpretation, however, sees Stevens's expression as one of utter desolation because Darlington *betrayed* him—not as a fellow citizen—but as a *lover* betrays another. All the nasty things Darlington did to Stevens suddenly stand out as personal betrayals. One such scene provided by the film is Spencer's humiliation of Stevens, not only in front of his beloved Darlington, but literally at the hands of Darlington, who allows Spencer to continue.

In the film, Spencer queries Stevens on the debt situation and the gold standard, the currency problem and the arms agreement between the French and the Russians, and North Africa and France. When Stevens cannot or says he cannot answer any of these questions—"I am sorry sir but I cannot be of assistance with any of these matters"—Spencer further humiliates and emasculates Stevens by declaring that "the good man is unable to assist us . . . and yet we still go along the notion that this nation's decisions be left in his hands and few millions like him. You might as well ask the women's union to organize a war campaign." Evocatively, Darlington's duplicitous look at Stevens is one of insensitive merriment—the callous spectator at a violent sport; all the while he is not sure that Stevens is not feigning stupidity. This look indicates that Darlington knows Stevens well enough to understand that he is enacting the part of the butler—never to challenge the aristocracy. Stevens is the feminine partner in the house of Darlington.

The film positions the interrogation after the scenes of the Jewish problem and the hiring of Lizzie as a result of a vacancy. The set-up of these scenes show that Darlington and his set are in the grip of the Nazis and that Stevens is being carried along with Darlington. The novel, however, positions the humiliation at the hands of Spencer directly after the Moscombe "gentleman" incident to show that Stevens's narrative had been hiding incidents from the reader. The film's sequencing works to the "Nazi plot" alongside of the Kenton and Stevens romance. Yet, once we see that Stevens's betrayal and humiliation is deeply *private*, then we see that Darlington, not Kenton, is the center of Stevens's life. It is because the homosexual desire is so strongly conveyed when we position Darlington at the center of Stevens's narrative that the film had to rework the ending of the story.

Pinter's version of the end of the film is similar to Ishiguro's text. Stevens, sitting on the pier at Weymouth after he has seen Mrs. Benn for the last time, is accosted by an older man who wishes to chat:

> MAN. You retired?
> STEVENS. No. Oh no. But perhaps I should think about it. I'm not sure I've got anything left to give, you see. I worked for Lord Darlington for thirty years. I gave him the very best I had to give. I don't think I have a great deal more to give.
> *The man is silent.*
> I think perhaps you're right. I should retire. You see, I've given all I have to give. I gave it all to Lord Darlington.
> MAN. Oh dear, mate. Want a handkerchief? I've got one somewhere.
> STEVENS. No, no thank you. It's all right.
> MAN. What did you do for him? This lord.
> STEVENS. I was his butler.
> *Pause.*
> No, truly. I think I've given all I have to give. I gave it all to him, you see.
> MAN. Listen mate. Take my tip. Stop looking back. Looking back'll get you nowhere. Why don't you look forward? Look forward to the evening. Believe me, it's the best part of the day. Honest. Take my tip. I know what I'm saying. The evening's the best part of the day.
> *The man stands.*
> See you again, then.
> *The man walks away.*
> *The lights suddenly go on the pier. Cheers from the onlookers.*
> *Music starts from the pier through the loudspeakers.*
> *The crowd moves up the pier.*
> *Groups of girls and groups of boys call to each other. Some of them, laughing chase each other through the crowd.*
> *Stevens sits still. He suddenly stands and looks at the brilliantly lit pier. He slowly walks towards the pier, gives a coin to the attendant in his booth, goes through the turnstile, and walks away from the camera along the pier until he is lost in the crowd.* [the end][50]

Jhabvala's ending, however, has been altered to bring closure to the romance between Kenton and Stevens. Postmodern humor might steal into the film text if such lines as, "No, truly. I think I've given all I have to give. I gave it all to him, you see," *remain* in the final version. In Jhabvala's ending, Stevens's confession of what sounds like homosexual love will *not remain*, nor will the gloomy peer scene with a stranger. As we have seen, despite the homosexual subtext of the novel, hints of which make it into the film, Merchant Ivory have clearly subordinated these elements to the film appealing to the heritage-loving mainstream American audience.

The last scene in the final version of the film, entitled on the DVD, "Darlington Hall renewed," indicates that the house and the butler's life work will be rehabilitated. With significance in terms of closure, Christopher Reeve's middle-aged Lewis resembles Fox's Darlington. The change of ownership, however, is marked as Lewis recalls the 1935 conference as he serves a ping-pong ball across an out-of-place ping-pong table. In twenty years Darlington Hall has gone from baronesses, lords, diplomats, and the elegant splendor of an international conference to an American serving a ping-pong ball across an opponent-less table. Perhaps this is Ivory's final metaphor: America's sole dominance at the diplomacy table; no one else is there to talk to or "play" with (Superman) Reeve's American because America has no worthy opponent. Couple this with the final image of the pigeon escaping from Darlington Hall as the camera moves ever farther away from the manor house and its grounds, and the feeling that America has arrived and England is receding is indelible. Despite the English-heritage features of the film, Merchant Ivory have reterritorialized the novel for American viewers, who will nostalgically connect to Reeve's Lewis and America's newfound dominance in world politics at the end of the Second World War.

CHAPTER 3

American Cowboy in England: *Possession*

This tendency of our minds to classify and register our experience in terms of the known must present a real problem to the artist in his encounter with the particular. Indeed, it may well be this difficulty which brought the downfall of the formula in art.

E.H. Gombrich
Art and Illusion

The previous chapter demonstrated how the film *The Remains of the Day* allows Americans to enjoy the subtextual pleasure of reliving their post–Second World War triumph as the only Western superpower. Through the magnification of Lewis's character from the book to the film, the film emphasizes the failure and wrongheadedness of British pro-Nazi sympathizers such as Lord Darlington and the success and clear-sighted vision of the Americans in the postwar era. The film adaptation in this chapter follows a similar strategy: make the British obsolete in their own "Deep England" through the heroism of an American. The adaptation of A.S. Byatt's Booker Prize–winning novel *Possession* by American filmmaker Neil LaBute in the 2002 film of the same title carefully reiterates the literary text so that it is a recognizable and predictable product for the American market, while seemingly remaining faithful to the "spirit" of the text through the setting, some of the cast, and even the overall plot structure. However, it is the reiteration into a recognizable product that betrays the subtle "transcoding" on the part of the film's narrative; and it is this transcoding that pulls the film into a stable set of citations.[1] Ryan and Kellner argue that films "transcode the discourses (the forms, figures, and representations) of social life into cinematic narratives. . . . films themselves become part of that broader cultural system of representations that construct social reality. That construction occurs in part through the internalization of representations."[2] Although not directly referring to film, Gombrich's statement—presented at the beginning of this chapter—that we "classify and register our experience in terms of the known" parallels Ryan and Kellner's assertion that we have internalized cinematic narrative structures and their accompanying forms of representation. Mainstream American audiences desire and enjoy a film when the film repeats known American cultural universals.

American mass audiences expect and enjoy citations that are easily "classified" and "registered." The most effective way to establish a one-to-one correlation is to control the context in which the statement is iterated. As discussed in chapter 1, for Austin, according to Derrida, to be successful he must actually first control, or as Derrida states, "totalize," the illocutionary, the context, so that the locutionary will be understood completely, leaving "no remainder." To leave a remainder would be to open up the possibility that a statement *might* be *misunderstood*. Analogously speaking, "Hollywood" has produced a mass-market audience that makes up the illocutionary field (a "conscious presence of the speakers or receivers who participate in the effecting of a performative, their conscious and intentional presence in the totality of the operation," according to Jacques Derrida in "Signature Event Context") that renders the iteration (the film) as 100 percent understood. If the audience *misunderstands*, then iteration fails—the film fails. Neither the film industry nor the audience wants the iteration to miss the mark. In this way, we can see that this system of communication is closed insofar that anything different, or anything that could produce a remainder, will not be allowed into the system; in fact, it will not be *understood* by the system.

The novel *Possession* is at once a Victorian-era love story reconstructed from the lost correspondence between the poets Christabel LaMotte—virtually unread until the post-1970s feminist critical reassessment of the literary canon—and Randolph Henry Ash—the Alfred Tennyson or Robert Browning of Victorian England—and at the same time a contemporary romance (that unfolds during the reconstruction of the Victorians' lost correspondence) between the academics, Maud Bailey, a successful feminist theorist and LaMotte scholar, and Roland Mitchell, a biographical, historical critic and Ash scholar. In the novel, the parallel nineteenth- and twentieth-century love stories revolve around the correspondence between Randolph and Christabel. It is the Victorians' love and desire for each other that propel the novel, not the twentieth-century couple's relationship. The Victorians' discourse of desire evident in the letters is one of productive desire; what they may "lack" in not being able, initially, to see each other is more than abundantly recuperated in the richness of the "papery" search for knowledge of the other: "*I am reluctant to take my pen from the paper and fold up this letter—for as long as I write to you, I have the illusion that we are* in touch, *that is, blessed*" (italics in original).[3]

Self-consciously titled *Possession: A Romance*, the text takes care that the reader notes that the novel is not in the realist tradition. Before the novel begins there is a quotation from Nathaniel Hawthorne's "Preface to *The House of the Seven Gables*" in which he makes the distinction between a realist novel and a romance: "When a writer calls his work a Romance, it need hardly be observed that he wishes to claim a certain latitude, both as to its fashion and material, which he would not have felt himself entitled to assume, had he professed to be writing a Novel."[4] Before the novel commences, Byatt has forced us to contextualize our reading experience as self-consciously presenting itself as metatextual exercise. The various genres and critical theories in the body of the narrative repeatedly force us to juxtapose the "story" with a metacritique. This continual barrage is part of the reason the novel has earned a reputation for being "postmodern." Byatt layers her novel with so many genres and critical positions that, at times, the novel is a critical challenge to the very act of reading. Yet, at the same time, Byatt gives the reader an "old-fashioned" narrative with a nineteenth-century textual mystery being revealed in the contemporary era. Concerning this critical full-court press in the novel, Byatt confessses: "It is the only one I've written to be liked, and I did partly to show off. I thought, why not pull out all the stops?"[5]

Possession is the exemplary contemporary novel that rewrites, discovers, rediscovers, or overwrites documents from the past. Referencing Byatt's novel, Suzanne Keen identifies "archive" novels as sharing "key traits":

> its character-researchers; its romance adventure stories, in which "research" features as a kernel plot action; its strong closure, with climactic [*sic*] discoveries and rewards; its depiction of discomforts and inconveniences suffered in the service of knowledge; its suggestion that sex and physical pleasure can be gained as a result of questing; its use of settings (such as libraries and country houses) that contain archives of actual papers; its revelation of material traces of the past holding the truth; and its evocation of history, looking back from a postimperial context.[6]

With *Possession*, the truth is revealed utimately in the person of Maud Bailey, but access to this truth must be pursued through the written word. Poems, letters, and journals are the *primary* texts in this labyrinthine novel. Byatt loves words, and she wants us to love them, too. So she creates a story of desire—a story we do not want to end. As lovers of words, however much we long to be satiated, we do not want the process of desire to end.[7]

In the novel it is Christabel and Ash who ignite our desire to read on. The reader discovers new documents as Roland and Maud discover the next text, the next clue. In this way, the contemporary couple knows no more than we do. The force of their desire is often evident in the text; it is not sexual, it is *textual*. Beyond easy forms of sexual desire, the postmodern Roland and Maud also know that their abiltiy to desire textual knowledge is similarily impaired—overcoded and contaminated. Maud tells Roland midway through the novel:

> We are so knowing. And all we've found out, is primitive sympathetic magic. Infantile polymorphous perversity. Everything relates to *us* and so we're imprisoned in ourselves—we can't see *things*. And we paint everything with this metaphor. . . . In every age, there must be truths people can't fight—whether or not they want to . . . we live in a truth Freud discovered. . . . However we've modified it. We aren't really free to suppose—to imagine—he could possibly have been wrong about human nature. (276)

This passage not only challenges us to read the narrative through the critical perspective offered by psychoanalysis—Freudian and Lacanian—but also to understand that we, too, like Maud and Roland cannot wipe away the film of interpretation from our own reading and just "see *things*." The Victorians, according to Maud and Roland in any case, could still see, imagine, and believe in the power of ideas and people.

Byatt levels her judgment against the contemporaries—and the reader—more than once in the text. The text assures the reader that she does "possess" the text—that closure and control are not possible. The text outwits us by always already acknowledging that our postmodern questions have been addressed: "Might there not, he professionally asked himself, be an element of superstitious dread in any self-reflexive, inturned postmodern mirror-game or plot-coil that recognises that it has got out of hand?" (456), and that we are readers who are "theoretically knowing" "in revenge proliferated sexual language, linguistic sexuality, analysis, dissection, deconstruction, exposure" (458). Byatt dresses down the professional postmodern reader, beats us at our own game, by *seducing* us, and accomplishes this by "leading us on." The text overtly discriminates between its own "papery" words and the empirical world "where words draw attention to the power and delight of words, and so *ad infinitum*, thus making the imagination experience something papery and dry, narcissistic yet disagreeably distanced, without the immediacy of sexual moisture or the scented garnet glow of good burgundy" (511). Yet, the irony is that the text is aware that it produces the world we know: "the book creates meaning, the meaning creates life."[8] The Foucauldian discourse from Maud above also reflects the fact that contemporary readers—and writers—desire discourse because discourse feeds our desire. According to Foucault, "We 'Other Victorians' " desire the opportunity to tell and write our desires: on the analyst's couch, in the confessional, in our autobiographies, and now in tabloids, "reality" shows, and talk shows: "the nearly infinite task of telling—telling oneself and another, as often as possible, everything that might concern the interplay of innumerable pleasures, sensations, and thoughts which, through the body and the soul, had some affinity with sex."[9] Although the reader sees and understands as the contemporary couple does, it is the Victorian couple and perspective that generate the text and through the text excite our desire to read—to read on, to find out *what happens.*

In the LaBute film the Victorians are secondary; we look darkly into the past at our Victorian ancestors. The focus, despite some clever camera tricks (sliding frame, fades), is squarely on the contemporary Roland, the American who discovers the lost correspondence, and Maud, his beautiful English accomplice. The audience's sympathy and interest resides with Roland while he pursues Maud and the lost Victorian "love story." Thus, the audience recognizes the love story within the love story unfolding, but the "real-time" story of Roland and Maud is central (though, ironically, the Victorians are passionate and unreserved, while the contemporary couple is detached and reserved). The Victorian love story, in fact, may be deterritorialized twice over: once according to American heterosexual cultural norms, and a second time according to norms of belated modernity, which channels the Victorians' productive desire into our own age's postmodern notion of desire as lack.

With the film *Possession*, LaBute, who not only directed the film but co-wrote the screenplay, has transcoded a particularly American cultural narrative into what otherwise appears to be a British (cultural) narrative. The familiar narrative is the genre of the classic Western conveyed through the heroic actions of the character Roland Mitchell.

The classic Western film, according to Will Wright, plays out the conflict of a deeper structure of core American beliefs. With the loner-hero playing the part of the "individual," the Western, in the end, reconciles willful individual freedom (in a capitalist market economy) with the community and social good:

> Valuable human experience, it seems, depends on open, trusting communication based on shared social needs, goals, and interests; it is in this context that the natural rewards of family, love, work, community are enjoyed. But the market demands that members of society identify themselves by independence and self-sufficiency. The values and goals of bourgeois society reflect the market principle of just exchange but are also grounded in the idea of the "good life," the achievement of equality, work, community, and mutual respect. The dilemma, then is apparent: the values of human experience, the norms of the institutional framework of society, the moral order based on social interaction, are all in conflict with values required by the self-regulating market.[10]

The film version of the character "Roland" is (re)cast as an American who has a mysterious past that causes him to avoid intimate social interaction. The very fact that he is an American, of course, makes him an "outcast" or outsider within the English academic social group. In this chapter I first look closely at the structure of the film, with special attention to the character Roland; in the second part of the chapter I discuss the film's Victorian citations and how they work into the whole structure of the film.

LaBute's sleight of hand is that he did not change the structure of the novel's narrative. Utilizing structural analytic terminology, LaBute changed the indices of the character Roland, but did not change his narrative function or the hinge points of the narrative. To understand the radical Americanization of Roland and how the filmic Roland sustains the genre of the Western, one needs to understand the literary Roland. The literary Roland simply is not available as a citation for most American viewers because he is so deeply embedded in the academic recession in the humanities that hit England in the 1980s (as well as in the United States). Early in the novel the text provides details of Roland's academic career: "In 1986 he was twenty-nine, a graduate of Prince Albert College, London (1978) and a PhD of the same university (1985). His doctoral dissertation was entitled *History, Historians and Poetry: A Study of the Presentation of Historical 'Evidence' in the Poems of Randolph Henry Ash*" (13). The dissertation title tells us a good deal about Roland and his career: he is, for the 1980s, an old-fashioned scholar who interprets Ash through his "sources." Apart from English majors exposed to critical theory, very few would know or be interested in these kinds of details. Also, Roland is a research assistant for an ongoing research project on Ash at the British Museum, which means he does not have a "job," a teaching position; the last university job opportunity went to his rival in the field, the suave, cunning, handsome Fergus Wolff. The lack of a university position out of graduate school and his background are the two biggest factors in Roland's ability to relate to others, especially to Maud Bailey.

The presentation of an English regional, lower-middle-class background in American film is virtually nonexistent. Americans recognize classic lower- and working-class film citations such as the cockney (Eliza Doolittle and her father in *My Fair Lady*), or regional working classes (beginning with *How Green Was My Valley* to the more recent *Brassed-Off* and *The Full Monty*); but an average male from a "depressed Lancashire cotton town," where his father was neither a union agitator nor the leader of the working men's brass band, but "a minor official in the County Council" (14–15) is not available to an American audience. The ability to relate to a "foreign" character must come from something normative or from something remarkable. The only remarkable part of Roland's past was his mother's insistence that he receive a "classical" grammar-school education, but overall "[s]he was disappointed. In herself, in his father, in him" (14). *Sight & Sound* reviewer Charlotte O'Sullivan characterizes LaBute's translation of Roland from British to American as the film's "worst betrayal" because "Byatt's dark, British smudge of a loser is lower class, stuck in a rut of academic mediocrity, friendless, chained to a bitter girlfriend and oppressed by a horrible landlady. In other words, he is everything Maud—beautiful, upper-class and critically lauded—is not."[11]

The fact that Byatt's Roland is such a "dark, British smudge of a loser" means that he must be changed in order to appeal to mainstream audiences. The best change, according to Labute, is to make Roland an American; and the best kind of an American in a British context is an "outsider" in a strange, foreign culture. LaBute utilized his own experience in the transformation of Roland's character, as he reveals:

> I turned Roland into an American because I knew less about the class structure in England than about being someone from another nation spending time in a different society. I did a fellowship at the Royal Court Theatre and poached a bit from there, just in terms of the way they looked at me as an American playwright—I felt louder and more aggressive than I have ever felt in my life. There was a sense of decorum that I tended to overstep without thinking about it, which I tried to imbue Roland with.[12]

The lone outsider bears a remarkable resemblance to the cowboy/gunfighter in the classic Western. Will Wright describes the classic Western as "the story of the lone stranger who rides into a troubled town and cleans it up, winning the respect of the townsfolk and the love of the schoolmarm."[13] LaBute's Roland is the lone American stranger who arrives in sleepy London; discovers or uncovers "trouble"; cleans-up Mortimer Cropper, the "bad guy" (and his accomplice, Fergus Wolfe), who happens to come from a university in the Western part of the United States; wins the respect of his London colleagues and the love of the schoolmarm, Maud Bailey. In fact, LaBute's film follows point-by-point Wright's sixteen structural steps of the classic Western, which means that the film maker has taken a citationally British narrative and deterritorialized it into popular mainstream American reterritorialized film citations.

According to Wright, it is the classic Western that is the prototype for all other Westerns, and the one of which we typically say, "all Westerns are the same." However, Wright identifies four periods of the Hollywood Western. First, the classic Western was made from 1930 to roughly 1955; second, the "vengeance variation" "overlaps the end of the classic period and continues until 1960"; third, "the transition theme" from the early 1950s "centers on a hero and a heroine who, while defending justice, are rejected by society"; fourth, "the professional plot" Western was made from 1958 to 1970, which "involves a group of heroes who are professional fighters taking jobs for money."[14] *Possession* corresponds point-for-point to the classic Western, though once Roland tells Maud about the letter, the viewer may be reminded of the third type of Western. The classic Western has three types of characters: the hero, the society, and the villains. Therefore, Roland is obviously the center of the narrative and the outsider, while Maud is a member of the English society who needs Roland to "save" her from the villains and restore normalcy to society. While this story is familiar in terms of films or books we know, Wright claims that this narrative resonates at a deeper level for Americans. I would add that LaBute has upped the ante even more by making Roland an American who struggles against *foreign forces.* In a post-9/11 world, American audiences are receptive to narratives that defend the "American way of life" in the United States and abroad. Thus, Wright's claim is that the Western plays out a mythical structural narrative (which I would qualify as culturally relative to American culture) that resonates with an audience (in recent years due to the terrorist attacks) desirous of repeating the glory era of the Second World War and the postwar years when the United States became a global leader. There is a certain cleverness in embedding narratives that play out these American myths in new contexts. In *The Six-Gun Mystique*, John G. Cawelti argues that the Western follows a game-like pattern, as well as ritual. The ritualist aspect allows the story to be told in new social or historical contexts thus affirming "certain basic cultural values, resolving tensions and establishing a sense of continuity between past and present. . . . the Western is effective as a social ritual because within its basic structure of resolution and affirmation, it indirectly confronts those uncertainties and conflicts of values which have always existed in American culture."[15] The fact that the American Western genre is used for an "adaptation" of an A.S. Byatt novel accentuates the paradox of the Hollywood appropriation.

As I examine Wright's points in relation to *Possession*, it will be evident that the film conforms perfectly to the structure of the classic Western. In terms of the Western, the opening shots of *Possession* establish Wright's first structural point, "the hero enters a social group."[16] The film opens with Henry Ash (Jeremy Northam) walking through a field, trees in the background, and a voice-over (presumably of him reciting a poem of his own). Northam's picture and voice fades into a Sotheby auctioneer's voice, the modern era, and we see Mortimer Cropper (Trevor Eve) and Hildebrand (Craig Crosby), a distant Ash relation. An original copy of the poem that we have heard recited is up for auction. Bidding starts at an exorborant 40,000 pounds; we see Cropper effortlessly, without astonishment, make a bid. The film then cuts to Roland Mitchell (Aaron Eckhart): he rides on the symbol of London transport, a red double-decker bus; stands in the open door; reads his well-worn paperback copy of Ash's poems; looks up, clenches his square masculine jaw with a look of firm determination, then turns as we view his virile profile. A long shot shows Roland hanging off the red bus as it makes a sharp turn; he jumps off before the bus comes to a complete halt. As Roland walks away from the camera past a signature red English calling box (phone booth), the most uninformed American viewer will recognize these as London citations—at the very least the viewer will know they are geographically "foreign." In these three scenes we have the three types of characters in the classic Western: Ash, the society—and it will be his and LaMotte's letters that are literally "saved"; Cropper, the villain (who eventually will be joined by Fergus Wolfe); and Roland, the outsider-hero.

The next scene at the British Library completes our introductory view of Roland, as we see that the "social group" privileges unique things: books, the institution of the library, and expensive acculturated objects (Sotheby's). The second structural point, "the hero is unknown to the society," is played out literally: the British librarian asks Roland as he walks away with Ash's "monster" copy of Vico, "Eeeh, who are you with again?" This scene is created for the film in order to establish the fact that Roland is "new" to this society and is an outsider who is not accepted. Choosing to make Roland an American requires an orientation scene; this plays out in the film in the following exchange:

> (English) LIBRARIAN. Eeeh, who are you with again?
> ROLAND. I'm aah Roland Mitchell.
> LIBRARIAN. Who?
> ROLAND. Professor Blackadder's research assistant.
> LIBRARIAN. Isn't that Dr. Wolfe?
> ROLAND. Was. Fergus got the lectureship at St. John's. Over me.
> LIBRARIAN. Of course he did. Oh, yes Dr. Wolfe mentioned you. You are that American who is over here.
> ROLAND. Well, I'm sure there are others. I mean, after all, you are our favorite colony.[17]

The nationalist clichés in this scene, from attitude to attire to accent, play upon familiar citations and stabilize what the American already knows about the English. Roland one-upping the tie-wearing bookworm librarian with "you are our favorite colony" not only creates humor, but smoothly reminds the American viewer that it is the *American* who is the superior person in spite of being on foreign soil. The citational value of Fergus getting the job at St. John's over Roland is very lucrative indeed because it can be perceived in several ways: one, that the English are biased against Americans; two, that there was some kind of dirty deal made to get Fergus the job; three, that Roland is "foreign" (which in this context is perceived as good) to the institution of "English Literature" (an American teach English poetry?); the fourth way is the most valuable citation because this scene shows that Roland conforms to a Western hero. As Robert Warshow makes lucid, "The Westerner is *par excellence* a man of leisure. Even when he wears a badge of a marshal, or, more rarely, owns a ranch, he appears to be unemployed."[18]

The next scene introduces Maud Bailey (Gwyneth Paltrow) and Fergus Wolfe (Toby Stephens), who, in contrast to Roland, look posh and sophisticated at Sotheby's. Fergus, who is eager to meet Cropper, introduces himself to the senior, well-heeled Ash scholar. In appropriate all-black attire (signature-black turtleneck), Cropper, with his American accent, makes a joke at Blackadder's expense. Inexplicably, Fergus quips to Cropper, "Well he's Irish you see, and enjoys being persecuted." This statement has no citational value at the level of representation—the persecuted-Irish notion might strike a chord with some American viewers (but not in a positive way)—yet the statement does have structural citational value: it bonds the "bad guys" together. Cropper *understands* Fergus. More importantly, Cropper understands that Fergus wants to "get ahead" and be successful.

The third structural point, "the hero is revealed to have an exceptional ability," occurs when Roland finds Ash's original, handwritten letters, which had been tucked away and undisturbed for over a hundred years. Roland's exceptional ability plays out at two levels: first, in his assiduous ability to look in the Vico in the first place; and, second, in his audacity in taking the letters out of the library. The second level is the one the film overplays throughout: the American who "steals," who "thinks he can take what he likes," or who "thinks he owns everything." This point is echoed when Roland seeks advice from his attorney landlord, Euan (Tom Hollander). An American audience perhaps would not completely appreciate the worth of the originals—despite the opening scene at Sotheby's—so it is reiterated by Euan, who, when told that he is holding the originals, exclaims, "Oh my God how much time do we have left? I will have to think up a defense for you." Roland emphasizes the fact that historians and critics know of no "other woman" in Ash's life—in direct contradiction to the letters Roland has discovered. In order to make the situation completely clear for the uninformed American, Roland explains to Euan: "See, Ash, supposedly, never even looked at another woman, I mean, not even glanced at another woman his entire marriage. Can you imagine what would happen if I could prove that Mr. Perfect Husband had this Shakespearean dark-lady-type-thing going?" Euan replies, in a very British accent, "That would be extraordinary. It would be rewriting history, old chap." As a hip young attorney, who is making "Peking duck" with his beautiful Asian girl "friend," Candy, the "old chap" quip not only harkens back to the mid-century British Hollywood films, but also linguistically, and hence culturally, delineates Euan from Roland.

Another point that is established during Roland and Euan's brief exchange is that when Roland makes a man-to-man comment about Candy, Euan asks, "Why, you interested?" Roland replies, "I told you I am off women." In the context of this conversation, and the fact that both Roland and Euan are obviously not homosexual, the audience is supposed to believe that Roland has had an unfortunate relationship with a woman—presumably in America. According to Warshow, Roland's character is a quintessential rendering of the Western hero who has given up women; Warshow theorizes that "his loneliness is organic, not imposed on him by his situation but belonging to him intimately and testifying to his completeness . . . .The Westerner is not compelled to seek love; he is prepared to accept it, perhaps, but he never asks of it more than it can give, and we see him constantly in situations where love is at best an irrelevance."[19] Thus, Roland, the loner, outsider-American who has a special ability to find the most important documents ever discovered in connection with the great Victorian poet Ash, easily fulfills the "exceptional ability" third point of the classic Western.

The fourth structural point, "the society recognizes a difference between themselves and the hero; the hero is given special status," is shown with the second and third points, but is furthered when Roland visits the British Museum where Blackadder (Tom Hickey) has his research project. The term "special status" as Wright uses it indicates that everyone in the society regards the hero as "different," and maybe different for different reasons. For example, Blackadder treats Roland like an undergraduate when he tells him of the untouched Vico in the London Library; Blackadder is certain that Roland (an ignorant American) could never discover something truly important—everything important has already been found. Blackadder, despite the film-version "Irish" identity and accent, fulfills the English bumbling-professor role (reiteration of Professor Welch in *Lucky Jim*?) for American audiences. The principle function, however, of this scene is Blackadder's mention of Cropper at Sotheby's; this reestablishes the image of Cropper-as-villain for the viewer. Another indication of Roland's special status is that he is admired by a minor character, Paola (Georgia Mackenzie), the young administrative assistant to Blackadder; Roland is friendly to Paola, but does not return her affection.

During the first few minutes of the film, the fifth point "the society does not completely accept the hero" has been developing. Apart from Euan, who finds Roland amusing, and Paola, who finds him attractive, our hero exists outside of the British Ash scholarship loop. This lack of acceptance is brought to a climax when Roland meets Maud Bailey. First, however, Roland seeks advice from Fergus concerning Maud before he meets with her. Fergus, now wearing his villain's black turtleneck, informs Roland that Maud "thicks men's blood with cold," then states, "or if you prefer the American vernacular, she's a regular ball breaker." Fergus, who had minutes before needled Roland that he was at the bottom of the scholarly "food chain," now appears threatened by Roland's interest in Maud. Fergus, as a bad guy, also provides a contrast to Roland in that he is *employed*; this scene reiterates the librarian's acerbic "Of course" in regard to the fact that Fergus Wolfe would be offered the lectureship over Roland. LaBute is compressing decades of Western-film citational value into a few short scenes. The English academic "society" views Roland as an outsider because they consider him a parasite or someone who is trying to insinuate himself into their world. Roland cannot get employment, not because he is foreign, but because the hero of the classic Western is never "employed" ("The Westerner is *par excellence* a man of leisure . . . . appears to be unemployed.").

With Roland-as-Westerner, Labute is iterating a known quantity to an American audience. However, Maud Bailey (Gwyneth Paltrow), a successful feminist academic and LaMotte scholar, does not appreciate Roland's situation or Western citations, and in her own distaste for this unemployed American, the American audience will recognize a snooty British attitude of supposed superiority. Therefore, with Roland and Maud, LaBute has created a systematic vehicle for American identification: the lone Westerner and the schoolmarm from the east, respectively. The audience always narcissistically identifies with the male lead, who carries the action forward, while it resents the Paltrow-as-spectacle, who arrests the action's progress.[20] The contrast of their initial meeting continues the incongruity of their characters: Roland's man-of-leisure, almost-infantile posture is set against Maud's uptight, properly responsible disposition. This initial scene occurs at the Lincolnshire train station as Maud finds Roland in his "leisure" pose waiting for her to give him a lift to campus; Roland resembles a student more than a peer (headphones, sloppy clothes). The audience's perspective of Maud as self-righteous and snooty continues when Roland shows Maud the original letters Ash wrote. She is shocked to be told she is holding the originals and exclaims, "[you have that] take-what-you-want attitude I've seen in other Americans." Roland helps Maud to finish "other Americans," confirming a well-known attitude by both parties. The next scene between Blackadder and Fergus hammers home this sentiment. When Fergus presses Blackadder to discover Roland's whereabouts, Blackadder testily replies, "He's an American, for God's sake, he's probably off trafficking drugs." These back-to-back scenes, along with the next scene at the Bailey's, when Maud announces that Roland is "on the dole," present a convincing package: for an American audience that does not find humor in these representations or characterizations of the cowboy-hero, there will be resistance and, through this, *identification*.

The sixth structural point is that "there is a conflict of interests between the villains and the society," which we can easily see unfolding through Fergus's initial jealousy concerning Maud and Roland, and then his divulging of information about the letters found at the Bailey's to Cropper. Wright makes the point that "in this conflict the villains always prove themselves to be far more capable of winning."[21] In *Possession*, not unlike a classic Western, the villains are underhanded and have no scruples when it comes to getting what they want. After an initial meeting in which Fergus offers Cropper (both attired fully in black) what he knows about Maud and Roland's mysterious investigation at Seal Court, they go to Seal Court to "buy off" Sir George. The seventh structural point confirms that Fergus and Cropper as "the villains are stronger than the society; the society is weak." Fergus betrays Maud by telling Cropper of their visit; this makes the bad-guy team stronger because Fergus has, in effect, infiltrated both sides—he is a double agent. A Western touch is added to a very English scene when Sir George yells "Hands up!" at Cropper and Fergus as he points a twelve-gauge shotgun at them. The cowboy lingo resonates with "Get off my property!" The "get off my land" of the Western is brought in to highlight the "property-rights" issue. Therefore, we see that Fergus and Cropper as "the villains are stronger than the society" because the "society" also includes Sir George. Cropper knows that Sir George is weak because he needs money to manage his disintegrating estate, and his wife is ill. In a competitive free-market economy, Cropper has more capital; and so, left unregulated, he wins—he will be able to buy out Sir George. From a "good-guy" position, the ability to buy and sell cultural artifacts and historical documents must be regulated and put into the "public domain." If not, then Cropper, the bad guy, with his huge capital resources will "win the day." Yet, regulation alters the "market forces" of capitalism and interferes with the laissez-faire policy that reemerged in America in the 1990s.

With the eighth structural point, "there is a strong friendship or respect between the hero and a villain," Wright admits that this is often symbolic: "This 'friendship' suggests some of the structural rewards of transforming male violence into female lust in the Western myth, and perhaps reveals some unconscious symbolism in the more standard Western."[22] While the Fergus–Maud–Roland love triangle is one possibility, the respect between the hero and villain is more clearly stated in the scene in Yorkshire in which Roland and Maud have retraced the Victorians' footsteps to the Thomason Foss Waterfall. Through Cropper's biography of Ash, Roland can confirm Ash's whereabouts on that fateful July in 1859. Roland tells Maud that Cropper has literally walked in the footsteps of Ash in order to write the poet's biography. Although Roland calls Cropper an "all-purpose asshole," he respects his work (at least to the extent that Cropper was the first to catalog all of Ash's movements). Maud's recitation of one of Christabel's poems places her at the waterfall with Ash. To verify Christabel's connection to the waterfall, the filmic Roland disrobes and jumps into the stream to discover whether, indeed, there is a cave behind the falls. Roland's stripping-down is portrayed comically as Maud mutters to Roland, who is already undressed and in the water, "I know this is an English repressive thing, but why don't we just ask someone." As Western hero, however, Roland must strip and jump into frigid water at this point to reaffirm to the audience that he is indeed a virile hero. Having Aaron Eckhart disrobe and plunge into cold water—"Mr. Darcy style"—is not only "eye candy" for what is likely a female-majority audience, but also displays the hero's body as capable of physical heroism.[23]

The ninth structural point, "the villains threaten the society," occurs in *Possession* when Roland overhears Cropper, Fergus, and Hildebrand Ash conspiring to dig up Ash's grave in order to retrieve the "black box" Ellen Ash buried with her husband. Due to necessity, the film has condensed and collapsed various actions and even characters to get to this point in the narrative. Wright asserts that the tenth and eleventh structural points of the Western are optional: "the hero avoids involvement with the conflict," and "the villains endanger a friend of the hero." However, the film teeters on fulfilling these two points when Roland apparently gives up the quest to know what happened to Christabel's child and writes a letter of apology to Blackadder. It is when Roland goes to the museum to leave Blackadder the apology and original Ash letters from the Vico that he overhears Cropper, Fergus, and Hildebrand discuss their plot to dig up Ash's grave. For the film's purposes, this scene conveniently draws Blackadder back into the story because if Cropper successfully gets the black box he will take the British cultural artifacts and history to the United States; since Blackadder represents the British interest by directing the Ash project at the British Museum, he is the one who will be wronged or "endangered." Also significant, we eventually discover that Maud's interests would also have been endangered.

The twelfth point, "the hero fights the villains" and thirteenth, "the hero defeats the villains," Wright asserts are absolutely necessary. The showdown at the cemetery turns farcical as Roland and his possé (Maud, Blackadder, Paola) close in on the villains just as they extract the black box. Cropper exclaims "I found it Fergus, I found it," when in fact he and Fergus found it together. When Cropper, the head of the bandit ring, attempts to escape with the booty, Roland chases him down. To sufficiently round out the "good-guys-get-the-bad-guys" scenario, Blackadder catches hold of Fergus and boots him while Roland catches and punches an already subdued Cropper. Maud runs to her newfound hero Roland and comforts him. Admittedly, the action happens very fast; but Roland as Western hero does not hesitate to do the right thing to bring order to society. According to Warshow, Roland must act decisively as the hero so as to fulfill his duty: "There is no suggestion, however, that he draws the gun reluctantly. The Westerner could not fulfill himself if the moment did not finally come when he can shoot his enemy down. But because that moment is so thoroughly the expression of his being, it must be kept pure."[24] Roland's hero status is thus confirmed by his decisive chase and punch. Indeed, the punch in the nose from Roland appears to be executed as punishment; taking the black box away from the villain is not enough, he must also be punished.

The fourteenth structural point is that "the society is safe." In the film Roland has not only secured the letters, but has restored a legitimate order to the English academic and literary society. The fifteenth point, "the society accepts the hero," occurs when the society witnesses the hero's fight against the villain. Therefore, the English academics get to see the brave *American* Roland duke it out and win. The fact that Cropper is also American presents an American subtext: the anomalous bad American exposed and beaten, the representative triumphant good American saves the alien English culture (because it was too weak to save itself). Finally, the sixteenth point, "the hero loses or gives up his special status," is fulfilled when it is revealed that Maud is the descendant of both Christabel LaMotte and Henry Ash. Maud and Roland's private inspection of the contents of the black box is unique to the film, but allows the revelation scene and the hero's loss of special status to be collapsed. According to Wright, "the hero marrying and settling in the now peaceful community, becoming just like everybody else—is the common ending throughout the classical Western."[25] The end of *Possession* implies that Maud, a descendent of Ash and LaMotte, will procreate with Roland and, thereby, combine the line of the great poets with Roland's heroic American bloodline, and thus, strengthen future society. The end of the film fulfills the "traditional" values of family and home that the classical Western advances, while the market economy represented by Cropper seems to falter. Of course, Cropper did not engage in "fair practices" of a regulated market economy, but engaged in unregulated market activity. An American audience would "unconsciously" recognize the difference, though the loser in the regulated economy appears to be the forgotten Sir George and his ill wife. In the end, the hero successfully gives back to "society" what is rightfully theirs: the letters will remain in the British Museum; literary and cultural history is restored to its rightful owners.

The Victorian Tableau

Enfolded in the American Western structural frame of the film is the Victorian love story minus the novel's extensive view of Victorian life. LaBute apologetically states that "huge chunks" of the novel had to go by the wayside in reference to the nineteenth-century narrative: "There were obvious passages that I knew I could not translate—huge chunks of their respective poetry and discourses on Victorian society and politics."[26] The Victorians function as time-frozen tableaux waiting to be uncovered by the contemporary eye of the camera. The Victorian tableau is consistently revealed inside of an actual written Victorian text that the contemporaries *unfold*: a text unfolds and we see Ash walking in the country; and, as it refolds, we are returned to the present in Sotheby's; or when the LaMotte–Ash correspondence is initially discovered, as the words unfold we glimpse the Victorians. The written texts in the film are invariably accompanied by scene cuts to the Victorians posing, often times, in a *tableaux vivant*: Christabel and Ash making love, Christabel and Blanche on the sofa, Ash and Christabel meeting near Trafalgar Square to arrange their rendezvous, Ash meeting Christabel at the seance. Therefore, for LaBute the Victorian tableaux are mere indices that *illustrate* the past as the contemporary couple, especially Roland, structurally moves the action forward. Thus, the *mise-en-scene*, or what I am calling the tableau, is the catch-all of the parallel story of the Victorians.

In like manner, the 1980s and 1990s popularity of heritage films depended on getting the "look" of the historical period, and LaBute fully participates in perfecting the style of dress, manner of gesture, attitude, and period details for the Victorian scenes. LaBute knows that achieving the look is essential in creating the past; as Andrew Higson explains, "The image of the past in the heritage films has become so naturalized that, paradoxically, it stands removed from history: the evocation of pastness is accomplished by a look, a style, the loving recreation of period details. . . . The self-conscious visual perfectionism of these films and their fetishization of period details create a fascinating but self-enclosed world."[27] LaBute supposedly "pored over" earlier period films, and paintings and drawings from the Victorian era to achieve *Possession*'s period look. In ferreting out these images, which contributed to LaBute's Victorian "look," we unfold easily recognized visual citational sources, which LaBute, in some instances, cannibalizes whole.

The idea that the contemporaries and the Victorians have equal time in the film is erroneous. What appears to be "parallel action" is the contemporary period "accessing" or imaginatively inventing through words little peepholes or pockets of the past, which the spectator gets to view. The Victorian story, though the more passionate and powerful of the so-called parallel stories, is subordinate to the "star power" of the contemporary couple who are following, basically, Roland's cowboy-hero trajectory. For instance, the need to put the star power on visual display is shown when the letters are read by Maud, and *Ash*, not Roland; though we see Roland, the American Roland's voice is not the voice of the letters. American Paltrow's English accent "works," whereas Eckhart's voice is too American. Before this scene, however, in the "Dolly-keeps-a-secret" scene, the film plays into our contemporary desire to fetishize the past—a past waiting to be uncovered, almost eager to be discovered. In the novel, of course, this coincidence is easily explained by the genre of the romance in which Byatt has carefully framed her novel. Even the former bedroom of Christabel, who died around 1900, has remained—miraculously—untouched for a hundred years. The water pitcher and bed clothes have not been moved; the doll babies in their cradle have been completely undisturbed, despite the subsequent generations of Bailey children growing up at Seal Court. Perhaps American film is deeply indebted to the romance since so many films rely on improbable circumstances and coincidences. The film therefore fulfills an American romantic fantasy: to silently trip through an English manor house—uncovering treasures and secrets long kept hidden.

In the film Maud remembers the "Dolly-keeps-a-secret" poem, but it is initially a false lead. In the book, the point of view is Roland's; Roland, frustrated, is characterized as feeling "as though he was prying, and as though he was being uselessly urged on by some violent emotion of curiosity—not greed, curiosity, more fundamental even than sex, the desire for knowledge" (92). Therefore, the novel's desire for knowledge finds its equivalant in the viewer's nostalgic desire for manor houses untouched for a century. The poem itself invites a future unknown Guest to come and "lay us to rest":

> The house is ready spotless
> Waiting for the Guest
> Who will see our white linen

At its very best
Who will take it and fold it
And lay us to rest. (42–43)

As the Guests, Maud and Roland will *un*fold the linen, read the hidden correspondence and "lay" Christabel and Randolph "to rest"; however, it is the audience who gets to *look* through that special peephole and *see* the past unfold.

LaBute's pockets of past are almost all direct copies of a certain style of Victorian dress, style, and manners. LaBute relies heavily on the "authenticity" of canvases of the Pre-Raphaelite painters and popular portraits of Victorian writers. LaBute claims to have viewed period films such as Ken Russell's black-and-white *Dante's Inferno* (1967). *Dante's Inferno* is a quintessential 1960s period film, with a Dante Gabriel Rossetti (Oliver Reid) who looks more "swinging London" than Pre-Raphaelite; the glaring 1960s periodization is more prominent because of the 1980s and 1990s heritage films' near-perfection of minute historical detail. Perhaps the primary success of *Dante's Inferno* in terms of "periodization" is the portrayal of the Pre-Raphaelite revival of "chivalry," which Dante Gabriel Rossetti enacts early in the film concerning his love for Elizabeth Siddal (Judith Paris). Undoubtedly, however, the deliberate attempt to saturate *Dante's Inferno* with a Pre-Raphaelite "look" is reiterated in the Victorian scenes in *Possession*. The iterative power of Pre-Raphaelite painting is clearly utilized by LaBute; after comparing a particular nineteenth-century painting to its corresponding film tableau, it is impossible to dismiss the image of the original from that of the tableau. Pre-Raphaelite citations, especially images of women, are generally recognizable to American audiences, even if they cannot "name" that "look." This "look" has been reiterated in popular American culture through the "San Francisco" music-scene posters (e.g., Wes Wilson, Bonnie MacLean), which were then reiterated on countless record-album covers (not to mention that Led Zeppelin's females always "look" Pre-Raphaelite—even the "Houses of the Holy" children look Pre-Raphaelite). The copy to original reasserts itself; it is only because Americans know the "bad" copies associated with pop culture that they can recognize the "look" as belonging to a former period. Americans know the look is retro.

In the film, Jennifer Ehle's Christabel is portrayed with very long reddish-brown hair and often wears green velvet clothes. While the novel Christabel is also always cloaked in green, the LaBute image of Christabel corresponds to any number of Dante Gabriel Rossetti paintings, including *The Blue Bower* (1865), in which the red-haired female figure wears green in contrast to the blue-patterned wall behind her; *The Beloved* (1865–1866), in which the ginger-haired female's head is wrapped in a green shawl that matches her dress (figure 3.1); in *Veronica Veronese* (1872), the sensual red-haired female not only wears luxuriant green velvet, but Rossetti referred to this painting as "chiefly a study of varied Greens."[28] Jenny Beavan's costume design for Christabel wearing a hood/shawl strikingly reiterates *The Beloved.* Culturally iconic, Rossetti's shawled woman is based on a passage from the ornate "Song of Solomon." Although Christabel does not

Figure 3.1 Dante Gabriel Rossetti's *The Beloved (The "Bride")* (1855–1856), Courtesy of the Tate Gallery, London/Art Resource, NY

have an entourage, she is the center of the frame as she walks toward Ash with her triangular hood drawn into the darkened space around her face; in contrast, her face is well lit, and we are attracted to the overall familiar iconic image of pre-twentieth-century chaste womanhood.

While Ash becomes the chief admirer of Christabel, he is not the first. Her lesbian lover Blanche (Lena Headey) is her first admirer and she does not use words to praise Christabel, but rather paint. We see Christabel sitting for Blanche in a scene that unfolds while Roland and Maud are reading aloud the correspondence. The canvases already painted and the one being executed are Pre-Raphaelite in style, color, and subject matter. Blanche's appearance, of course, must not be seductive to an American audience; therefore, Blanche is cast in the "spinster-who-can't-get-a-man" role. Her dresses are drab, her hair is always pulled-back, and most telling of all she wears "granny glasses" (Americans are unconsciously reminded of such characters as "Granny" from *The Beverly Hillbillies*)—a deliberate mark of her lack of heterosexual appeal (figure 3.2). Blanche's painting style is Pre-Raphaelite, and in figure 3.2 we can see one of her own tablauex: a man reaching out to a woman brushing her hair, with a second

Figure 3.2 Blanche Glover (Lena Headey) in front of her painting, *Possession* (2002), Courtesy of Universal Studios Licensing LLLP

Figure 3.3 Christabel LaMotte (Jennifer Ehle), posing, *Possession* (2002), Courtesy of Universal Studios Licensing LLLP

woman standing between them. The triangular configuration we see again, but in this painting we can see that Christabel is the figure on the right. Similar in tone, Rossetti's *Dante Meets Beatrice* (ca. 1855) features the poet Dante meeting Beatrice (in the afterlife); the viewer's focus is concentrated on Beatrice's hair and head, which is similar to Blanche's preening image of Christabel as the woman on the right side of the canvas. Also, in figure 3.2 we have the foreshadowing of the future action in which Ash reaches out to Christabel while Blanche stands in the middle; the viewer also "naturally" responds to Blanche's painting as representative of heterosexual courtship, and, because of the three figures, perhaps unrequited love or betrayal. In the foreground of this frame, Blanche pleads with Christabel to return their private life to what it was before Ash's letters began arriving.

As Blanche's model, holding a letter from Ash, Christabel wears an uncharacteristically low-cut dress with jacket (figure 3.3), a reiteration of Edward Burne-Jones's *Clara von Bork* (1860) (figure 3.4). This painting is one of a two-set illustration of the English translation of Johann Wilhelm Meinhold's romance *Sidonia the Sorceress* (1847), in which Clara is the good woman and Sidonia von Bork the evil woman (the first dies at the hands of the second; the second is burned

Figure 3.4 Edward Burne-Jones' *Clara von Bork 1560* (1860), Courtesy of the Tate Gallery, London/Art Resource, NY

at the stake as punishment). Christabel is the adored Clara, while Blanche becomes the evil Sidonia. One does not need to know the particulars of the story to understand the subtle iterative power; LaBute establishes Christabel's antithesis: the evil, unattractive, *lesbian* Blanche. In contrast, Christabel's ornate brocade dress, displayed decollage, and hair unbound make her heterosexually attractive to the viewer, overturning the contemporary bias toward the would-be repressed Victorian. Certainly, the contrast between Christabel's heterosexual appeal and Blanche's dour appearance is not lost on the spectator accustomed to affiate or empathize with the beautiful woman in heterosexual society.

The film does not linger long on the relationship between Christabel and Blanche so as not to turn the audience off of Christabel (who is actually bisexual before the word is coined) because she is a lesbian. Yet, LaBute creates one very striking tableau of Christabel and Blanche that indicates unquestionably the nature of their relationship. This peephole tableau shows Blanche reclining on a sofa with her head on Christabel's lap (figure 3.5). The scene is a striking reiteration of Simeon Solomon's erotic *Sappho and Erinna in a Garden at Mytilene*

Figure 3.5 Blanche Glover (Lena Headey) and Christabel LaMotte (Jennifer Ehle) reclining, *Possession* (2002), Courtesy of Universal Studios Licensing LLLP

Figure 3.6 Simeon Solomon's *Sappho and Erinna in a Garden at Mytilene* (1864), Courtesy of the Tate Gallery, London/ Art Resource, NY

(1864) (figure 3.6). *Sappho and Erinna in a Garden at Mytilene* was not the kind of painting that was publically shown in its own era; rather, this painting and others like it by the "practising homosexual" Solomon, "were circulated in the form of photographic reproductions to wider audiences than the small circle of Solomon's close friends."[29] Thus, the painting's depiction of the lovers, like Christabel and Blanche, would have been a secret, considered vile, "a love that bears no name." Moreover, the *Possession* film tableau reiterates the ambivalence of the painting. Although Sappho was Erinna's mentor, they were "sister" artists together, much like Blanche and Christabel. Thais E. Morgan depicts the Solomon painting as portraying Sappho's dominance of Erinna: "Sadism of the Sadeian kind may be represented by Sappho's aggressive embrace and partial disrobing of the apparently reluctant Erinna in Solomon's painting . . . .Sappho's neck cords stand out tensely as she leans into Erinna who tries to delay the dominant woman's impulse by putting her right knee up between them."[30] Blanche as the forceful Sappho figure and Christabel as the resisting Erinna reiterate Christabel's moving away from a homosexual relationship toward a heterosexual relationship with Ash.

Moreover, LaBute or others involved in the film may have discovered a great deal about the Pre-Raphaelites, including the fact that Solomon executed a pen-and-ink drawing *Erinna Taken from Sappho* (1865), which depicts a *male* figure embracing the partially nude Erinna while the scorned Sappho watches. As noted above, Blanche's painting in the background in figure 3.2 functions as a foreshadowing of the triangular homosexual/heterosexual relationship of *Erinna Taken from Sappho*. In figure 3.5 Christabel strokes Blanche's hair as she surreptitiously reads from a secretly received Ash letter. The fact that Blanche opens her eyes to see Christabel lost in reverie as she reads Ash's words opens up the counter-betrayal on the part of Blanche: she steals and hides Ash's letters to Christabel—the discovery propels the consummation of Christabel and Ash's relationship. The film presents repetitive citations that approve of the heterosexual, though adultrous, union as they reterritorialize homosexual desire. Because we already have heterosexual codes in place, the audience will "naturally" approve of the heterosexual couple, and the film is loaded with cultural reiterations that reinforce that approval.

Anyone familiar with A.S. Byatt's text might connect her cover art, Edward Burne-Jones's *The Beguiling of Merlin* (1870–1874), with the "look" of the film's Victorians. Perhaps LaBute chose to recreate, reiterate, and repeat the Pre-Raphaelite "look" because of the original cover art of the Byatt text. While Arthurian legends were very much a part of the Pre-Raphaelite mentality, the Arthurian legend does not figure in the novel *Possession* at all—except, of course, in the "quest" motif of the contemporary action. The connection, therefore, must be made at the level of "beguiling," which in this painting is a kind of "possession." However, LaBute has no practical use for this image (with his Western-genre focus); thus, we encounter a different kind of paradox when we look at Byatt's original cover, and the film's promotional paraphernalia. A film that relies on the iterability of Pre-Raphaelite citations abandons the one visual connection from book to film concerning this "look." Instead, the film's promotional releases feature the contemporary couple, or more precisely, the recognizable "star power" of Paltrow and Eckhart. In the Paltrow and Eckhart portion of the poster, Big Ben glows white against a dazzling sky and cityscape. Looking "contemporary," Big Ben and the House of Parliament appear "hip" and exciting to even the average movie goer; the streaks of light and seared paper below the stars' visages connotes fast-paced action and sexual attraction. This poster is reiterative of countless other "high-concept" formula-film promotions. In direct correspondence with the film, Northam and Ehle are not only "second billing," but also are presented as much smaller, blurred figures falling off the bottom right of the film's promotional poster. Northam appears to whisper in Ehle's ear, but the supposed look of rapture (eyes closed, mouths slightly open) suggests intimacy. The smaller presentation of these figures alludes to a subtextual subplot. Indeed, if the Victorian couple are truly a "parallel" story, then "equal" billing would reflect equal time in the film; but clearly the Victorian story is of lesser importance; appropriated to fit into a recognizable American narrative formula and repackaged into a "high concept" narrative "which is very straightforward, easily communicated, and easily comprehended," *Possession*'s promotional images are predictably "high concept."[31]

While Jennifer Ehle's Christabel is presented as a series of Pre-Raphaelite "looks," Jeremy Northam's Ash depends more on "literary" citations. The character of Ash bears a resemblance to Pre-Raphaelite John Everett Milais's *John Ruskin* (1853–1854), which shows Ruskin standing in front of a running stream in black attire with a hint of a white shirt. While Ash is often in a simple black suit, tie, and white shirt (walking in the country, writing at home), we also see him more lavishly attired. While it is difficult to quantify the specifics of a reiteration, Ash's character is almost a replica of a famous portrait of a young, good-looking Charles Dickens known as the "Nickleby Portrait" (1839), painted by Daniel Maclise (figure 3.7). The most striking detail is Dickens's exaggerated pout, his top lip jutting out, aligning with this nose, a pose reiterated by Northam's Ash (figure 3.8). The somewhat-annoying posing Northam must do to achieve this "pout" is so consistent with the Dickens portrait that we can only surmise that LaBute thinks it the quintessential trait of the dashing and brilliant Victorian poet/writer. The fact that Dickens is the one Victorian writer every person in America has read—or supposedly been forced to read in school—and that this portrait is famous and often reproduced means that the iteration is likely to be familiar at some level. The cliché of the Victorian writer, with Dickens as a perfect example, who is duped into a passionless and unhappy marriage is also familiar to many. This stereotype in *Possession* allows the reader to feel some empathy for Ash. The fact that Ellen and Ash never actually consummate their marriage is merely hinted at in the film; perhaps contemporary Americans would not believe this was possible *even* in Victorian marriages.

Therefore, virtually all the Victorian peephole scenes feature Ash's pout, Christabel's lavish green persona, and the well-shot English

Figure 3.7 *Charles Dickens* by Daniel Maclise (1839), Courtesy of the National Portrait Gallery, London

landscape scenes. The consummation of Ash and Christabel's love is romantic and passionate, but not "sexy" in the contemporary sense. Still wearing her slip, Christabel mounts Ash; this scene is sexy "enough" for the Masterpiece Theatre audience, but not for the average American viewer accustomed to more nudity. This scene is an approximation of what a contemporary can imagine a Victorian doing while

Figure 3.8 Randolph Henry Ash (Jeremy Northam), profile, *Possession* (2002), Courtesy of Universal Studios Licensing LLLP

having sex. As Sue Sorensen points out, LaBute "does provide nicely charged erotic scenes between the handsome Northam and Ehle as Ash and Christabel, but these are shopworn in their presentation of Victorian corsets slowly unlaced and four-poster beds agreeably rumpled. Generally, LaBute seems uncomfortable with sexual pleasure."[32] Yet, the paradox of the Victorians being passionate, and *fertile*, while the contemporaries, acclimated to sex around every corner, cannot form a relationship, is ultimately proven (even after the end of the film's revelation scene), in large part because there is little "chemistry" between the "stars" Paltrow and Eckhart.

The novel's postscript is played out in high heritage style with Ash's walk in the country (near Seal Court) to find Christabel; instead of Christabel, Ash finds May Bailey. The final effective long shot and the camera's movement away from the past—literally in this film—is a technique used in the heritage-film genre. Higson points out that this kind of manipulation, typically provides the audience a more "aesthetic" take on the scene:

> There is also a preference for long takes and deep focus, and for long and medium shots, rather than for close-ups and rapid cutting. The

> camera is characteristically fluid, but camera movement is dictated less by a desire to follow the movement of characters than by a desire to offer the spectator a more aesthetic angle on the period setting and objects that fill it.[33]

The setting and objects in the final scene are the English countryside of Seal Court and the manor house, which we see in perspective as the long shot moves farther away from the ground. The camera's view is, and has been, contemporary; thus, this final scene assures us that Ash knew of his daughter and understood that Christabel had done the right thing for their age: passed off their child to her married sister, to be raised as the couple's biological daughter. Therefore, the spectator knows that overall the past did all right for itself: Ash died knowing he had a daughter, while Christabel watched her grow up as her niece. It is not perfect for the contemporary audience, who want the Oedipalized nuclear family happily united (perhaps Ellen Ash could die soon after Blanche drowns herself); but the audience understands the Victorian situation to be limited and so the conclusion to be a "happy ending."

From our analysis of LaBute's *Possession*, we can conclusively understand how the film radically deterritorializes and reiterates the literary text into a different context of meaning by employing the Western genre that repeats familiar citations, reterritorializing the film into a *recognizable* and predictable product for American audiences. Even with what is effectively two endings—one, Roland and Maud's reading the correspondence and, two, the film's enactment of the novel's postscript—the Western-genre formula is dominant as the contemporary society *and* the Victorian "society" are restored; and, as Cawelti argues, the bridge between the past and present are solidified. Contemporary American viewers are brought into the film and given the satisfaction of a "feel-good" recognizable American narrative—despite the foreign setting and foreign "source" material. As a good old-fashioned American formula film, *Possession* is, as we have seen, surprisingly successful as a British academic novel transfigured through deterritorializing the British citational values into reterritorialized American Western codes. Additionally, the film is successful in conveying a philosophy of identity that ensures that we never have to "think" about the film since it never puts into question America's cultural "superiority" or belief system.

CHAPTER 4

Cinema's Romance with the Colonial: *The English Patient*'s "AntiConquest" Adventure

This chapter explores the imaginative hold that British colonial, imperial history of the Empire has had on the American imagination. The global hegemony over knowledge and naming that white European males exerted for hundreds of years over the colonial world (from Africa to the Far East to the Americas) is analogous to the postwar capitalist and military dominance the United States has displayed. Hollywood reproduces the American's fantasy—global American hegemony—through historical and literary figures borrowed from this older European tradition.

The genre of the adventure film has several manifestations; this chapter focuses on one primary strand that involves the quest motif under the auspices of "anticonquest" colonialism. In *Imperial Eyes: Travel Writing and Transculturation*, Mary Louise Pratt discusses the "anticonquest" as those "strategies of representation whereby European bourgeois subjects seek to secure their innocence in the same moment as they assert European hegemony."[1] The film *The English Patient* (Anthony Minghella, 1996), adapted from Michael Ondaatje's 1992 Booker Prize–winning novel of the same name, seemingly updates the imperial adventure interrupted by war and a dramatic love story. Commercially successful, winner of nine Academy Awards, including Best Picture, the film was directed and its screenplay was written by Anthony Minghella, who utilizes a simple formula for success: deterritorialize the "foreign" contingent (Kip the Sikh), and feature the passionate, "tragic" love affair between the two upper-class English characters (Ladislaus de Almasy aka the English patient, and Katharine Clifton); then frame the action in the adventure mode with spectacular panoramic, empire desert scenes (and "present-day" romantically ruined Italian scenes)—the reterritorialization is complete.

The fact that critics repeatedly frame the film in terms of Almasy and Katharine Clifton, and then in terms of territorialization on a global scale—colonialism, a brewing world war—tells us that most see the narrative frame in terms of the story in the *past*, that must unfold in the *present*, the Italy of 1945. Often, however, critics and scholars are not sure about dates or timelines; this confusion, I believe, happens because the film delivers the historical, colonial adventure quietly, though faithfully, alongside the "romance" of Almasy and Katharine. In "Mapping the Other: *The English Patient*, Colonial Rhetoric, and Cinematic Representation," Alan Nadel theorizes that the colonialism has been so naturalized that "*The English Patient* presents an extended rhetorical argument about the dimensions of colonial discourse in such a way as to connect that discourse to the codes of cinematic representation, thus revealing the seductive quality of colonial discourse as a form of cinematic romance from which the rhetorical tenets of mainstream cinema allow no escape."[2] If this is the case, then the colonial discourse in *The English Patient* is more powerfully seductive than the often-steamy sexual affair between Almasy and Katharine. But the discourse of colonialism is so deeply ingrained that we are unaware of its operation, of its hold on us. Barbara Kennedy's attempt to assess the film with Deleuzian language plays into the seductive logic of the colonial discourse: "Set in 1939, the story unfolds of the disastrous, passionate and obsessive love affair between Count Almasy and Katharine Clifton, set within the confines of a world fascinated by, embroiled in and organised through 'territorialisation.' Map-making, sovereignty and ownership are highlighted through acts of sanctioning, sectioning and segregation across endemic moral codings."[3]

It is my contention that the film's success relies on two stable (sub)generic formulae that provide the context for audience empathy and participation. In the first, the filmic Almasy undergoes a leading man make-over transforming him into an adventure hero; second, Almasy as desert-map maker is a recognizable European colonial figure as he participates in the colonial enterprise of the "anticonquest" hero along the lines of Richard Burton (*Mountains of the Moon*, 1990) or T. E. Lawrence (*Lawrence of Arabia*, 1962). These two subgenres are part of the same Hollywood tradition that goes back to the black-and-white swashbuckler and Robin Hood films starring Errol Flynn and forward to films such as *The Raiders of the Lost Ark*, starring Harrison Ford. The third convention that *The English Patient* seemingly exploits is the romance, but, as we shall see, I believe this hyped aspect of the film to be actually part of the genre of the colonial adventure, and thus, is only *marketed* as a romantic drama to increase ticket sales. The romance is absorbed by the adventure formula.

According to Pratt, explorers interested in scientific, historical, anthropological, and even linguistic, knowledge created "natural" histories, detailing "a rationalizing, extractive, dissociative understanding which overlaid functional, experiential relations among people, plants, and animals. In these respects, it figures a certain kind of global hegemony, notably one based on possession of land and resources rather than control over routes."[4] These distinctively European models of knowledge and power provided a rationale for explorers such as Almasy as "natural history provided a means for narrating inland travel and exploration aimed not at the discovery of trade routes, but at territorial surveillance, appropriation of resources, and adminstrative control."[5] As the previous chapters have shown, British literature narratives are appropriated to fit into recognizable American narrative formulae so that often complex and "foreign" narrative content can be repackaged into a "high-concept" narrative "that is very straightforward, easily communicated, and easily comprehended."[6] Despite the film's length and complexity, *The English Patient* participates in recognizable film tropes. While the romance between Almasy and Katharine is the narrative centerpiece, the colonial desert-adventure story propels the lovers' fate. In fact, it could be argued that Almasy's sudden heroic status in the film frames the narrative first and foremost as an adventure story. As Brian Taves argues in *The Romance of Adventure: The Genre of Historical Adventure Movies*, "the love interest is also more important to adventure films than to such other action genres as westerns, war, or crime films. Love forms a subplot that parallels the main themes, placing the woman in a perilous situation that provides the hero with the opportunity he seeks to prove his nobility, chivalry, courage, and altruism."[7]

As Maggie M. Morgan points out, the film is "brilliant in its own right, but radically different in its interests, the film diverged from Ondaatje's revised history of World War II."[8] Sensitive to the changes made from novel to film, Minghella, in an interview with Angela Baldassarre, states, "There's this unnecessary ruthlessness that occurs when you can't have another two hours of the film, and so you make thousands of decisions, but we made them collectively. But they were made in the spirit of trying to appreciate a book that we all loved and at the same time understand the fact that ninety percent of the audience going to see this film wouldn't have heard of *The English Patient.*

I hope they run off and buy the book after seeing the film. Our first obligations as filmmakers is to tell a story."[9] Concerning the film's focus in relation to the larger focus of the novel, David Williams states, "So the first effect of linearization in the film is really to reduce the story of the man to obituary. 'History' has become the narrative of a doomed love affair."[10] By this, Williams refers to the narrative frame created by the English patient's unfolding memory, which reveals the past as the film cross-cuts to the desert or to Cairo, which are both spatially and temporally distant from the Italian ruined monestary at the end of the Second World War. Our history lessson develops on the condition that the burned patient can continue his recollection. History, at many levels, is subservient to the all-consuming "tragic" love affair between Almasy and Katharine.

The film's astonishing success makes it a poster child for capitialist axiomatics; the film has single-handedly created a new industry of material about the "real" English Patient: interest in one of the last colonial outposts—the North African desert of the 1930s—and, of course, further increased sales of *The English Patient* as well as Ondaatje's other texts. Minghella's *The English Patient* evidences the delicate balance of deterritorializing the novel in order to reterritorialize it into film. The novel's Booker Prize honors are deserved for the author's presenting not only a poetic linguistic *tour de force*, but also for the risks taken by centralizing the interiorization of the narrative in Kip, the Indian sapper; Hana, the war-broken nurse from Toronto who administers to "the English Patient" in his final days; and the odd middle-aged thief, also from Toronto, who was a friend of Hana's father. The novel is often cited as being "Canadian postmodern" because it not only participates in the questioning of the event, but also puts into question the narrator or "teller" of the story. Referring to Ondaatje's earlier work, Ajay Heble theorizes that "Ondaatje makes problematic the split between subject and teller, between the person being framed and the narrator doing the framing. His suspicion of history thus takes the form of showing how the utterer (Ondaatje) is implicated in the utterance (the texts themselves), how the teller is, in fact, part of the subject."[11] The camera cannot capture this complexity; and, in fact, the adventure genre, if anything, reproduces the colonizer's vision in contradiction to the noncolonial perspective presented in the novel. Also, the full irony of the title is lost in the film; in the novel, Hana, Kip, Almasy, and Caravaggio each have their "own" chapters: none of them are English either. The film's shift away from Kip and Hana toward the more bankable "English" characters, the Cliftons, and even Madox to some extent, gives the film a colonizer perspective. While I do not wish to disrate the film's success, it is important to know what the film needed to deterritorialize in the novel in order to successfully reterritorialize the film for Hollywood. There are two key events omitted from the book—one each from the two major generic formalae Minghella utilizes.

The first key event to go under erasure is the novel's ending, which must be avoided by the film. The colonial adventure, however "anti-conquest" it initially appears, would be ripped apart by the insertion of the novel's final events—the dropping of the atomic bombs on Japan, and Kip's reaction to this event. Oddly enough, producer Saul Zaentz took issue with Onjaatje's novelistic portrayal of Kip's reaction to the dropping of the atomic bombs in 1945. Zaentz is quoted as saying concerning Kip's reaction to the news of Hiroshima, "I told Michael I didn't think the atom bomb thing was right. I was in the war. I was there, nobody knew what the atom bomb was all about. Even the high ranking people didn't know."[12] This statement seems odd coming from a producer and seems more likely to be motivated by the fact that Americans do not like to be reminded—especially in the midst of a great adventure-romantic-drama film—that their military incinerated thousands of Japanese citizens in 1945. The colonial "bad-guy" image is for the English and the Germans in this film.

The second key sequence from the book that must undergo erasure is the three-year gap between Geoffrey Clifton's suicide and attempted murder, Almasy's subsequent departure from Katharine in the Cave of Swimmers (1939), and his eventual return (1942) when he and her remains burn and fall to the ground. As noted in the previous chapter, the marshalling of sympathy (and obvious drama) of the airplane *shot out* of the sky by *Germans* at the beginning and end of the film is a formula for successful viewer appreciation; the fact that the plane caught fire of its own accord (due to its age and dilapidation) in the novel is much less forceful or dramatic than its being shot out of the sky. The time difference between Almasy's parting from Katharine and returning for her is shortened from three years to three weeks—fueling the drama, or "melodrama," as Raymond Aaron Younis notes. Younis believes that the film's shift from Hana's centrality in the novel to Katharine's in the film is used to exploit the romantic melodrama:

> Melodrama has been associated with explorations of "inner voice" . . ., that is, of inner turmoil and conflicts and of strong emotions . . . . It has also been argued that this genre employs linear narrative with flashbacks and "parallel action" to explore characters in

> moral and emotional terms even as it highlights the "irrational forces of desire" . . .; that this genre interrogates notions of pleasure and fantasy reveals the contradictions within middle class ideology . . ., and embodies these in ways which many can recognize and know . . . .[13]

If Younis's formulation is correct, then the film very easily slides into American middle-class expectation. Melodramic tension is created because the audience (American, middle-class) extends hope that Almasy can still reach Katharine "in time" to "save her." The ultimate Hollywood ending would be that he does save her and they survive the war, but we know that Katharine is dead; so the most we hope for is that he reaches her while she is still alive. The romantic plot has to be considerably rewritten for Almasy to attain heroic status; and in the interest of a successful climax, Minghella knows that the novel's presentation of Almasy's act of necrophilia in the Cave of Swimmers is not "blockbuster" material.

The Historical Colonial Adventure

The desert of the Sahara has historically been a place of deterritorializations; the sand erases the human mark of attempted reterritorialization. Almasy, Madox, and the "International Sand Club" try to map the desert, claim it, even while they overtly state that they are not making national, territorial claims. In the novel, the English patient explains:

> By 1932, Bagnold was finished and Madox and the rest of us were everywhere. Looking for the lost army Cambyses. Looking for Zerzura. 1932 and 1933 and 1934. . . . There were rivers of tribes, the most beautiful humans I've met in my life. We were German, English, Hungarian, African—all of us insignificant to them. Gradually we became nationless. I came to hate nations. We are deformed by nation-states. Madox died because of nations.
>
> The desert could not be claimed or owned—it was a piece of cloth carried by the winds, never held down by stones, and given a hundred shifting names long before Canterbury existed, long before battles and treaties quilted Europe and the East.[14]

Despite the fact that the desert cannot be mapped by his team in the 1930s, he knows, and narrates for the reader, the fact that those aborginal to the desert territory have already found their way through it: "This was a world that had been civilised for centuries, had a thousand paths and roads" (140). The key word is *civilised*, versus mapped, or reterritorialized. While white Western explorers are finding "the source of the Nile," or "jars at Abu Ballas" (140), the indigenous people have long since touched or "civilised" their own territory: "The ends of the earth are never the points on a map that colonists push against, enlarging their sphere of influence. On one side servants and slaves and tides of power and correspondence with the Geographical Society. On the other the first step by a white man across a great river, the first sight (by a white eye) of a mountain that has been there forever" (141). While the novel *The English Patient* exposes the colonialist reterritorialization as myopic and exploitive, the film blindly reterritorializes this Hollywood convention.

Indeed, scholars and critics of the film *The English Patient* argue that the film invites the viewer to share in and enjoy the colonizing discourse. The viewer maintains the privileged white eye of the Western camera. Nadel argues that the viewer is invited to partake in the exalted perspective of the colonizer in *The English Patient*: "Just as the codes of mapping are thus rhetorical devices providing colonial narratives with a scientific ethos, so the codes of cinematic representation, especially in mainstream Hollywood-style cinema, are rhetorical devices providing the illusion of omniscience or, to state it differently, the ethos of objectivity to narratives that subordinate the deigesis to the desires of the spectator."[15] And so, territorial mapping is actually occuring at two levels: the narrative level of British and European colonials in the desert attempting to use modern advances in cartography to map the space of the desert, and the objectifying perspective of the film, which marginalizes the territory of North Africa to a space to be filled up by colonials. Like so many other colonial adventure stories, the Western perspective obliterates the indigenous point of view. Although Minghella attempts to successfully "naturalize" his film perspective, the reaction by some has been anything but "natural." Representing "Otherness," in this instance, Palestinian poet Hussein Barghouti's perspective "sees" something quite different from what the millions of American viewers who "fell in love" with the film saw: "Did you see *The English Patient*? Foreground action: white people, noble fine feelings, strong full of laughter, walking in gardens, taking showers, standing up. Background action: Arabs, shifty, mysterious, dirty, untrustworthy, sitting down."[16] This focus is consistent with the genre of the historical, colonial adventure film.

According to Brian Taves in *The Romance of Adventure: The Genre of Historical Adventure Movies*, "the occupying race, not the rebelling natives, is portrayed as representing the move toward a freer society and believe that they are bringing enlightenment to primitive lands."[17] The historical adventure film typically takes place between the medieval period and the First World War, "after the fall of the ancient world," and the "genre allows the viewers to escape from their contemporary world into a historical past where right and wrong are presented unambiguously, when morality was drawn in sharp relief dividing heroes and villains."[18] Although the colonizing adventure in North Africa presented in *The English Patient* takes place in the 1930s, viewers in 1996 and after understand quite well that the Sahara Desert was one of the last unmapped colonial territories left on Earth before the Second World War. Yet, in the film the "Arabs," or "rebelling natives," are only mentioned explicitly as a people with an aptitude during the farewell dinner in Cairo, 1939. Almasy, arriving late, drunk, and obviously in pain concerning his break-up with Katharine, embarrasses himself and everyone present:

> ALMASY. I believe I'm rather late.
> MADOX, *ignoring the drama of this entrance.* Good, we're all here? A toast, to the International Sand Club—may it soon resurface.
> THE OTHERS. The International Sand Club!
> ALMASY, *raising his glass.* The International Sand Club! Misfits, buggers, fascists, and fools. God bless us, everyone.
> *The others drink, trying to ignore his mood.*
> ALMASY. Oops! Mustn't say *International.* Dirty word. Filthy word. His majesty ! Die Fuhrer! Il Duce!
> CLIFTON. Sorry, what's your point?
> ALMASY, *not responding.* And the people here don't want us. You must be joking. The Egyptians are desperate to get rid of the Colonials . . .
> *To an embarrassed Fouad.*
> Isn't that right, Fouad? Some of their best people down on their hands and knees begging to be *spared* a knighthood . . .
> *To his host, Sir Hampton.*
> Isn't that right? Isn't that right, Sir Ronnie?
> *Ronnie Hampton shrugs. They're all very uncomfortable.*[19]

While we have seen minor characters such as Kamal and Al Auf participate in the desert exploration, the fact that they might be defiant colonial subjects has not been central. The theme of supposedly international cooperation is highlighted several times in the film. A key prewar remembrance of the English patient's is his farewell in the desert to Madox. Madox responds: "We didn't care about countries. Did we? Brits, Arabs, Hungarians, Germans. None of that mattered, did it? It was something finer than that."[20]

The fact that Almasy was an actual person, and that members of the British Geographical Society are fictionally presented as well, lends creditability to *The English Patient*'s inclusion in this genre: "adventure dramatizes the exploits of actual historical figures or famous incidents that fall into its generic domain, the challenges faced in the past of kings and battles, rebellion, piracy, exploration, the creation of empires, and the interplay of power politics between the individual and national authority. Only in this genre does Hollywood combine these subjects."[21] My argument is that Minghella's changes to the character of Almasy from novel to film make the film fit comfortably into the historical, empire adventure genre, and a great part of the film's box-office success can be attributed to these changes; as Taves argues: "Adventure is important not only as a major Hollywood genre but also because it deals with the western world's past attempts to broaden civilization and to develop responsible self-government in a political philosophy that reflects the American experience."[22] Taves maintains that Americans typically correlate other times and countries in adventure films to their own "American Revolution."[23] In contrast, I do not think that a typical American who views *The English Patient* thinks of America's colonial break from Britain. Rather, a more typical response is that Americans had virtually nothing to do with North Africa in the 1930s and that this is a *commendable* fact; and this laudable "hands-off" policy ties in well with the omission of the American dropping of the atomic bomb on Japan.

As the film unfolds, we know that American military might is quietly behind the eventual German retreat, but American forces are not represented *at all* in the film. For some American viewers this cinematic portrayal of wartime sweeping desert-shots, nationalist causes, and iconoclastic heroes might remind them of David Lean's *Lawrence of Arabia* (1962), which won seven Academy Awards including for Best Picture. Reviewers of the film acknowledged Almasy's likeness to Lawrence and other colonial "anticonquest" adventurers. According to Bronwen Thomas, Almasy's discovery of the "Cave of Swimmers" qualifies this comparison: "Minghella departs slightly from the novel in portraying the discovery of the cave as a personal triumph for Almasy, casting him in the same heroic mould as a Lawrence or a Livingston."[24]

In addition to Arabs who inhabit North Africa, the book, and to a significant lesser extent the film, represents another British Colonial Other: Kirpal Singh, who serves in the British Army as a sapper. While in England during his training with Lord Suffolk, he is dubbed "Kip" by white English soldiers making fun of the Indian recruit. The film's primary reterritorialization of the novel and of colonial identity is the shift away from Kip and Hana as the central focus to Almasy and Katharine because it does more than simply choose one pair of lovers over another; it realigns the entire narrative and, hence, the entire film into the predictable and acceptable. In noting this shift from Kip and Hana to Almasy and Katharine, Bronwen Thomas concedes that "to the cynical, this might smack of knee-bowing to the Hollywood machine, and the commercial wisdom that a relationship between a Sikh and a French-Canadian might not have the same appeal as that between a swarthy European and an English rose," but that "for many critics, too, it is the relationship between Almasy and Katherine [*sic*] that constitutes the heart of the story."[25] It must be assumed that Thomas's reference to "many critics" is to the critics of the film who view the Almasy and Katharine love story to be central; and, of course, in the film it *is* central, and so quoting film critics is rather redundant. We only know Katharine through Almasy's fleeting memories, which are supposedly remembered (has he *really* forgotten his name?) in nonchronological fragments that we have to piece together to form the chronological narrative of the English patient's past. Although it might be argued that Katharine is objectified on screen, all the characters are to some extent objectified; but when we know what truly happened to Katharine Clifton, through flashbacks in the form of a visual memory, then we will have the key piece of the English patient's past. At that point we will know if Almasy was a spy in the desert, a double agent, if he intentionally murdered Geoffery Clifton, and what connection Caravaggio's story ultimately has with Almasy's actions. This discourse drives the narrative. Conversely, Hana and Kip become incidental characters in the film—present-time sideline action that we can dip into when the intensity of the Almasy/Katharine affair becomes too much.

Race theorists in the West often discuss the idea that "(w)hites have difficulty perceiving whiteness, both because of cultural prevalence and because of its cultural dominance."[26] In the film, Hana must tell the English patient that Kip is racially and ethnically different. In the following scene Hana's description and the worldly English patient's correction of her misidentification of Kip's true background educate American viewers—the majority of whom would not, along with Hana, know the difference between a turban wearer and an Indian:

Hana looks down from the patient's room, watching the tents go up. Kip glances up at the window. Hana, suddenly shy, backs away.

HANA. He wants us to move out, says there could be fifty more mines in the building. He thinks I'm mad because I laughed at him. He's Indian, he wears a turban.

THE PATIENT. No, he's Sikh. If he wears a turban, he's Sikh.
HANA. I'll probably marry him.
THE PATIENT. Really? That's sudden.
HANA. My mother always told me I would summon my husband by playing the piano.[27]

This scene also shifts our understanding of Hana's focus. Before the ruined monastery she was traumatized; now she is playing the piano and thinking about her future husband. Hana's character, in tandem with Kip's, gives the film a parallel romance—this one, unlike Almasy and Katharine, is "lighthearted," definitely less compelling and passionate. The status of this romance is evident in the *lack* of media coverage in the form of representations of the couple's togetherness; the only consistent media representation of Kip and Hana is of them on his motorbike, which, given their expressions and the general associations of being on a motorbike (youthful, fun, carefree, European), one knows that this is not the primary story of the film. In fact, the viewer never seriously has to think about the miscegenatic situation between Hana and Kip because of its lack of intensity and triviality. The novel, however, presents the idea of miscegenation through Caravaggio encouraging Hana and Kip to abandon their posts, "The correct move is to get on a train, go and have babies together" (122). This advice is given in the context of *class*—according to Caravaggio, only the rich and well placed have anything to gain by continuing to fight the war. However, discussions between Hana and Kip about ethnic and national differences are not broached in the film so as to keep this relationship nugatory. These are indeed supporting characters.

Moreover, we simply cannot have a cinematic "romance with the colonial" if the white Western perspective fails to absorb Kip. However, in the novel we are given Kip's perspective and know that he is fully aware of his racial difference. As an Indian among whites in England, Kip assumed a kind of invisibility until at Erith he defuses the new type of German bomb that killed his beloved Lord Suffolk, Miss Morden, and Harts. After his success,

> He knew he was for now a king, a puppet master, could order anything, a bucket of sand, a fruit pie for his needs, and those men who would not cross an uncrowded bar to speak with him when they were off duty would do what he desired. It was strange to him. . . . But he knew he did not like it. He was accustomed to his invisbility. In England he was ignored in the various barracks, and he came to prefer that. . . . It was as much a result of being the anonymous member of another race, a part of the invisible world. (196)

This quotation parallels race-studies findings that suggest that the dominant race, white in the American or European context, excludes the "Other" or "Black" because it is outside of the illusion that white is the norm. The color of skin and the Western perspective is even played out in the presentation of the burned Almasy. In conceiving of the English patient's prosthetic make-up, Jim Henson's Creature Shop did not derive its look from the book's discription of the burned Almasy. On the first page of the novel we are told that "[e]very four days she washes his black body . . . .Above the shins the burns are worst. Beyond purple" (3), and later when the English interrogate the burned man: "Everything about him was very English except for the fact that his skin was tarred black, a bogman from history among his interrogating officers" (96). Despite the fact that the novel variously refers to Almasy's burned skin as black or ebony, the film makes the burned Almasy a hairless, yellowish creature (similar, in fact, to that lovable, blockbuster extraterrestrial, E.T.).

Near the end of the novel, Kip, who always has radio earphones on while he works, finds out about the Americans dropping the atomic bombs on Japan. His reaction is fierce—wielding a rifle he goes to the English patient's room to kill him: he and his people are responsible for the bombing of the "brown races." The patient implores Kip to kill him; Kip, of course, cannot. Although awakened to his own difference and his unchangeable Otherness, he is not like his older brother who, Kip tells Hana, "*sided with whoever was against the English*" (italics in original). Kip's original affection for Lord Suffolk is transferred to the English patient; and so, the impact of the bombing is poured into the patient. Addressing the patient, Kip blames him for this new kind of bomb, which the sapper cannot defuse:

> I grew up with traditions from my country, but later, more often from *your* country. Your fragile white island that with customs and manners and books and prefects and reason somehow converted the rest of the world. You stood for precise behavior. I knew if I lifted a teacup with the wrong finger I'd be banished. If I tied the wrong kind of knot in a tie I was out. Was it just the ships that gave you such power? Was it, as by brother said, because you had the histories and printing presses? (italics in original) (283)

Kip's tirade in the novel directly attacks the "anticonquest" colonizer, as he points out that his brother had warned him to "[n]ever turn your back on Europe. The deal makers. The contract makers. The map drawers" (284). Despite the "ebony pool" of his skin color, the

English patient who is not English is representative of the West, as Kip answers Caravaggio's "He's not English," with "American. French. I don't care. When you start bombing the brown races of the world, you're an Englishman. You had King Leopold of Belgium and now you have fucking Harry Truman of the USA. You all learned it from the English" (286). Kip abandons his post in Italy and begins his return to India on his motorbike. A quintessential statement in the text is "[h]is name is Kirpal Singh and he does not know what he is doing here" (287). His name, in other words, is *not* Kip, and he is never going to be English; his postcolonial awakening is quick and sweeping. The film cannot translate this total rejection of the West; and to give Minghella credit, the final cut of the film does not even try.

Because the film has to wrap up each character's story in the villa, it needs to do something with Kip. Instead of the Americans' dropping of the atomic bomb, Kip's sapper partner, Hardy, gets blown-up with a remaining undiscovered mine during the Allies' victory celebration. The disclosure that Hardy had an Italian fiancée wounds Kip. The day after Hardy's death, Kip confides his pain to Hana in the following exchange:

> KIP. I was thinking yesterday—yesterday!—the Patient and Hardy; they're everything that's good about England. I couldn't even say what that was. We didn't exchange two personal words, and we've been together through some terrible things, some terrible things.
> *Still incredulous*
> He was engaged to a girl in the village!—I mean—*looks at Hana* —— and us—he never once. . . . He didn't even ask me if I could spin the ball at Cricket or the Kama Sutra or—I don't even know what I'm talking about.
> HANA. You loved him. (96–97)

In this scene we still have Kip conflating the English patient with England, but that is about all that remains of the original parting scene. Kip's sensitivity makes him a more complete character at the very moment he will exit the film; but Hana, the wise Western female, is the person who tells Kip that he feels so badly because "you loved him [Hardy]." This scene and its tremendous reduction of emotion reproduces a colonial perspective; in all likelihood, most viewers will barely remember this scene—it dissolves just like Kip, like Hana and Kip, and then Hana—before the last dramatic scene of the film featuring Almasy and Katharine.

Minghella could have taken a chance on the audience's reaction to a full presentation of the character Kip—rounded him out; given him an interiority similar to that in the book; deterritorialized a new film space with an attractive, thoughtful Indian (beyond the clichéd turbaned "wiseman" from the East) who has emotional as well as political motivations. Kip could have revitalized the adventure drama, updating its tired standards, even the anticonquest genre, by having a central role in the film. Rather, Minghella uses Hana and Kip as a nonessential light-hearted reterritorialization. As Thomas Schatz's points out, "A film genre develops when the audience encourages the repetition of a film narrative."[28] Therefore, "Kip the Sikh" must quietly fade away at the end of the film instead of providing the sharp political edge that he does in the novel.

Romantic Drama

Even as I have constructed the idea in this chapter that the film *The English Patient* is a "romantic drama"—quoting the critics as partial support—I am still, conversely, convinced that the film is principally, if not solely, a colonial adventure film. The film *appears* to be a romance because it is marketed as such; yet the colonial adventure almost always has a romantic supplement that allows the hero (pirate, adventurer, soldier) to step outside his homosocial world, display his manliness, and impress his filmic beloved (and the entire female audience). In *Adventure, Mystery, and Romance: Formula Stories as Art and Popular Culture*, John G. Cawelti theorizes that there is a male bias toward the adventure and a female bias toward the romance. The adventure is the "standard" or the universal: "The interplay with the villain and the erotic interests served by attendant damsels are more in the nature of frosting on the cake. The true focus of interest in the adventure story is the character of the hero and the nature of the obstacles he has to overcome."[29] Cawelti's argument is that these stories are universals in the mythological sense: "This is the simplest and perhaps the oldest and the widest in appeal of all story types. It can clearly be traced back to the myths and epics of earliest times and has been cultivated in some form or other by almost every human society."[30] Unlike Taves's version of the adventure, with distinctions between each of the subgenres, Cawelti's account of the adventure is basically of the quest variety. From this formulation Cawelti links the romance to the adventure as the female "equivalent": "The feminine equivalent of the adventure story is the romance."[31] If I were to update this duality, we might characterize the separate genres, as put forth by Cawelti, as part of the heterosexual norm, which capitalism, as well as the state, finds useful to maintain in America. If this is the case, then these generic biases are part of the axiomatic in our capitalist culture.

Cawelti's discussion is most pertinent in terms of *The English Patient* when he states, "Romances often contain elements of adventure, but the dangers function as a means of challenging and then cementing the love relationship."[32] *The English Patient* certainly can be perceived as a romance wherein the challenges presented to Almasy (walking from the Cave of Swimmers, fleeing English soldiers, returning to the Cave) are the fulfillment of "cementing" true love. If we begin down this path, however, then we must immediately take the genre to the next level—the level of the romantic tragedy—and the film encourages us to do so. The intensity of Almasy and Katharine's love will not let them live; and, of course, Geoffrey steps—flies in—to insure this outcome. The love affair is doomed, "it simply cannot continue to exist in the fictional situation either for social or psychological reasons and consequently the passion itself brings about the death of one or both of the lovers."[33] Like the most famous doomed lovers in the English language tradition, Romeo and Juliet, Almasy and Katharine find themselves unable to "exist"; Geoffrey's suicide and murder attempt seals this fate in a protracted and agonized fashion. According to Cawelti, the fact that lovers can never be together reflects a more "sophisticated" type of love story that goes beyond a happily-ever-after marriage plot. But given the fact that the severely burned English patient is narrating the details of his affair years after the Tiger Moth's crash, there is no way to turn the film into a "happily-every-after." For the remainder of this chapter, I want to ferret out the possibility that—surreptitiously—the audience has been fooled: both Almasy, as the archetypal outsider-turned-hero, and Katharine, who is "spirited," independent, and married into the military, fit the colonial adventure script perfectly. And yet, the film is marketed as—has sold well as—a dramatic romance (coupled with tragic romance); Hollywood has successfully marketed the "high-concept" aspect of this commodity to fit into our capitalist heterosexual, colonial axiomatic.

While it is fairly straightforward to understand the bankability of the "English-patient-and-the-English-married-woman" romance as gaining a central place in the film, critics never focus enough on the trauma that Hana has suffered to understand that she is not suitable for "leading-lady" status. The film streamlines and collapses all relationships into the male/female binary. We see the filmic Hana is no longer grieving for her father, she is grieving for her boyfriend/fiancé; the father connection is again squelched when the prior relationship with Caravaggio (her father's old friend from Toronto) is silenced, and she meets Caravaggio for the first time at the villa; and, of course, there is no filmic mention whatsoever of her wartime abortion. When in the novel Hana tells Caravaggio about her war experience, he is an "uncle" figure, an old friend of her now-dead father, "I courted one man and he died and the child died. I mean, the child didn't just die, I was the one who destroyed it. After that I stepped so far back no one could get near me."[34] The film presents Hana's emotional state with an equivalent at the very beginning when she first finds out that her boyfriend/fiancé has died; then her good friend, Jan, is dramatically blown-up in a jeep (by a road mine not yet sapped). Since neither of these incidents are in the novel, we must interpret them as equivalents—quick shorthand to bring us into the full horror and grief of Hana's wartime world. In this brief exposition of Hana, the audience can understand that the villa, a citadel on the hill, which the camera catches her looking at, is her much needed respite from the war, death, and dying. The English patient is presented as an excuse for her "time out" from the war, but in the novel the English patient is fodder for a much deeper psychological trauma pertaining to her father. At the very end of the text, Hana writes a letter to her stepmother, Clara, and reveals the details of her father's death: "*His unit had left him, burned and wounded. So burned the buttons of his shirt were part of his skin, part of his dear chest . . . . He was a burned man and I was a nurse and I could have nursed him. Do you understand the sadness of geography? I could have saved him or at least been with him till the end*" (italics in original) (295–296). This poignant revelation speaks directly to the many thematic layers of "geography" in the novel—from map making, to being born in Hungary and not in England, to, of course, the expanse of desert separating Almasy from Katharine in the Cave of Swimmers, as well as, at the end of the novel, Hana's longing to be with Clara in Canada, far away from "Europe."

Taking center stage, however, is Katharine who is initially ignored and even disliked by Almasy, but who, in the telling of the story of Canduales, wins Almasy's heart. Katharine's role is magnified from the novel, but it is also formulated to work inside the colonial adventure. First, as Taves points out, "Movies do not concentrate on the hero's wooing but on the dramatic moment when at last he finds true love. Often he falls for the one woman who is not immediately seduced by his charm; she is hostile to the untraditional person who courts her, and the two make an unlikely pair."[35] While Almasy never actually courts Katharine, she is initially not seduced by his charm; in fact, the film plays out several little scenes in which Katharine openly resists the "untraditional" behavior and habits of Almasy. Women come into the adventure story via a man—a father, husband, or brother. Katharine plays out her connection in the adventure film almost too perfectly. According to Taves, "While women in empire are rare, they are independent individuals, frequently born or married into military families. When danger threatens, they may be urged to leave for a less dangerous area but insist on fearlessly staying."[36] First, Katharine is perfectly scripted as the wife of an army intelligence officer. In the novel, Caravaggio informs the English patient that the youthful, boyish Geoffrey Clifton was not quite what he had seemed to Almasy: "Clifton was with British Intelligence. He was not just an innocent Englishman . . . . As far as the English were concerned, he was keeping an eye on your strange group in the Egyptian-Libyan desert. They knew the desert would someday be a theatre of war" (252). The narrative is the same in the film except that, while they are lost in the desert, Katharine divulges to Almasy the fact that Geoffrey is not simply in the desert for a lark, before, in fact, they begin their affair. This incident, getting lost in a sand storm after a vehicle wrecks, Minghella creates for the film that plays out, in the second instance, the perfect way in which Katharine has been scripted as the lover of the adventure hero. She could have returned with Madox to get help, but insists on staying in the desert because she is not injured.

In the novel, Katharine is only narratively presented by the English patient as he remembers his past, and he invents and actively imagines events in her life of which he has no knowledge. One of the most confusing of these passages is the narrative concerning her meeting Geoffrey at Oxford. Almasy's narrative begins unraveling late in the text when he attempts to tell Caravaggio about the airplane crash. He recounts that Katharine's "glare was permanent" after getting her to the Cave of Swimmers, and in this he realizes "I will be the last image she sees" (258). From this statement Almasy begins to digress into the myth of the "jackal in the cave who will guide and protect her, who will never deceive her" (258). As this jackal or ghost, he tells Katharine—through telling Caravaggio—that he was there when "you met Geoffrey Clifton at two a.m. in the Oxford Union Library" (258). Similar to Tireseus who watches the typist and clerk in *The Waste Land*, Almasy recounts this meeting: "My arms folded, watching your attempts at enthusiastic smalltalk. . . . both of you have found your fates" (259), which in the patient's version happens to include "Wepwawet [the jackal] or Almasy" (258).

Unhinged, the English patient cannot bear Katherine's death, and so invents a story so that their destinies unite. The reader does not know whether this story is something that Almasy imagined at the time, or whether he has spent years working on it, and Caravaggio is the first person to hear his tale. In another part of the novel, the English patient describes a ritual he performs as he prepares Katharine's body for removal from the Cave of Swimmers; from this disclosure we might surmise that he is thinking of Wepwawet at the time of her death. The film, of course, must make a straighter path—the Cliftons are old family friends; as Clifton tells Almasy, "I've know Katharine since she was three, we were practically brother and sister before we were man and wife." This change functions to take the edge off the adultry Almasy will commit with Clifton's wife in the film. The plot of fate from the novel has an equivalent in the Canduales story.

The film frames Katharine's camp-fire recounting of the Canduales story during a game of spin-the-bottle inside of Hana's reading Herodotus to the English patient in the villa. Minghella weaves the women's voices together: Hana's hesitant, awkward, mispronounced reading dissolves into Katharine's confident, posh-accented telling of the story of Candaules's betrayal of his wife through allowing—encouraging—Gyges to observe his wife's beauty. The screenplay borrows heavily from the text, though in the novel Almasy is talking to Caravaggio: "This is a story of how I fell in love with a woman, who read me a specific story from Herodotus" (233). The film utilizes the frame—the story in Herodotus—to open up the English patient's memory; the memory, or flashback, is of the utmost importance because it establishes the parellel between the Canduales–Gyges–wife story with the Geoffrey–Almasy–Katharine triangle. The plot actually is more-closely aligned in the film if we understand Geoffrey to be "showcasing" his wife; Geoffrey's action is similar to Canduales's: "The vanity of a man to the point where he wishes to be envied." Katharine, like Canduale's wife, is "exposed" to Gyges/Almasy and, therefore, challenges him to slay Candaules/Geoffrey or kill himself.

Apart from the Canduales story, the film principally uses Herodotus's *Histories* as a kind of scrap book; and as Alan A. Stone pointed out in a review after the film's release, "[t]wenty-five centuries later, Herodotus reads like a postmodern, constructing historical reality as a series of narratives told by different people from different perspectives—the right book for the English patient, though not a big selling point for the moguls at Twentieth Century Fox."[37] Voyeuristically, early in the film Katharine looks through Almasy's copy of the *Histories*, not for Herodotus's history but for Almasy's past. Finding even his baby picture among the loose papers and photographs in the text, Katharine, along with the audience, begins to understand or see a "soft" side to the remote and terse desert-consumed man. The turning point arrives when she reads the letter "K" in his book and surmises that he is writing about her. After a night in the desert trapped in a car together, Almasy allows Katharine to paste her cave paintings into the book. Years later Hana finds a Christmas cracker in the text's pages; on it Almasy has written, "December twenty-second—Betrayals in war are childlike compared with our betrayals during peace . . . . for the heart is an organ of fire," which opens onto the scene of the Christmas party in 1938.[38] Herodotus, therefore, functions as either a bookmark of the past, or, often concurrently, a door in the present onto which the past opens. *The Histories* text functions as a conduit between time and space, and, hence, creates a convenient link between scenes.

Ostensively, the novel presents Herodotus as Almasy's ancient double. Jacqui Sadashige situates Ondaatje's use of Herodotus as one that provides the author an "Ur-text for the exoticism and its role in the naturalization of Western imperialism" beyond that of the other intertextual references in the novel, such as Kipling's *Kim* or Forster's *Passage to India*.[39] Sadashige characterizes Herodotus's *Histories* as the ancient analogue to modern colonialism: "*The Histories* is multi-generic or hybrid work, situating the rise of Athenian imperialism within both a broader history of Greco-Persian conflict and the cyclical rise and fall of political regimes."[40] While Almasy identifies with Herodotus as an explorer and as a storyteller, his own book, *Recentes Explorations dans le Desert Libyque*, is "succinct and to the point" and only "seventy pages long" (235). A few pages later, Almasy repeats that his book "had been stern with accuracy" in order to insure that he did not write Katharine or Katharine's body into his pages—she is now so intertwined with his every thought and association with the desert. In this way, Sadashige conflates Ondaatje with his character Almasy, "[c]onsidered to be both the father of history and the father of lies, and prone to include both fanciful and factual tidbits of ethnography and geography in his writings, Herodotus, at one level, is the mirror image of Almasy."[41] Rather, Herodotus is the "mirror image" of Ondaatje, who weaves lies and "factual tibdits" into his narrative, which creates a series of fictional discourses of half-truth, half-lie—and, thus, all fictional lies. No doubt Almasy admires Herodotus for his nomadic posture and for his storytelling, which, according to Almasy, leads the reader down one blind alley after another. At one point early in the villa life, the English patient asks Hana for his copy of *The Histories* and then, characteristically in his relationship with Hana, takes the opportunity to act as pedagogue:

> I have seen editions of *The Histories* with a sculpted portrait on the cover. Some statue found in a French museum. But I never imagine Herodotus

> this way. I see him more as one of these spare men of the desert who travel from oasis to oasis, trading legends as if it is the exchange of seeds, consuming everything without suspicion, piecing together a mirage. "This history of mine," Herodotus says, "has from the beginning sought out the supplementary to the main argument." What you find in him are cul-de-sacs within the sweep of history—how people betray each other for the sake of nations, how people fall in love . . . (118–119)

Of course, at this point in the novel the reader does not know anything about Katharine and Geoffrey or maps of the desert, and, so, these words about betrayal, love, and nations will only later gain their full significance. The territory—the novel—has also done its share of deterritorizing and reterritorializing history and geography, as well as fictionalizing "real" people.

After the success of the film, the "real" people whom Ondaatje fictionalizes become a source of popular interest. For example, John Bierman, in *The Secret Life of Laszlo Almasy: The Real English Patient*, reveals that Almasy was known as "Lasci to his family, Teddy to his friends," and that the "real" person, and the fiction man "are very much alike in one thing: they are equally enigmatic, equally elusive."[42] Similar to the fictional person, Almasy was a Hungarian desert explorer and scholar who is accredited with helping German Lieutenant General Erwin Rommel across the Egyptian desert. Critics of Ondaatje's fictional Almasy and Minghella's screen rendering of the "English patient" object to the glossing over of Almasy's role in helping the Nazis. Moral philosopher Thomas Hurka argues that "this utter denigration of the political that makes *The English Patient* immoral. . . . There was not just some political end at stake in the Second World War; there was resistance to Nazism, a movement threatening millions of innocent people. Yet the movie treats even this end as morally inconsequential."[43] Bierman points out that Hurka's accusation is irrelevant because Almasy was a "reserve officer in the Hungarian Air Force and Hungary was an ally of Nazi Germany, so that it is surely stretching an otherwise legitimate point to characterize his conduct as 'betrayal.' "[44] Bierman also stresses that it is difficult to know if Almasy was not a "double agent": "Was he, as the British suspected, a pre-war spy for the Italians or, as the Italians suspected, a pre-war spy for the British? Perhaps he was both; perhaps he was neither."[45]

One aspect of the fictional presentation of Almasy that is completely false is the explorer's healthy heterosexual appetite. Bierman make this plain in his biography: "the lean, hawk-nosed Laszlo was to remain a lifelong bachelor . . . certainly not without charm, but with no interest at all in the opposite sex," speculating that, "Childhood memories of his parents' scalding rows and the trauma of their divorce may have been a factor in his inability to relate to women and his evolving homosexual inclinations."[46] The historical Almasy's homosexuality, apparently, was a well-known fact among those associated with him. Lady Dorothy Clayton-East-Clayton, wife of Sir Robert Clayton-East-Clayton (Ondaatje modeled his fictional Katharine and Geoffrey Clifton on her and her husband) knew of Almasy's orientation. Bierman notes that Ellie Clayton, wife of Pat Clayton, a British desert-expedition colleague of Almasy, and Lady Dorothy, "both conceived an aversion to him [Almasy], having 'immediately detected his homosexual tendencies and his capacity to induce distrust in some of those who knew him.' "[47] Further widening the gap between the "real-life" Almasy and his relationship with a British female, and the fictional Almasy and his relationship with Katharine Clifton, is the fact that

> Lady Dorothy [Katharine] publicly declined to shake Almasy's hand on more than one occasion. As for Ellie Clayton, she too "simply couldn't stand him," as her son Peter would recall many years later. It is not at all clear how the two women were so quick to spot Almasy's sexual orientation. He had acquired a public reputation as a womanizer on the look-out for a wealthy wife, but whispered and unsubstantiated Cairo gossip hinted otherwise, suggesting that he patronized the "rough trade" that was readily available in the capital's back-street bars and boy brothels.[48]

Ondaatje's presentation of Almasy makes him heterosexual but does not make his role as "spy" completely lucid. Minghella, however, cleans up the ambiguity of Ondaatje's Almasy by showing the "spy" transaction to the audience. The maps are given to the Germans because the English betray him—and by extension also betray Katharine. This, of course, evokes sympathy for Almasy's plight and brings the audience into full acceptance of his heroic status *despite* the fact that he betrays the Allies. A series of scenes sets up the audience's acceptance of Almasy-as-traitor. After walking for days to get help for Katharine, whom he left in the Cave of Swimmers, Almasy arrives in El Taj. When he attempts to solicit help from an English army officer, he is put through the typical bureaucratic procedure of being asked for his papers. Almasy's indifference to the brewing war and nationalistic boundaries and identities will prove to cost him his freedom and his ability to return to Katharine in a timely fashion. In the film,

Almasy imprudently gives his very Hungarian-sounding name to the English officer:

> ALMASY, *gulping the water, trying to summon his thoughts.* There's been an accident. I need a doctor—to come with me. And I need to borrow this car. I'll pay, of course, and I need, I need morphine and——
>
> OFFICER. May I see your papers, sir?
>
> ALMASY. What?
>
> OFFICER. If I could just see some form of identification?
>
> ALMASY, *brain racing.* I'm sorry, I'm not making sense, forgive me. I've been walking, I've—there's a woman badly injured at Gilf Kebir, in the Cave of Swimmers. I am a member of the Royal Geographical Society.
>
> OFFICER. Right. Now if I could just take your name.
>
> ALMASY, *trying to control his feelings.* Count Laszlo de Almasy.
>
> *The officer is writing this down. A glance at his Corporal.*
>
> OFFICER. Almasy—would you mind spelling that? What nationality would that be?[49]

This scene parallels the narrative the English patient relays to Caravaggio in the monastery. Caravaggio, too, begins to feel sympathy, against his better judgment, for Almasy. The above flashback-scene ends with Almasy knocked unconscious. In the next scene we see him being transported in chains in a jeep, where he tries again to get the English to listen to him. The corporal mocks him, calls him Fritz, and when Almasy responds in dismay, the soldier states in substandard English, "That's your name innit? Count Fucking Arsehole Von Bismarck? What's that supposed to be then, Irish?"[50] These scenes effectively establish the necessary sympathy for Almasy and his heroic cause to save Katharine, so that when he strangles the young soldier on the train in order to escape we know he must.

Almasy is a scholar and, at best, a knowledgeable, self-sufficient desert traveler, not a swaggering, masculine figure; yet this seeming lack of manliness does not disqualify him from reaching heroic stature. Among Taves's definitions of the various heroic types in adventure film, one is the explorer who is able to "discover and map new, uncharted lands," but who also comes "with a readiness to face the perils of nature and the unknown. Exploring and annexing territory requires an imaginative mind and the ability to inspire others."[51] As an aristocratic European "count," Almasy is also an outsider among the British Royal Geographic Society members, who regard him as different. Madox, for example, in the novel, attempts to warn

Almasy that the "great English web" was watching him, and knew of his affair with Katharine, "the club of bodyguards watched over her husband and kept him protected. Only Madox, who was an aristocrat with a past of regimental associations, knew about such discrete convolutions. Only Madox, with considerable tact, warned me about such a world" (237). The adventure genre can embrace the "outsider, living apart in rugged surroundings with a devil-may-care demeanor," but he will be transformed—"the adventure makes them aware of higher values."[52] Love and honor will override the English web, which eventually incorporates a larger web of the Allies, so that when Almasy betrays the English and the Allies, we understand that it is necessary.

Ultimately, then, when the scene shows Almasy uncovering Madox's "Tiger Moth," and handing over his work, the desert maps, to the Germans, the prone English patient explains to Caravaggio: "I did get back. I kept my promise. I was assisted by the Germans. I had our expedition maps. And after the British made me their enemy, I gave their enemy our maps."[53] This scene is the act of the avenger adventure-hero who "is attuned to the moment, boldly, and with a touch of fatalism, risking all, banking on luck and instinct to point out the road to be followed."[54] Therefore, Almasy's love for and loyalty to Katharine causes him to avenge the very people for whom he was exploring the desert and making maps. Mitigated by the actual facts of Almasy's giving the maps to the Germans, Caravaggio no longer wishes to kill the English patient; thus, likewise, if the man who lost his thumbs (he believes) because of Almasy's betrayal can forgive or at least understand him, then the viewer obviously can feel the same way. The dramatic unfolding of the events of 1939 has primed the audience for the emotional climax of Almasy's return to the Cave of Swimmers.

In the film, Katharine is still alive when Almasy leaves her (not so in the novel). The film must have this as a basic premise or the film would become forty-minutes shorter; we must have the return of our adventure hero in a time-frame that allows that audience to hold out hope that he will find Katharine *alive*. With such fast-paced action and scene and time shifts, the audience is tense, and primed for Almasy's heroism to be rewarded by Katharine's dying acknowledgement of his loyalty and devotion. Knowing that she died, we do not expect a happy ending, but a final reunion and acknowledgement, emotionally and psychologically is what the audience wants—needs. Instead, we get a voice-over of Katharine's last words, written in the cave as she dies with the dying light. Inconsolable, Almasy weeps as he wraps her in the white parachute to take her home—faithful to her and loyal to his promise not to leave her in the desert. Minghella achieves a great emotional climax in these scenes—perhaps melodramatic—but the audience enjoys a catharsis worthy of the best Acadamy Award--winning "tear-jerkers." The glory and success of the film is that it maintains its suspense and tension even though we actually know what happened—or what is likely to happen as the past unfolds in the English patient's flashback. The final desert scene is heightened by the German troops firing on the English Tiger Moth—the irony of course is that the Germans enabled Almasy to find and fuel the English airplane—and the film comes full circle with a replay of the burning airplane falling out of the sky.

It is not difficult to understand that Minghella's ability to hold his film together is dependent upon the audience believing that Almasy can get back to the Cave of Swimmers before Katharine dies; and so, the reduction from three years to three weeks is cinematically acceptable. The novel's nonlinear presentation of the events surrounding Katharine's death scrambles and confuses the reader; yet, the effect of the prose manifests Almasy's intense passion, grief, and madness. The film's reduction of the novel to a formula replicates both sides of the Searle/Derrida debate: the filmmaker radically reiterates the literary text at all levels—narrative, plot, circumstances—into a different context of meaning (in order to satisfy a mass-market audience), while at the same time repeating familiar citations that reconstitutes the film into a *recognizable* and predictable product (also in order to satisfy a mass-market audience). We have discussed the various ways the reiteration has transformed the text, but the most telling is the "cleaning-up" of Almasy's reputation as a spy and mysterious "foreign" figure, which are at the heart of the novel. First, the reader simply never knows exactly what to believe concerning Almasy's involvement with the Germans; and, second, never adequately accounted for is the mysterious necrophiliac ritual Almasy performs in the Cave of Swimmers. Dropping what does not fit into the Hollywood formula allows the film to be easily encoded into the Hollywood axiomatic of predictable adventure film. The narrative outline of El Taj in 1939 stems from the novel:

> "Too much happened at El Taj in 1939, when I was rounded up, imagined to be a spy."
>
> "So that's when you went over to the Germans."
>
> Silence.
>
> "And you still were unable to get back to the Cave of Swimmers and Uweinat?"

> "Not till I volunteered to take Eppler across the desert."
> "There is something I must tell you. To do with 1942, when you guided the spy into Cairo . . ."
> "Operation Salaam."
> "Yes. When you were working for Rommel."
> "A brilliant man . . . . What were you going to tell me?"
> "I was going to say, when you came through the desert avoiding Allied troops, travelling with Eppler—it *was* heroic. . . . What I want to say is that they did not just discover Eppler in Cairo. They knew about the whole journey. A German code had been broken. . . . We watched you the whole way. . . . You became the enemy not when you sided with Germany but when you began your affair with Katharine Clifton" (italics in original). (253–255)

The film streamlines this passage into the three weeks of Almasy's journey to El Taj and back, which erases the three-year gap from the novel. The time gap is three years; but from the above passage when Almasy imagines himself a jackal (we know that Katharine was dead, or nearly dead), when Almasy leaves her, again the text is deliberately vague; this is after the crash of 1939: "I leaned forward and put my tongue against the right blue eye, a taste of salt. Pollen. I carried that taste to her mouth . . . . It was almost too late. I leaned forward and with my tongue carried the blue pollen to her tongue. We touched this way once. Nothing happened" (259–260). When her tongue twitches, "the terrible snarl, violent and intimate, came out of her upon me. . . . Her neck flipping this way and that" (260). The reader assumes that this is her "death rattle" because Almasy then carries her out of the cave, into "the communal book of moonlight" (261). In another passage in the novel, Almasy tells the reader that he painted Katharine the colors of the desert before he left her in 1939—we have to assume that this was a postmortem ritual to "return" to nature, or to the Earth ("ashes to ashes").

Second, what becomes an issue is what happens in those three years when the English watch Almasy help Rommel. The English, in order not to reveal that they had broken a German code, *allow* Almasy to transport Eppler across the desert; yet, they do not listen when he begs for help for Katharine. Caravaggio questions the English patient's memory:

> "Are you telling me the English did not believe you? No one listened to you?"
> "No one listened."
> "Why?"

> "I didn't give them a right name."
> "Yours."
> "I gave them mine."
> "Then what——"
> "*Hers.* Her name. The name of her husband."
> "What did you say?"
> He says nothing.
> "Wake up! What did you say?"
> "I said she was my *wife*. I said *Katharine*. Her husband was dead. I said she was badly injured, in a cave in Gilf Kebir, at Uweinat, north of the Ain Dua well. She needed water. She needed food. I would go back with them to guide them (italics in original). (250–251)

Therefore, what becomes apparent is that Katharine Clifton is the one ultimately betrayed by the English: they know of the affair; they know that Geoffrey was supposed to pick up Almasy; and when Almasy claims Katharine is injured, they do nothing for the *English woman*. In fact, the English do go back to the location Almasy gives them because they later find Geoffrey's grave, but do not find her (though they are told where to look for her). In the novel it is the El Taj treatment by the English that leads Almasy to betray the English. The three years of subterfuge that Almasy must endure, we are to believe, is Almasy's vengence upon the English. Similar to Herodotus, however, Ondaatje's mosaic presentation of events, subchapter cul-de-sacs, and retelling of the same event or time-frame, does not yield clarity.

The final deterritorialization connected to Almasy is the film's omission of his 1942 necrophiliac ritual with Katharine upon his return to the Cave of Swimmers. Our filmic adventure hero would be turned into a gothic-like subhuman had Minghella been at all faithful to Almasy's 1942 return to the Cave of Swimmers. Knowing that he must face Katharine's corpse, Almasy prepares himself:

> He reached the shallow well named Ain Dua. He removed all of his clothes and soaked them in the well, put his head and then his thin body into the blue water. His limbs exhausted from four nights of walking. He left his clothes spread on the rocks and climbed up higher into the boulders, climbed out of the desert, which was now, in 1942, a vast battlefield, and went naked into the darkness of the cave. (169)

Again, unhinged, exhausted, grieved, Almasy must collect the remains of Katharine. From this passage we assume he wishes to leave the desert, which is no longer pure, but a battlefield, behind him, and cleansed he can claim Katharine, the only woman he ever loved, the woman he has traveled three years to get to. But Almasy is thinking of Katharine as she was during their affair—in the prime of her physical beauty:

> I approached her naked as I would have done in our South Cairo room, Wanting to undress her, still wanting to love her.
>
> What is terrible in what I did? Don't we forgive everything of a lover? We forgive selfishness, desire, guile. . . . You can make love to a woman with a broken arm, or a woman with a fever. She once sucked blood from a cut on my hand as I had tasted and swallowed her menstrual blood. There are some European words you can never translate properly into another language. *Felhomaly.* The dusk of graves. With the connotation of intimacy there between the dead and the living. (170)

We do not actually know if Almasy made love to Katharine three years after her death, but even in fantasy, this passage speaks to the intensity of their union—a love beyond death. A few pages later, the above passage seems fabulous considering that when the airplane begins to fall apart mid-air, "a spark from a short, and the twins at her knee catch fire," "He is flying a rotted plane," and Almasy describes Katharine: "She collapses—acacia twigs, leaves, the branches that were shaped into arms uncoiling around him. Limbs begin disappearing in the suck of air" (175). In the film this macabre sight is translated into the Germans gunning down the Tiger Moth with the recently dead Katharine draped in the front cockpit.

The film is a stunning success because of its participation in the Hollywood adventure genre and for its visual quality (a topic we have not fully explored here). The adventure, in its many guises, is capable of blockbuster stature, and this film delivered for Miramax. Although England with its hedgehogs and wet gardens is not represented, the range of beautiful scenery from Italy to the Sahara desert (where, reportedly, the "Saul Zaentz Highway" had to be built so that the crew could get the equipment to the rocky area where the Cave-of-Swimmers scenes were shot) has character-like status, not unlike that in the heritage film of the previous chapter.

CHAPTER 5

Cool Britannia for Sale: *Trainspotting* and *Bridget Jones's Diary*

> *One of the criticisms that has recently been thrown—thoroughly unjustly—at our new Government is the charge that we are somehow only interested in the "popular" in the arts, and not in serious and high culture. Why, they say, is the Prime Minister seen sharing a glass of wine with Noel Gallagher at 10 Downing Street? Why is there talk of "Cool Britannia" and the impression given that anything modern is good and anything traditional is bad? Why is attention always concentrated on movies and pop music and never on the rest of the country? Have we not failed to notice that culture is something rather different from entertainment? This argument is complete nonsense.*
>
> *The Rt. Hon Chris Smith, MP*
> Creative Britain

Irvine Welsh's debut novel *Trainspotting* (1993) became famous and fashionable in the United States with the Miramax Film's release in 1996. However, John Hodge's screenplay of *Trainspotting* is only minimally based on Welsh's novel; the film *Trainspotting* narrowly presents one strand of events to the exclusion of several others found in the novel. The overwhelming popularity of the film's discourse is analogous to Foucault's idea of the discourse of the author, in which a false or misleading "mystique" of the author overshadows subsequent interpretations: "It points to the existence of certain groups of discourse and refers to the status of the discourse within a society and culture."[1] The film *Trainspotting* "defin(es)" the "form" and "characteriz(es)" the "mode of existence" that the discourse on the novel is likely to take.[2] The Cool Britannia image of the film *Trainspotting* belies the complexity, politics, and sorrow of the novel. In a different manner, but with similar results, Helen Fielding's *Bridget Jones's Diary* (1996) is always already subservient to the discourses produced around not necessarily Fielding but the image of "Bridget Jones," and the equally famous, "Bridget Jones Syndrome."[3]

In the United States, *Newsweek* declared London to be "the coolest city on the planet" in its November 4, 1996 issue.[4] The article recalled that Americans have not been this much in love with the old city since the 1960s "Swinging London." This time, though, the 1990s "Swinging London" was not only swinging but cool, hip, and postmodern, all the while retaining for Americans its savoir faire Old World style. Still, similar to the 1960s "Swinging London," the 1990s "Cool Britannia" featured a general air of optimism, with emphasis placed on youth culture and its icons: in music with Britpop featuring Oasis and the Spice Girls; in fashion with then twenty-nine-year-old Phil Treacy, thirty-five-year-old John Galliano at Dior, and twenty-seven-year-old Alexander McQueen at Givenchy. Even the institution of monarchy suddenly looked attractive to Americans when it focused on Princess Diana and the young princes William and Harry. Yet, London was cool in 1996 because it had *money*, and recently refurbished international finance connections. As the *Newsweek* article stressed, "London is happening because London is rich. The British economy has seen three years of sustained growth. And since the Thatcher revolution, the City has consolidated its position as a center of international finance."[5] The article, however, was quick to say that there was disparity between rich and poor, and that the boom could not last—"Better get there soon."[6] The *Newsweek* article, if anything, was simply announcing in print what Americans already knew through the media arts. One did not have to travel to London to see *Trainspotting* released earlier in the year, or hear the bands Oasis, Blur, or the Spice Girls—they were everywhere.

Former British Secretary of State for Culture, Media and Sport Chris Smith, MP, argues in *Creative Britain* that New Labor, led by Blair's landslide victory in May 1997, supports "creativity and culture" because of their "enormous impact" on the "modern economy of Britain."[7] New Labor changed the Department of National Heritage to the Department of Culture, Media and Sport to update the image of Britain. According to New Labor, Britain is not a heritage museum, but a nation of creative people helping to grow the new economy with music, art, and performance. Smith argues that by "changing the name, we also set out four key themes for the work of the Department, and they stand as a useful guide to the nurturing of creative activity and enjoyment that I regard as the proper business of government. The key themes are *access*, *excellence*, *education*, and *economic value*" (italics in original).[8] This kind of populist theme is key to New Labor's agenda. Before the election, Tony Blair, in *New Britain: My Vision of a Young Country*, states that responsibility and accountability are for all sectors of British society. Responding to the Conservatives' touting of "enterprise culture," Blair counters that "enterprise is just another word for the quick buck":

> The Thatcherites used to boast they were anti-establishment. But the trouble with them is that they never wanted to bust the establishment, just buy their way into it. And the new establishment is not a meritocracy but a power elite of money-shifters, middle men and speculators—people whose self-interest will always come before the national or the public interest. So it is hardly surprising that fifteen years of sleaze in high places has given birth to the yob culture. Tory philosophy is the most effective yob-creation scheme ever devised.[9]

Blair's wide appeal to youth culture as counter-yob works to reverse Thatcher's view of yob culture. *Yob* is not a word Americans use, but it basically means a person who disregards the traditional values of society. Yet, the yob spectrum is fairly wide—one could be seen as a yob for being counter-cultural in dress or attitude or a yob for breaking the law or being intentionally offensive or abusive in public. At the very worst, yob describes the soccer fanatic who trashes trains, buses, and other public places; who fights with the opposing team's fans; and whose interest lies more in getting drunk and becoming violent than watching the soccer match. By making Thatcher's middle-aged civil servants and public officials the true yobs of British culture, Blair appeals to the disenfranchised, who would otherwise be labeled yobs by the "establishment." If Blair can convince youths that they are not really yobs but "creative Britain," then he can help to turn the image of certain sectors of British society into something more positive.

However short lived, Cool Britannia embraced the youth sectors formerly regarded as yob and gave them a place and a voice, all the while promoting a new vision or image of Britain. Chris Smith's concluding remarks in *Creative Britain* indicate that while some may consider Noel Gallagher, for example, a yob, Smith argues that popular cultural "enterprises" like the pop band Oasis are good for the British economy:

> When James Stirling builds a new edifice in Stuttgart, or Damien Hirst is lionized in New York . . . or the scriptwriter of *The Full Monty* is hounded round a clamouring Hollywood for his next movie, or

> British bands play to what seems like half the world in Japan, these are not just the evocation of a new British style and part of a new British identity; these are economic transactions too. As a nation, we have been slow to wake up to this truth, but the evidence is now becoming incontrovertible. Creativity, culture, national identity and the nation's future wealth are all inextricably bound up together. It is skilled, creative people that make the difference. And the proper role of government is to *enable* that to happen (italics in original).[10]

The price tag attached to the national identity card for New Labor could appear crass or cynical. Euphemistically put, contemporary postmodern society is "more knowing," as Byatt states. Yet, however crass, cynical, or self-serving, New Labor also appears sophisticated. Popular culture has overtly sold itself as a culture of images—is it not time for politics to *acknowledge* the same sell tactics? Cool Britannia is not simply rock bands or fashion designers, it is a new awareness that many postmodern techniques can work together to imprint an updated image of Britain: from a Wall Street–like image of financial coups, to elegance and style, to the gritty and seeming rebellion of "counter" culture. Perhaps more than any one element, Cool Britannia as posited by New Labor *is* inclusion, not in terms of *acceptance* of difference, but, rather, inclusion to make sure that there is some facet of society that sells to everyone, "something for everyone" in "New Britain." Now, *that* is cool and postmodern.

The two films in this chapter embody the spirit of Cool Britannia in different ways, but both are equally seductive. With the film *Trainspotting*, Americans encounter a replay of 1960s drug-and-pop-music culture updated for 1990s youth culture. The "Swinging London" montage in *Trainspotting* is a pastiche that most twentysomething film-goers would not recognize *as* pastiche or parody. The sophisticated play of postmodern imagery—the screaming colors of painter Francis Bacon's palette that director Danny Boyle uses—the surrealism, and garbage-heritage play on "heritage" indicate that this episodic film will not conform to Hollywood conventions. Yet, contrary to its exotic, foreign appeal, the film is full of American cultural citations as well as American ethical, morals beliefs. According to film scholar Murray Smith:

> For all its "Scottishness," the impact and appeal of America—its glamour and vitality—is everywhere in *Trainspotting*. Most elusively, the "romanticism" of Renton's final break with the gang, his decision to ditch the past and reinvent himself in a new place, has a deep resonance with the American dream. This is, of course, a dream as much for

non-Americans as Americans; as Lesley Fiedler once put it, the world is full of "imaginary Americans."[11]

The film *Trainspotting*, in fact, opens with the dynamic and forceful boom-boom beat of "Lust for Life" by Iggy Pop (America's *only* "real" punk rocker), which begins the film on an energetic note. This appeal cannot be ignored: repackage American culture—including its most famous junkies, Iggy Pop and Lou Reed—and sell it back to America. Capitalism's ever-expanding axiomatic is at work.

With the film *Bridget Jones's Diary* (2000), we get the other-side-of-the-tracks look at Cool Britannia starring, ironically perhaps, the Texan Renee Zellweger as the quintessential English girl, Bridget Jones. Helen Fielding's novel has been identified as a pastiche of Jane Austen's *Pride and Prejudice*, as well as an overwriting of such famous American novels as *Fear of Flying* (1974), by Erica Jong, and *Sex in the City* (1996), by Candace Bushnell. Similar to *Trainspotting*'s "romantic" ending, *Bridget Jones's Diary* shows us that modernism has failed, and in its place is the postmodern "return of the repressed"—the longing for a premodern way of life—a desire to "return to a non-alienated condition, understood as something we have left behind us in the past."[12] In 1996, Martin Wroe's article defined that year's (British) film audience neatly as being in either the Janespotter *Sense-and-Sensibility* camp or the Trainspotter *Trainspotting* group of film-goers, which demarcated the nation's cultural, economic, and generational gaps. Each film, according to Wroe, can be summed up: "One is about insensible smackheads in Edinburgh, the other about sensible bonnet-heads in middle England. One is about chemical highs, the other about romantic highs." And, according to Wroe, the film-goers can be summarized too: "Trainspotters are younger, Janespotters older. One audience comes out speeding, the second weeping."[13] The parallels of plot and characterization in the novel *Bridget Jones's Diary* to *Pride and Prejudice* are "Janesque"—even double-dipping by folding into *Bridget Jones's Diary* the BBC broadcast of *Pride and Prejudice*, which featured Colin Firth as Mr. Darcy—despite the fact that the setting of Fielding's novel is completely contemporary. Yet, *Bridget Jones's Diary* is not principally Janesque, since Bridget has a career, has sexual relations, drinks and smokes, and above all has an awareness that she is trapped between the feminism that helped to grant her greater economic and personal freedom, and femininity—the quantity that makes her yearn for a stable relationship and is marked by her "nesting" impulse. This "Bridget Jones Syndrome"—being caught between greater gender equality and freedom, and the desire to be partnered—casts Bridget as a representative of contemporary woman decidedly trapped between prefeminism, and postmodern postfeminism. In fact, I argue that the distinction between the "Janespotter" and the "Trainspotter" is deconstructed by the film *Bridget Jones's Diary*.

Contextualizing the *Scottish* Novel

According to Andrew Macdonald, the film *Trainspotting* is a "buddy movie," which explains the narrow focus of the film on the exploits of Mark Renton and his small group of friends.[14] With substantial help from the film soundtrack, the film's focus on a group of young men from Edinburgh's youth subculture makes the mystery occupation of "trainspotting" commonplace (Primal Scream's "Trainspotting"), and heroin use seem hip and attractive, though it can be argued that the film does not promote drug use (the film opens with Iggy Pop's infectious "Lust for Life," and continues buoyed by songs like New Order's 1982 dance hit, "Temptation"). Welsh's title is only mentioned once in the text in "Trainspotting at Leith Central Station." With the hobby of trainspotting, identifying as many different trains as possible is the primary "goal"; and, in this way, the "hobby" lacks a specific teleology: trainspotting is open-ended and may be likened to heroin use (or life itself).

Despite the pop-culture image, it is my contention that the novel *Trainspotting* enters into a discourse with the Scottish literary tradition, and through its use of a nonlinear, nonstable narrative rhizome structure severely critiques Scottish life and culture. Taking a very harsh view of the Scottish past and present, the novel effectively demonstrates the lack of connection between individuals, the lack of a genuine cultural or literary past, a self-loathing, and a hopelessness by *enacting* the rhizome structurally. While representation in the text almost always presents these characteristics—from baby Dawn's death from neglect, to Tommy's succumbing to heroin and eventually testing HIV positive, to Dodi's racially motivated beating—the rhizome further heightens the effect of despair and tragedy through "a model that is perpetually in construction or collapsing . . . a process that is perpetually prolonging itself, breaking off and starting up again" without heed to purpose or end.[15] Welsh amplifies the despair and hopelessness of his out-of-work Scottish characters in the 1980s by presenting their narratives rhizomatically; one might even question the categorization of the text as a novel, rather than simply a collection of sketches about a group of people more or less from the same economically depressed working-class Edinburgh suburb. With no past or future of its own making, the rhizome structure of the novel presents as a mirror image the rhizome-like cultural, linguistic, and national identity of Scotland.

Edwin Muir's seminal 1936 assessment of Scottish literature connects spatially and thematically to *Trainspotting*; Muir argues that there is no Scottish literary tradition, even in terms of the tradition's most famous novelist, Walter Scott:

> . . . and so I was forced to account for the hiatus in Scott's endowment by considering the environment in which he lived, by invoking the fact—if the reader will agree it is one—that he spent most of his days in a hiatus, in a country, that is to say, which was neither a nation nor a province, and had, instead of a centre, a blank, an Edinburgh, in the middle of it.[16]

Muir posits that Scotland lacks a genuine literary heritage because it can boast of only a few individual writers (Walter Scott; Hugh MacDairmid), and no sustained national literary tradition. Written in English, *Trainspotting* can be read as a response to a colonized culture, society, economy, education system, and literary tradition that are conducted in English, rather than Gaelic or Scots; in terms of a Scots or Gaelic heritage, it is a vacant past, and what is there has been falsely "imagined" for economic reasons (by non-Scots). As Hugh Trevor-Roper argues in "The Invention of Tradition: The Highland Tradition of Scotland," the Highlands, for example, were culturally dependent upon, and, until the seventeenth century, ruled by the Irish. Trevor-Roper maintains that the Highland "hereditary bards, physicians, harpers (for their musical instrument was the harp, not the pipes) came from Ireland," and "even under the oppressive rule of England in the seventeenth and eighteenth centuries, Celtic Ireland remained, culturally, an historic nation while Celtic Scotland was, at best, its poor sister. It had—could have—no independent tradition."[17] The only Scottish literary production to emerge was the "Kailyard" tradition, which ironically indicates the very lack of an original, vibrant Scottish tradition. Cairns Craig defines "Kailyard literature" as a substandard tradition of "inherent sentimentality" that, with "its flight from the realities of industrial Scotland, becomes both the symptom of the state of the national imagination—a national imagination without a state—and the sickness to which Scottish writers will continue to fall victim whenever they try to engage with the nature of modern Scotland."[18] "A national imagination without a state" is compounded by the loss of a national language with which to express the national imagination. While Walter Scott wrote in English, Hugh MacDairmid attempts to reinvigorate Scottish poetry by using Scots, but acknowledges the duplicity of his identity, “Curse on my dooble life and dooble tongue, /—Guid Scots wi’ English a hamstrung.”[19] While Welsh certainly rejects a sentimental view of Scotland and a supposed “Scots” culture, an awareness of duplicity, a “dooble life and dooble tongue,” are presented in the text. The primary narrative voice, that of Mark Renton, has an interior monologue in which he does not “blame” the English for colonizing Scotland and creating centuries of “doobleness”; he blames the Scots for being colonized by the English:

> Ah hate cunts like that. Cunts like Begbie. Cunts that are intae baseball-batting every fucker that’s different; pakis, poofs, n what huv ye. Fuckin failures in a country ay failures. It’s nae good blamin it oan the English fir colonising us. Ah don’t hate the English. They’re just wankers. We are colonised by wankers. We can’t even pick a decent, vibrant, healthy culture to be colonised by. No. We’re ruled by effete arseholes. What does that make us? The lowest of the fuckin low, the scum of the earth. The most wretched, servile, miserable, pathetic trash that was ever shat intae creation. Ah don’t hate the English. They jist git oan wi the shite thuv goat. Ah hate the Scots.[20]

This passage is often referred to (and, as we will see, even makes it into the film in a different context) because of the recognition that the English conquered and colonized Scotland in the past, and, thus, a postcolonial interpretation reads the English-are-wankers as the most important feature of the passage. The subtext of the passage is that the Scots have a national crisis of identity. The by-product of the crisis produces individuals such as Begbie who, in their inferiority, are defensive, racist, and fearful of difference; the cruel behavior that accompanies this kind of individual eventually drives certain characters to despair and accounts for some characters’ solutions to hopelessness: heroin use and alcoholism.

In fact, the dominant strands of narrative are those that present fear of or hate for Others. When we focus on these discourses, we read beyond the fashionable, hyped, and now clichéd club culture popularized by the film version. From the above passage Renton tells the reader that challenges come from foreigners, whose skin color makes obvious their difference (“pakis”); HIV-positive people probably infected by contaminated needles—but ultimately the contamination is blamed on male homosexuals (“poofs”); and, more generally, non-Presbyterian Scots; tourists; women; and anyone generally perceived as different by virtue of class, education, or life outlook ("what huv ye"). In a novel that is culturally and linguistically aware of its place in what it describes as a culture of "wretched, servile, miserable, pathetic trash," multiple strands of narrative emerge to amplify the rhizomatic connections; narratives continuously repeat and reconnect with discourses involving self-loathing and hate, which are often directed toward those who are, or are perceived to be, different.

Leith, once a separate town, lies north of Edinburgh (incorporated into the city in 1920), and historically was a vital port. Scotland's traditional industries include shipbuilding, mining, and other "heavy industries." After the Second World War, these industries went into decline; by the 1970s and 1980s, Leith was a severely economically depressed area. John W. Books theorizes that a "dependency" view of Scotland's economic downturn "would concentrate on how the actions of the British Government in first creating heavy industries like shipbuilding and then closing them (mines and other heavy industries) kept Scottish development dependent on the centre (London) working through the centre of the periphery (Edinburgh)."[21] In the 1990s and into the twenty-first century, the new dependency is on the multinational corporation that comes into Scotland, builds a plant (electronics, computers), and employs hundreds of Scots, but sends profits and products elsewhere. However, the 1980s *Trainspotting* precedes the multinational-corporation phenomenon that was brought about by the policies of the Thatcher administration (1979–1990). Thatcher broke the trade unions and ushered in an era of "free trade" and economic reform. The working classes saw Thatcherism as initiating an era of economic down-turn as she worked to eliminate their jobs, introduced a poll tax, engineered the Falklands War, and welcomed yuppie values. The reader can easily ascertain the novel's political position when Renton thinks of Margaret Thatcher to ward off premature ejaculation in "The First Shag in Ages." Alan Freeman frames Thaterchism in *Trainspotting* in terms of late capitalism's commodity culture:

> The trainspotters exemplify Late Capitalism's replacement of work with leisure, of action with consumption, of meaning with system, of life with lifestyle. Commodity culture is inscribed with values of corporate capital, the kitsch, the ersatz, with passivity and expendability. "No future" was the battle-less cry of the Sex Pistols and the punk generation with which Renton identifies, both symptom and diagnosis of commodity

> culture. Unable to act in history, Welsh's characters correspondingly suffer the segmentation of their experience.[22]

Although Freeman does not distinguish between those narratives that differentiate their commodified views (Renton's views are markedly different from Sick Boy's, for example), he does sum up the economic and cultural paralysis that affects all the narratives in the novel. However, Freeman fails to distinguish Edinburgh's unique position relative to, say, Leeds or Manchester; having been colonized and brought into a union with England in 1707 *does* distinguish Edinburgh—Leith—as more vulnerable, and apparently more expendable, to London's economic policies. The one answer to economic and culture stagnation is Scotland's, and more precisely Edinburgh's, tourist industry, which does not touch the community of Leith (no tourist would want to visit Leith in the mid-1980s), and which is dependent upon the commercially viable kilts-and-bagpipes image of the happy Scotsman that Renton, in particular, rails against throughout the novel. According to Freeman, the characters' failure to act in history is reflected in the "segmentation of their experience." That is, I would argue, the narrative structure of the novel because, precisely, segmentation *is* the characters' postcolonial identity.

Admittedly, *Trainspotting*'s language is defiant—certainly to anyone who holds a "high-art" concept of the literary novel—and so, predictably, several critics have argued that language in *Trainspotting* works to undermine the authority of the traditional English novel. In "Contemporary Scottish Novelists and the Stepmother Tongue," John Skinner posits that Welsh's use of language is not strictly "Scots"; his manipulation of various dialects and individual idiomatic verbal characteristics gives Welsh's novel a power and a range lacking in "Scots." Skinner illustrates his point by comparing *Trainspotting* to James Kelman's Booker Prize–winning novel, *How Late It Was, How Late* (1994), written in Scots: "Rather than abandoning Standard English, like Kelman's *How Late It Was, How Late*, *Trainspotting* merely overturns conventional linguistic hierarchies by marginalizing the language. Welsh's metropolitan Scots is actually far more impressive in range and variety than the more homogenous Glaswegian demotic forged by Kelman."[23] While there is a certain thumbing one's nose at London by Kelman (who gave his Booker Prize acceptance speech in Scots), Welsh's practice of moving in and out of Leith-speak, utilizing various voices but primarily Renton's, then into cockney in the London bar and standard English (Renton), proves that the "original" (proper English) can be copied, however poorly, so that it ceases to have the authority of originality. According to Andrew O'Hagan, Welsh "has accused James Kelman, for example, of sanitising the way people talk—airbrushing out their racism, their sexism, their self-defeating naffness about people. It's true to say that the characters in the fiction of Kelman and Gray and Janice Galloway speak as people do in the West Coast of Scotland—but they don't say the things that people *say* there" (italics in original), which may be a way to "airbrush" their literary productions for an English-reading public. If it is true that a Scottish novel must be written with London in mind (it is true, generally speaking, of contemporary Irish novelists), then this is another instance of Scotland's dependency—economic, cultural, and linguistic—on the (former) colonial "centre."[24]

In *Devolving English Literature* (1992), Robert Crawford argues that Deleuze and Guattari's *Kafka: Toward a Minor Literature* "contains material likely to be stimulating for anyone interested in questions of how an un-English identity may be preserved or developed within English Literature."[25] Yet, Welsh's presentation of difference does not promote an idea of "un-English identity" or a pro-Scottish identity. Rather, the text repeatedly emphasizes the inferiority of the Scots and their inability to identify themselves without reference to the English, and without use of the English language. When Renton discusses Kierkegaard or his own attempts to read books or discuss psychiatric theories, he uses standard English. Muir believes that the Scottish mind is "doobled" because it thinks, reasons, and critiques in English, but feels in Scots: "For, reduced to its simplest terms, this linguistic division means that Scotsmen feel in one language and think in another; that their emotions turn to the Scottish tongue, with all its associations of local sentiment, and their minds to a standard English which for them is almost bare of associations other than those of the classroom."[26] Welsh, of course, rejects Scots, and one who glances at the novel for the first time would hazard that he has primarily rejected English, too. Yet, Welsh has not rejected the English language; the characters in the book *must* speak English because their schooling, television, music, and other forms in the symbolic are in English. What Welsh forces upon the reader in terms of language is "understanding" a Leith-speak vernacular that is phonically accurate and consistent.

Welsh's interaction with the *lack* of an indigenous literary tradition furthers its lack of coherence and presence. The novel accomplishes this through its rhizome nonhierarchical, narrative structure: narratives begin, splinter, connect to a new narrative, the first narrative reattaching perhaps later in the narrative, perhaps not—all seemingly random and nonhierarchical. The narrative structure helps produce the effect of randomness, chaos, and pointlessness, which, unexplored and unanalyzed, is in fact the sum of the novel. The theorist Gilles Deleuze can help us frame Welsh's discourse of randomness and (in)difference. Deleuze's concept of the rhizome promotes a philosophy of difference because it is nonrepresentational and operates on the "plane of consistency," which resists any kind of universalization. The first characteristic of the rhizome is that it makes random connections in opposition to an organizational plane that plots, orders, and produces hierarchies. Second, the rhizome is heterogeneous in formation and stratification. Third, connected to its heterogeneity is its multiple alliances, which do not seek unity on a plane of organization. *Trainspotting* does not try to unite the multiple discourses and narratives; we can make the connections, but the connection is in the interpretation rather than in any kind of *a priori* intentionality. Fourth, the rhizome is an asignifying rupture; it never ends—it keeps attaching, and reattaching. An exception to the novel's randomness—maybe its greatest flaw, one could argue—is that the novel's ending is too neat and tidy because it provides too much closure. Or, one may argue that the novel in fact never ends—Renton departs for Amsterdam and the narrative could continue *ad infinitum*, especially if one interprets Renton as the main character. A fifth characteristic is that the rhizome maps a new cartography; one could argue that Welsh's novel is indeed "path breaking," especially in terms of the use of language. Sixth, the rhizome rejects "decalcomania," or the transference of one thing on to another; the decal simply transfers the image already mapped or drawn. Yet, the novel is a copy, supposedly, of a certain group or class of people in Leith, Scotland, whose vernacular, in particular, is both a copy and a seeming "original" in literature. The novel's imbrication of the rhizome—a systemless system that keeps renewing itself heedless of a linear or horizontal configuration—is a paradigm, but not a stable one, that Welsh uses to mirror his interpretation of the fragmented, unoriginal, and often violent Scottish identity.

Among the several derogatory references to people of color, there are those that target women of color. Early in the text Johnny Swan shares his fantasy of going to Thailand to have sex with women and notes that it is a place "whair ye could live like a king if ye had a white skin n a few crisp tenners in yir poakit" (12). Also early in the text, Sick Boy's interior narrative in the section, "In Overdrive," relays his thoughts while he cruises the festival scene for women. Sick Boy, Simon, who carries on a conversation in his head with Sean Connery, steps in to help with "[g]ood old-fashioned Scoattish hoshpitality" "two oriental types" who appear lost looking at a map:

> —Can I help you? Where are you headed? ah ask. *Good old-fashioned Scoattish hoshpitality, aye, ye cannae beat it, shays the young Sean Connery, the new Bond, caus girls, this is the new bondage . . .* —We're looking for the Royal Mile, a posh, English-colonial voice answers back in ma face. What a fucking wee pump-up-the-knickers n aw. *Simple Simon sais, put your hands on your feet . . .* (29)

This passage presents a colonial triangle: the "Scoat," the English-colonial (voice), and the "oriental." Simon feels racially superior to the "oriental" until he hears her "posh" English voice, which symbolically castrates him (in a colonial power dyad). Emasculated and perhaps imagining an era when as soldier for the Crown these women would have feared and revered him, Simon cannot compete with the "posh," postmodern "English-colonial voice," and so, immediately fantasizes the "oriental" women as subservient—bending over so that he can have sex with them. This short strand of narrative features the intersection of sex, power, postcolonial (oriental) wealth, and images of past colonial military campaigns. Indexing the fact that Scots supplied the colonial military armies for centuries is a discourse that has multiple tentacles that connect throughout the text. As we will see, Renton muses later in the text, "Anybody will tell you: the Scots make good soldiers" (190).

Perhaps the most disturbing racist and sexist episode in the novel occurs in Stevie's narration of "Victory On New Year's Day," which takes place during the Scottish celebration of Hogmanay. As his sole narrative, Stevie's discursive strand is seemingly randomly placed, and his voice speaks from both within and without the Leith group of friends. Stevie, who now lives in London, has returned for the holidays, and is reluctantly dragged from one new-year's party celebration to another. Stevie is in love with Stella, who is not with him in Leith, and whom he must meet at the train station after the Hiberians (Hibs) and Hearts match. Renton, Stevie, and the other "lads" are all Hibs supporters, and this is an ongoing topic in the text.[27] Stevie, wearing a Hibs scarf, is caught up in a crowd of Hearts fans who taunt him with " 'Hibby bastard' and 'fenian cunt' " (49), then punch him in the mouth, and kick him. Rather than finish Stevie off, as Begbie might, the Hearts fans find victims whose otherness is much more apparent and threatening:

> He thought they were going to come back for him, but they turned their attention to abusing an Asian woman and her two small children.

> —Fuckin Paki slag!
> —Fuck off back tae yir ain country.
> They made a chorus of ape noises and gestures as they left the station.
> —What charming, sensitive young men, Stevie said to the woman, who looked at him like a rabbit looks at a weasel. She saw another white youth with slurred speech, bleeding and smelling of alcohol. Above all, she saw another football scarf, like the one worn by the youths who abused her. There was no colour difference as far as she was concerned, and she was right, Stevie realised with a grim sadness. It was probably just as likely to be guys in green who hassled her. Every support had its arseholes. (49–50)

Stevie's attitude toward the Asian woman is surprisingly sensitive, and his limited ability to think beyond football team "support" makes his observation more poignant. This passage is more poignant because the reader recognizes that Stevie's ability to be different is a great achievement given the fact that he has no reason, outside of human kindness, to be different than either the brutal Hibs or cruel Hearts supporters. For Stevie to momentarily feel what the woman feels, that "[t]here was no colour difference," is true insight on the part of this character who had just left the side of Begbie at the football match. Hearts fans make a "chorus of ape noises and gestures," which indicates that it was a group of Scots, not an isolated individual; indeed, Stevie sarcastically refers to them as "sensitive young men," which indicates their plurality as well as their gender. This passage also tells us that "Paki" is a derogative term that stands in for any person of racial Asian origin. The Hearts fans are not interested in a "Paki's" country of origin; Indian, Pakistani, Chinese or Korean—everyone of color is a "Paki slag" and everyone of them should "[f]uck off back tae yir ain country." In *The New Scots: The Story of Asians in Scotland*, Bashir Maan states, "By 1980, the Asian community in Scotland stood at about 32,000. This carefully estimated figure includes Pakistanis, Indians, Chinese, Bangladeshis and Vietnamese."[28] The overall population statistics for Scotland have been just over five million for the last several decades. Therefore, it is odd that such a small minority (granted that the minority population is most concentrated in the cities), has an effect on the imagination—the fantasies, both sexual and cruel—of the white males in the novel.

The novel also presents complex relationship issues, especially the father-son issue, which attaches to the narratives of Renton and his father, as well as Billy and his father, even Dode and his absent father, and culminates with Begbie and his father in "Trainspotting at Leith Central Station," near the end of the text. Renton, who is returning to Leith from London for the holidays, narrates this section. Running into Begbie, he decides to join him drinking; they stop to urinate at the old Leith Central train station, "now a barren, desolate hangar, which is soon tae be demolished and replaced by a supermarket and swimming centre" (308), when an old man approaches them:

> An auld drunkard, whom Begbie had been looking at, lurched up tae us, wine boatil in his hand. Loads ay them used this place tae bevvy and crash in.
>
> —What yis up tae lads? Trainspottin, eh? He sais, laughing uncontrollably at his ain fuckin wit.
>
> —Aye. That's right, Begbie sais. Then under his breath:—Fuckin auld cunt.
>
> —Ah well, ah'll leave yis tae it. Keep up the trainspottin mind! He staggered oaf, his rasping, drunkard's cackles filling the desolate barn. Ah noticed that Begbie seemed strangely subdued and uncomfortable. He wis turned away fae us.
>
> It was only then ah realised thit the auld wino wis Begbie's faither. (309)

Walking silently until they come upon a lone man, Begbie hits him in the face and boots him a couple of times. The anger, the hate, and the self-loathing that Begbie embodies always translate into violence upon the other. "Trainspotting at Leith Central Station" pulls together and makes lucid the various strands of discourse that focus on hate, especially self-hate, and fear of anything different—people, places, ideas, even football clubs. I do not wish to suggest that the novel has closure, but "Trainspotting at Leith Central Station" consolidates the title of the text with a multiplicity of discourses, including Leith's economic depression and cultural stagnation, which breeds individuals like Begbie. Renton's stealing of the drug money from his mates in London and the novel's conclusion with Renton "contemplat[ing] life in Amsterdam" end the story of Renton and his friends once and for all. Renton states that he could never go back to Leith or Scotland if he takes the money. Therefore, we might have a second novel that concerns Renton in his new life, but we will not have this group of "mates" again. Moreover, we will not have the mates' story with Renton taking place in Leith or in Scotland because that is the one place that Renton can never visit again. What "Trainspotting at Leith Central Station" illustrates is that Begbie is destined to be like his father, the "auld wino"; and if real changes do not occur in this culture and society, Begbie's son with June will be a repetition of the same of his father, and his father's father: Begbie as model Scottish progenitor.

The theme of trainspotting, Scotland's past, and the economically depressed area of Leith are central to the attitude and behavior of each character we have considered. The complex, overlapping, and often-disconnected strands of *Trainspotting* produce a discourse preoccupied with debunking mythic Scotland by presenting how specific social, cultural, and economic situations foster and promote racism and fear of difference and change. The rhizomatic or nonhierarchical structure of the narrative mirrors the effect of randomness, chaos, and gratuity of the inner life of many of the characters, their interactions with others, and their fragmented postcolonial identity. The novel's rhizome produces a Scotland that, "instead of a centre" has, as Muir states, "a blank" because the rhizome builds-up, breaks-down, attaches, and reattaches continuously, never allowing a meaningful "centre" to form and stabilize the text. *Trainspotting* enacts the rhizome to depict, or even to cope with, the situation for those economically stymied by Thatcher-era policies and opportunities, and culturally adrift with a borrowed language and an invented heritage.

From Rhizomatic to Cool Britannia

Perhaps if Michelangelo Antonioni's 1966 *Blow-Up* captured the "look" and energy of 1960s London, then one might argue that *Trainspotting* (1996) captures the media-hyped "look" and energy of 1990s Britain. Screenwriter John Hodge, director Danny Boyle and producer Andrew Macdonald, however, could not create a rhizomatic structure, nor could they delve into the economic, institutional, political, or nationalist problems of the novel. Hodge took the shortest and safest path to the screenplay: sex, drugs, and rock and roll. These topics are typically best developed with male protagonists; since the novel is nearly 100-percent male, all Hodge needed to do was choose which males he would develop. Mark Renton (Ewan McGregor) is an obvious choice. Simon "Sick Boy" (Jonny Lee Miller), Spud (Ewen Bremner), and Begbie (Robert Carlyle) are developed to form the "drug-deal" ending (Second Prize is dropped completely), with Tommy (Kevin McKidd) as a subplot. Swanney (Peter Mullan) is not shown in his true light; author Irvine Welsh cameos as Mikey Forrester. The boys, especially Mark and Tommy, will need sexual partners; so, Diane (Kelly Macdonald), the underage school-girl Mark meets at a club, becomes his girl-beyond-her-years lover and confidante, and Tommy's "downfall" will be blamed on his "losing" the homemade sex-video featuring sex with Lizzie (Pauline Lynch). Drugs, alcohol, and rock and roll pervade the entire film. The Hodge,

Boyle, and Macdonald team had worked together to put out *Shallow Grave* (1993), when Macdonald was encouraged to read *Trainspotting*. Macdonald is quoted as saying, "I've always been very anti-adaptations. I think the best cinema work generally comes from original screenplays. *Trainspotting* was kind of different, because it wasn't really a novel."[29]

The trio also claim that they could have easily gone to Hollywood but wanted to stay in Britain to do a project like *Trainspotting* and not a "genre" film: "After *Shallow Grave*'s success, Boyle was asked by Twentieth Century-Fox if he'd like to read the screenplay for *Alien 4*. 'No, definitely not!' was his instant response."[30] Part of the legend that surrounds the making of *Trainspotting* is that it was made on a small budget, 2.5 million dollars, funded by Channel 4 in Britain. The cult status of the film derives to some degree from its origins: no big Hollywood money financing the project. While this is true, in Britain alone Polygram spent 1.25 million dollars marketing the film for release.[31] Macdonald was adamant that the film *not* be marketed as an "arthouse" film, but rather marketed as a cross-over. In this way, the soundtrack was important to the success of the film, as Macdonald "felt that the music was extremely important in the positioning of the film, telling Screen International that 'British youth culture is fashionable at the moment, and the rise of "Britpop" has been phenomenal. We want the film to tap into the same audiences.' "[32] Though given an "18 certificate in the UK," it was marketed to the sixteen- to twenty-four year-olds, which shows the film's awareness as fitting into the then-surging "British youth culture," eventually dubbed Cool Britannia. The fact that the novel had already sold well to a 1980s generation (that was now mostly thirtysomething) meant that the film was marketable to an older audience as well. The soundtrack, again, contributed to wider generational marketability.

Indeed, a large part of *Trainspotting*'s success as a cinematic experience can be attributed to the film's attention to detail. Editing, camera angles, color scheme, costumes, location, and soundtrack carry the weight that a film narrative might—for the very reason that MacDonald states above, "*Trainspotting* was kind of different, because it wasn't really a novel." Before I discuss the loose nature of the episodic narrative, and the final tacked-on "drug-deal" plot construction, I want to consider the use and, to a large extent, the success of the film's editing strategy, *mise-en-scene*, and soundtrack.

The energy that *Trainspotting* generates comes in part from the numerous and rapid scene cuts in the film. The scene changes follow a fast or slow tempo, depending upon the action. The sound track and voice-over by Renton also contribute to control the tempo of the film. Martin Stollery believes that the film "is full of playful editing experiments":

> As with the cinematography, these often serve narrative or thematic functions as well as being exercises in style for its own sake. Editing often works with the rhythm and tempo of actors' performances. Frantic editing just before and during Spud's interview takes its cue from Ewen Bremner's manic performance. The editing here responds to the way he fidgets, delivers his dialogue very quickly and uses his whole body to express nervousness and excitiability. Renton and Sick Boy's escapade with the air rifle in the park, which precedes this sequence, is edited more slowly. This matches the calmer tone of the performances at this point. Although often rapidly edited, *Trainspotting* varies its edition rhythms from sequence to sequence according to what is being represented.[33]

Another obvious example of the editor Masahiro Hirakubo's control over the tempo is the very beginning of the film, when Renton, Spud, and Sick Boy are running from the police. Before the film begins, we have the heavy drum-and-bass beat of Iggy Pop's "Lust for Life," which functions like a "hit" of speed as it pumps up the audience—revs us up and gets us ready for the mostly fast-paced adventure. We are deliberately slowed down, ripped off our high when Renton overdoses and Swanney drags him to a desolate road and calls a cab to take him to a hospital. Lou Reed's mournful "Perfect Day" accompanies Renton's psychic and cinematic fall through the floor into his grave. "Lust for Life" accompanies the film's high, while "Perfect Day" brings us down—the addict's inevitable "coming down."

In terms of the *mise-en-scene*, Boyle very carefully controlled every aspect, especially the indoor scenes of the "shooting gallery." These scenes were filmed in a former cigarette factory in Glasgow that the crew painted in Francis Bacon colors—bright dark reds and greens—despite the potential negative connotations of Bacon's work, which presents a nightmarish world of bodies on toilets, groping or wrestling with each other, and screaming, gashed mouths. The 1980s were marked by Thatcher's government (1979—1990); until the 1997 success of New Labor, Conservatives held the majority. Despite the 1980s down-and-out atmosphere of *Trainspotting*'s subject matter, director Danny Boyle rejects the gritty realism of the 1980s, and the 1990s reaction to Thatcher's 1980s policies typical of such filmmakers as Ken Loach, Mike Leigh, or even Stephen Frears. Instead of a dose of reality that was sure to be a downer, Boyle states he was conscious of not repeating "bleak shots of housing estates":

> But since the book's take on this sordid subject matter is a celebratory one, Boyle thought that a grim, documentary-style approach would be inappropriate. The stance also suited the director's desire to depart from the established aesthetics of English filmmaking.
>
> Says Boyle, "British cinematic culture as a very strong tradition of dogged realism, and that's something we fought against. We didn't want this to be the kind of drug film that has a lot of bleak shots of housing estates as its context. The book is about the spirit within the characters, which is what we tried to capture. It's meant to be from [the addict's] point of view, rather than that of outsiders who don't do heroin."[34]

The surrealism of the film, especially the famous diving-into-the-toilet-for-the-suppository scene, takes us away from the dreary, miserable, and depressing world of the heroin addict. In the hands of Ken Loach, we would have been made to taste the feces—to scoop with our hands into the toilet's nastiness. Boyle's director of photography, Brian Tufano, did provide a realism in that most of the camera angles are shot low-angled to emphasize that the film is from the "skag-head's" point of view. Tufano states that "Addicts spend a lot of their time flat on their backs on the ground. In a lot of the scenes, we couldn't have gotten much lower unless we'd dug a hole and gone just below ground level."[35] While the viewpoint is supposedly of the addict, Boyle chose colors for the *mise-en-scene* that were "meant to subliminally counteract the general feelings of repulsion that audiences experience while watching scenes depicting heroin use."[36]

Perhaps the primary aesthetic—and marketing—tool for the film is the soundtrack. Both the diegetic and nondiegetic music is used to set the tone of the scene, control the rhythm of the action, and even to supply a narrative. The music is not particularly British, despite the "Britpop" image eventually used to market the "Britishness" of the film. Murray Smith notes that when we hear *American* Iggy Pop's "Lust for Life," we also hear Renton's voice-over; Renton's voice-over had to be *Americanized* in order for non-*Trainspotting*-initiated audiences to understand his Edinburgh vernacular. Despite Macdonald's claim that the film is tapping in on the "Britpop" phenomenon, Smith theorizes that the film has been highly Americanized:

> For all its "Scottishness," the impact of America is everywhere in *Trainspotting*. The appeal of American culture to European culture is a

> long-established and diverse phenomenon, depending on associations of abundance, glamour, dynamism, social mobility, expressiveness, openness, directness, and modernity. . . . As Andrew Higson has written, Hollywood has become "an integral and naturalized part of the popular imagination of most countries in which cinema is an established entertainment form."[37]

Indeed, if there is one thing that emulating Hollywood can help one with, it is how to market oneself as an autonomous entity.

The packaging of *Trainspotting*—not only promotional posters and trailers for the film, but the re-release of the novel, and especially the film soundtrack—has the consistent, "cool" look of a generic grocery or drug-store product. According to Karen Lury, the orange, silver, black, and white package became iconic in its own right as a "brand." Lury argues that, in contrast to a film such as *Shopping* (Paul Anderson, 1994), which critiqued commodity culture that worships "brand" or "label" status, *Trainspotting*, on the contrary, "rather than a commentary becomes a brand itself, offering a distinctive visual aesthetic, its extension into the market of posters, T-shirts, video sales and CDs supported by two key promotional campaigns."[38]

In the United States, Miramax marketed the film, but EMI's subsidiary, Capitol Records (Hollywood, CA) put out the distinctively "Trainspotter"-looking soundtrack. In "Banking on Film Music: Structural Interactions of the Film and Record Industries," Jeff Smith argues that Hollywood benefits in two significant ways by investing in music subsidiaries: "First of all, film companies earn millions of dollars in ancillary revenues from the outright sale of records and sheet music. Second, through their ownership of publishing and record ventures, film companies also derive additional monies from their control of various copyrighted materials."[39] Perhaps more important for the mystique of *Trainspotting* is the promotional value: "soundtrack albums serve as an effective means of circulating a film's title and imagery through rack sales and retail displays."[40] In addition to the film *Trainspotting*'s packaging and promotion as a "brand," Lury argues, the successes of the soundtrack and subsequent CD sales came about because the music was eclectic and offered something new—utilizing the music of not only Americans but that of different periods of rock- and pop-music history: from the 1970s (Lou Reed, "Perfect Day," 1972); 1980s (New Order, "Temptation," 1987); and the newer "Britpop" of the 1990s (Pulp, "Mile End," 1995). In this way, the soundtrack appeals to a larger demographic, introduces the older music to a younger audience, and evades the mistake of narrowly defining itself as a "statement" about a particular generation (and thereby rendered "dated" in a few years time).

Derek Paget argues that there is an "additional dimension" opened up with the nondiegetic music used in "The-Worst-Toilet-in-Scotland" scene and the "pearl-diving" scene, in which Renton dives into the worst toilet in Scotland to retrieve his suppositories, although this music is not on the original released soundtrack:

> As Renton goes through his "cold turkey" shopping list, the screenplay adds "soothing music" to Welsh's original list—cueing music from Bizet's "Carmen." It is heard throughout the scene with Mikey Forrester. After diegetic sound for the betting shop, "Carmen" returns as elegant and ironic counterpoint at the moment Renton capitulates to his junkie need and sinks himself into the repellent toilet pan. The final, triumphant, chord sounds as his feet disappear from view. The pearl-diving music, Brian Eno's "Deep Blue Day," then underscores the contrast between underwater peace and tranquility and surface vileness.[41]

Paget's description captures the nature of the diegetic and nondiegetic music to successfully dictate the audience's response to the film. *Trainspotting* may, in fact, be one of the few successful *cinematic* experiences from the group of novels made into films in all of *Britain Colonized*. Not taking the gritty realist route, the film is more open to the various cinematic techniques that make the film an aesthetic experience. When Irvine Welsh was asked if he was "glad that [the filmmakers] haven't taken the social realist approach," he responded in the affirmative:

> I think I would have been a wee bit despondent if—not to knock Ken Loach of anything because I think that he's brilliant at what he does—if they had made it in the Loach fashion because I don't think we need another Ken Loach. I would have been disappointed if it had been a worthy piece of social realism. I think there's more to it than that. It's about the culture and the lifestyle in a non-judgemental way.[42]

Certainly the film hangs most assuredly on the lifestyle and subculture of the characters in the film. Welsh refused to intervene in any way with the film, and when asked about his own cameo role, he quips, "It stops the author from criticizing the film because you can't say, 'Oh, my God, they've ruined my book,' because you've been a part of the whole process and you've joined in."[43] Welsh is noncommittal about the more-serious issues in the book, and believes that by the time the film was made, the Edinburgh "culture" he wrote about had evolved from his 1980s representation.

If we look at one passage taken from the book and used in the film we can see that the political, economic, and national identity issues opened in the novel are not broached in the film. The "English are wankers" quotation is used against the film's only "heritage" scene. Tommy persuades Spud, Sick Boy, and Renton to get on a train which they do not know, we surmise, was taking them to the highlands—to the mountain country in Scotland. When they get off the train, they are portrayed as completely in awe of the countryside—*not* for its beauty, but for its *foreignness.* Stunned, the three former addicts are not sure what to do, so when Tommy starts off on a trail and queries why they are not following, Spud states: "I don't know, Tommy. I don't know if it's . . . normal."[44] The "braveheart" Scotsman (*Braveheart*, Mel Gibson, 1995) happily roaming the highlands is pointedly *unnatural* for three of these "natives." Referring to the scenery, Tommy asks the others, "Doesn't it make you proud to be Scottish?" Renton counters with the famous, "wankers" diatribe:

> RENTON. I hate being Scottish. We're the lowest of the fucking low, the scum of the earth, the most wretched, servile, miserable, pathetic trash that was ever shat into civilization. Some people hate the English, but I don't. They're just wankers. We, on the other hand, are colonized by wankers. We can't even pick a decent culture to colonized by. We are ruled by effete arseholes. It's a shite state of affairs and all the fresh air in the world will not make any fucking difference.[45]

In this context the hatred that the Scots hold for others ("pakis, poofs, and n what huv ye") and their self-hatred as a nation ("Fuckin failures in a country ay failures") is completely omitted. The speech is not only linguistically cleaned up, it is turned into an expression of *personal self-hatred* that motivates their boredom, drinking, and smack use. Most Americans cannot separate English politics from Scottish politics, nor do they know much about England's colonization of other parts of the British Isles (except for what they see in films such as *Braveheart* and *Michael Collins*); therefore, *Trainspotting* audiences will take this invective as simply typical of Renton's role as the slightly intellectual one of the group who is also a rebel in regard to society. As a commentator on Scottish culture, Renton's speech in the film does not tell us anything about Scottish politics, nationality, economics, or xenophobia.

This scene can be connected to the London scenes for American viewers. The Swinging-London-pastiche's style is such that in the context of the grubbiness of the main characters, we are supposed to view this as ironic or humorous. Yet, the move to London by Renton is analogous to the traditionally clichéd image of an American from Iowa or Kansas moving to New York City to "make it big." In fact, this is exactly the way the film presents Renton's move—he is going to make it big, or, at least, make lots of money. Renton's voice-over indicates that this is not the 1980s of the novel, but the 1990s of London's "Cool Britannia" economic boom:

> I settled in not too badly and I kept myself to myself. Sometimes, of course, I thought about the guys, but mainly I didn't miss them at all. After all, this was boom town where any fool could make cash from chaos and plenty did. I quite enjoyed the sound of it all. Profit, loss, margins, takeovers, lending, letting, subletting, subdividing, cheating, scamming, fragmenting, breaking away. There was no such thing as society and even if there was, I most certainly had nothing to do with it. For the first time in my adult life I was almost content.[46]

This information tells us a great deal, not only about Renton, but also about the world he is leaving for his new life in the city. The most striking piece of information coming from this former skaghead is that capitalism is *exciting*. The very words are exciting: "profit, loss, margins . . . fragmenting, breaking away." All this is so exciting that Renton admits, "for the first time in my adult life I was almost content," which is monumental considering that boredom and lack of opportunity is what the film has been presenting as the reason for drug addiction. This passage, then, tells us that London is the land of opportunity; and not only can you get off drugs there, you can find yourself there—find out what makes you happy. This step in Renton's development is actually Renton's "deep resonance with the American dream," which Smith indicated was part of the plot of the final drug-deal. Without this episode of Renton as successful capitalist, audiences, especially American audiences, would be less supportive of Renton's final action.

Therefore, whether the English are wankers or not, the "English" London episodes are the ones in which Renton is most happy—even clubbing with Begbie in London was fun for Renton. Of course, it is at the club in London that Renton echoes Diana's "the world is changing" discourse. Begbie ends up with a transvestite—while the audience sees the action unfold, Renton's voice-over persuades us that even boys and girls are changing: "music is changing, drugs are changing, even men and women are changing. One thousand years from now there'll be no guys and no girls, just wankers. Sounds great to me. It's just a pity that no one told Begbie."[47] When Renton teases Begbie, Begbie threatens him with a knife, "Now, listen to me, you little piece of junky shit. A joke's a fucking joke, but you mention that again and I'll cut you up. Understand?"[48] The scene is interrupted by a knock at the door; it is Sick Boy. Attempting to fulfill his "American dream," Renton is bogged down by his friends: a psychopathic armed robber, and a cold-hearted pimp and pusher. These are core scenes that draw the mainstream movie-goer into the plot of accepting Renton's betrayal of his "mates."

The London scenes work to set-up Renton's regime of self-improvement, which American audiences typically like because he is considered a "loser" before he joins "society." The fact that Renton consciously says he does not believe there exists "such a thing as society and even if there was, I most certainly had nothing to do with it," indicates that he knows he has sold out to capitalism. And yet, it is fairly obvious that he was always already trapped in consumer capitalism before moving to London. This statement marks Renton's passage from "loser" to capitalist success-story. The viewer might register the irony in Renton's gratuitous self-defense, "I most certainly had nothing to do with it"; or the viewer might think that his "estates agents" job *is* a scam, and he is still slightly outside of "society." Either way, we have seen his character change, evolve, and attempt to "make good" in the big city. When Tommy's funeral brings them all back to Leith, the "drug deal" is established. Critics have noted the influence that certain directors have had on Boyle's style. Quentin Tarantino is often mentioned, and as Stollery observes:

> Miramax, the company which distributed *Trainspotting* in America, had previously distributed the commercially successful *Pulp Fiction*. . . . Miramax's trailer for *Trainspotting* emphasized the drug deal towards the end of the narrative and the overall style of the film. Emphasizing the drug deal as an objective for the characters within the narrative downplays the more unconventional aspects of *Trainspotting*'s narrative which mainstream audiences might be wary of . . . .Highlighting style and crime in *Trainspotting* also suggested the film would appeal to audiences who had enjoyed films directed by Tarantino.[49]

The drug deal is marketed as the climax of the film, and from an American perspective, the escape from his so-called friends is more evidence of Renton's "success." Initally, Renton is forced into the drug deal because Begbie knows Renton has a savings account with over two-thousand pounds in it. The audience sympathizes with Renton's attempt to "make good," and now understands that he is being forced to participate in the world he had resolutely resolved to leave behind. The fact that Begbie is not only wanted for armed robbery, but is a certified psychopath, and Sick Boy a heartless pimp and pusher, makes Renton's betrayal of them acceptable. While we feel for Spud, we also know that Renton feels for him, too. Spud sees Renton take the money, but does not call out or stop him, which, in turn, makes us feel more sympathy for Spud. For extra "happy ending" feel-good closure, Renton sends Spud his bus locker key, which Spud uses and happily finds his share of the drug deal cash.

The actual closure comes through a tidy recapitulation of the opening voice-over by Renton. The opening voice-over rejects consumer culture for "junk culture," but the final voice-over sardonically states "I'm going to be just like you" and take the job and buy the washing machine. In a way, the ending is a postmodern send up—no story, no moral, but the film hopes that you have enjoyed the ride:

> RENTON, *voice-over.* So why did I do it? I could offer a million answers, all false. The truth is that I'm a bad person, but that's going to change, I'm going to change. This is the last of this sort of thing. I'm cleaning up and moving on, going straight and choosing life. . . . I'm going to be just like you: the job, the family, the fucking big television, the washing machine, the car, the compact disc and electric tin opener, good health . . . looking ahead, to the day you die.[50]

Renton not only does not offer an alternative to consumer culture at the end of the film, he *embraces* consumer culture. One could interpret Renton's closing voice-over as completely ironic, and believe he will return to his former addiction, at least until his money runs out. But to buy into this interpretation is against the spirit of the film. Remember, not only is Renton totally sick of his friends and their way of life, he is also *excited* by capitalism—by the idea of making and possessing money. Renton's savings account indicates that he did not simply squander his money; rather, the savings account tells us that Renton enjoys "earning" and hoarding the money from his job in London. Lastly, it should be fairly simple to see that the Scottish novel *Trainspotting* has been transformed into a vaguely British film *Trainspotting* in order to cash in on the Cool Britannia phenomena. "Creative Britain" of New Labour is more than happy to embrace the vast citationality of the packaging of *Trainspotting*—however much it displays yob culture and appeals to a yob audience.

Jonespotting in Cool Britannia

The novel *Bridget Jones's Diary* exists on two literary planes. The first plane is that of reworking the woman's romance novel through the diary genre. Alison Case argues in "Authenticity, Convention, and *Bridget Jones's Diary*," that Fielding's novel participates in the convention of "feminine narration," which "is characterized by the exclusion of the narrator from the activity of shaping her experience into a coherent and meaningful story."[51] With the diary form, Bridget supposedly narrates "what happened" and perhaps produces commentary on the events, but she is powerless to change "what happened." Addressing the genre from a wide, historical perspective, Trevor Field in *Form and Function in the Diary Novel* posits that there are two primary issues with this diary: "First, verisimilitude, or the likelihood that a given character would be able to write the diary in question, must be respected; while the very fact that the text is a purported reproduction of a particular form of writing means certain mimetic devices will be used."[52] With *Bridget Jones's Diary* the reader is peering into the innermost thoughts of the diarist, Bridget, and she, overall, can be interpreted as "realistic." If this is the case, then the novelist herself has successfully utilized the genre's conventions. Thus, the diary form combined with the "feminine narrative" of lack of control in the creation of the story result in fictional naiveté that, when executed well, can produce not only a powerfully realistic novel, but one in which the reader's sense of superiority to Bridget is a primary pleasure for the reader.

Yet, this "lack of control" is not restricted to female narratives. According to H. Porter Abbott, "the diary method of narration has been functionally linked to that collection of conventions Ian Watt called 'formal realism.' "[53] The astonishing success of the tried-and-true genre of the "marriage plot" by a 1990s woman inscribed into her diary is due to Fielding's ability to make Bridget "real," or her novel seem otherwise "artless": "In purporting to give the truth of a real, not an invented, consciousness, the diary strategy favors a conception of the real as artless, and thus in a familiar paradox it has become a formal attribute of the absence of form."[54] The text is sophisticated in its "artlessness" or lack of literary artificiality. As Case states, the identification, "what feels right and convincing and appealing to readers about this voice has as much to do with gendered literary convention as it does with any kind of verisimilitude to contemporary women's lives."[55] Yet, this literary "verisimilitude" reiterates a literary form that not everyone, especially feminists, wish to see reinstituted in the postmodern era; as Daphne Merkin in "The

Marriage Mystique" states: "What's really bothering people about 'Bridget Jones' is that it signals the return of what is referred to in English-lit classes as the Marriage Plot."[56]

This point brings us to the second literary plane of *Bridget Jones's Diary*—that of the contemporary dubbing of the novel as "Chick-Lit." Broadly speaking, there are two forms of contemporary "Chick-Lit": the avowed pro-feminist type, and the postfeminist variety. The pro-feminist variety is postmodern enough to use the nomenclature of "postfeminism," though it is not antifeminist. Cris Mazza, co-editor of *Chick-Lit On the Edge: New Womens Fiction Anthology* (1995), claims in a recent issue of the American magazine *Poets & Writers* that her text was the first to utilize the term "Chick-Lit." Claiming to be "Postfeminist," Mazza declares in her introduction that her book is not an antifeminist text, but also "**not**: my body, myself my lover left me and I am so sad all my problems are caused by men . . . but watch me roar what's happened to me is deadly serious society has given me an eating disorder a poor self esteem, a victim's perpetual fear . . . therefore I'm not responsible for my actions."[57] These words are presented in different print fonts so that the emotive aspects of the statements can be more fully realized. The different fonts themselves could be seen as either different voices speaking—when the font changes the speaker changes—or the printed word's being "feminized" or made "girly" through this kind of "expressionistic" print. If the latter, then the very real feminist strand of thoughts is deflated—or ironized.

The fact that the term "Chick-Lit" gets picked up by popular media (and the tag "Chick-flick" is also coined for a woman's film) mystifies Mazza, who states concerning the title of the anthology: "This was the ironic intention of our title: not to embrace an old, frivolous, or coquettish image of women, but to take responsibility for our part in the damaging, lingering stereotype."[58] One must assume that the "damaging, lingering stereotype" is that of a "frivolous, or coquettish image of women" and not of the strident burn-your-bra feminist image of women. A fully realized parody of "Chick-lit" would be able to infiltrate and undermine the frivolous faithfully, much in the same way that *The Remains of the Day*'s character Stevens's closeted irony spills into postmodern humor. Apparently, the commercial book publishers to whom Mazza refers missed the irony but liked the title. According to Mazza, *Bridget Jones's Diary* is just one of the many books by women that her book's term helped launch:

> What we couldn't anticipate was that less than 10 years later our tag would be greasing the commercial book industry machine. I've

> conducted no extensive research into culture and society to explain why chick lit was "originated" all over again, about three years after *Chick-Lit* was published. But a stroll through any bookstore confirms that chick lit's second incarnation looks not at all like its first. Somehow chick lit morphed into books flaunting pink, aqua, and lime covers featuring cartoon figures of long-legged women wearing stiletto heels.[59]

Since *Bridget Jones's Diary* is chief among the list of the "second incarnation" of Chick-Lit, we need to ask ourselves why Mazza, for instance, wishes to demarcate her pro-feminist version of "Chick-Lit" from the so-called commercial-industry version of "Chick Lit" epitomized by Fielding's novel. To answer this question we must unpack the various meanings of postfeminism, especially in the context of *Bridget Jones's Diary*.

One way into the issue of the status of "Chick-Lit" is to look at the way "Bridget Jones" has become a *zeitgeist* of the 1990s. "Bridget Jones" has turned into the "Bridget Jones Syndrome" or "Bridget Jones Effect," which most critics describe as a "backlash" to 1970s and 1980s feminism. In the 1990s, feminism became the "f-word" that no one dare repeat. On the one hand, Bridget's own experience in the novel is one that is familiar with old-style feminism; but she does not care much for it, especially if it gives her a butch appearance: "there is nothing so unattractive to a man as strident feminism."[60] Feminism in the 1990s has the power to scare off potential heterosexual mates:

> *Bridget Jones* became a bestseller because women recognized within its irony their own experiences of popular culture, and especially the tensions between the lure of feminist politics and the fear of losing one's femininity. This perception of the incompatibility of feminism with having a meaningful heterosexual relationship has unfortunately been perpetuated beyond reason to its current status as self-evident "truth."[61]

On the other hand, at the beginning of the text when Bridget first meets Mark Darcy at the Alconbury's New Year's Day Turkey Curry Buffet, she tries to impress him by answering his question—"Have you read any good books lately?" (14)—by saying that she has read Susan Faludi's *Backlash*. This answer indicates that she knows that a serious female, an intellectual in the publishing business, *should* be reading a book such as *Backlash*. Also, the fact that Bridget has actually been reading the then trendy, nonintellectual, *Men are from Mars, Women are from Venus*, but is too embarrassed to admit it, tells us a great deal about what she knows about feminism. Pro-feminists interpret Bridget as antifeminist or representing an antifeminist stance in society. As Mazza might put it, Fielding's character Bridget displays "an old, frivolous, or coquettish image of woman." Yet, it is my contention that Bridget in *Bridget Jones's Diary* is neither pro-feminist nor antifeminist in the "old" image of woman, but is quintessentially postfeminist in a postmodern world that always already has her trapped by a gendered set of life-options.

Thus, readers, especially women readers, identify with Bridget because she represents this gendered set of life-options so well; yet, commentators and critics on both sides of the feminist debate want to make an example of Bridget to further their own particular agenda. Bridget is a "poster child" of the 1990s woman because she is caught in the middle of two eras—neither perfectly formed. One American reviewer picked up the fact that Bridget is caught between two eras, "Some idealists might see such a woman as a troubling role model, but who are they kidding? I mean, we really do act like that. Bridget Jones is a fair compromise between the '70s-style feminist and the '50s-era debutante—the '90s woman."[62] First, she embodies the seemingly fully emancipated woman of the postfeminist era of expectations: educated, liberated, sexually active, career-oriented. Second, she also embodies, at the same time, the pre-feminist set of expectations in regard to her body, potential partner, domestic space, and social life. Because Bridget is more typical or more average than her U.S. fictional "sisters," such as the neurotic Ally McBeal or the supersexed Samantha Jones from *Sex and the City*, she appeals as an "everywoman" figure. There is no doubt, however, that in the United States, Ally McBeal and the woman characters from Bushnell's novel paved the way for Bridget's Atlantic crossing.

Or, maybe for Americans, Bridget's precursor is Betty Friedan. In *The Miseducation of Women*, James Tooley connects Betty Friedan's "feminine mystique" to "the Bridget Jones Syndrome" and states that "the novel argument of this [Tooley's] book is that a much more serious injustice is being perpetuated against girls, that allows them to pass through schooling unscathed and with flying colours—unlike for boys—but which kicks in when they are older, when they reach Bridget Jones' certain age."[63] Unfortunately, Tooley does not spell out exactly why boys do not go through school equally well, "with flying colours," as girls, or the lesson boys apparently learn at an early age that girls do not. Are we to understand that Tooley is inferring that girls are "passed" through the system because they are girls? One wonders where Tooley has been hiding—if anything, in the United States in any case, females do not seem to be the recipient of any special educational benefits. In any case, Tooley utilizes Bridget as representative of her society in order to make his own case that feminism has failed females:

> Some readers might think that I am getting rather carried away with this character, who, whatever her charms, is after all only a fictional creation. Perhaps I am taking her predicament too much to heart? But it turns out four million women are not wrong. Survey after survey, not to mention anecdote after anecdote, all point in the same direction. Women's magazines are full of stories about women's current unhappiness and surveys to explore why. *Top Santé*—"the UK's best-selling health and beauty magazine"—for instance, revealed in its summer 2001 survey that "only nine per cent of working women (and four per cent of women with pre-school children) say they choose to work full-time" . . . .'78 per cent of all working women" would quit their jobs tomorrow if they could and similar percentage think that their work is damaging their health, "causing ailments such as headaches, constant exhaustion, backache, anxiety, forgetfulness, insomnia, irritable bowel syndrome and migraine." "Family life," says the report, "is being driven to breaking point" by women's current lifestyles.[64]

Needless to say, Tooley's argument is fairly transparent. Postmodern, high-tech lifestyles with, as Bridget's mom says, "too many choices," too many over-committed people—especially working parents—affect both women and *men*. While it is kind of Tooley to emphasize the plight of the female in the twenty-first century, I am sure that at least " '78 per cent of all working' " *men* "would quit their jobs tomorrow if they could." Indeed, Bridget Jones represents women at the end of the twentieth century; although men's problems in our era are different, she also manages to tell us a lot about what it is like to be either gender in our era.

Connected to being human in our era is the fact that irony and parody are the core strategies of postmodern literature. Therefore, it seems that critics on both sides of the feminist debate who bash Bridget are missing Fielding's self-confessed plundering of plots, satire humor, and girl hyperbole. While intentionality is not particularly fashionable, we need to remember that the character who would eventually be "Bridget" emerged from a weekly newspaper column in which even Fielding thought would be absurd to write:

> I was asked to write a newspaper column as myself. I said no because I thought it was hopelessly exposing and embarrassing. But I offered instead to make up a comic, exaggerated fictional character—one that

> I'd been playing with for a sitcom: the girl who's the embodiment of the banana skin joke, optimistic, with grand aspirations: "I'm not going to sleep with him"—cut to her in bed with him. The irony is that everybody thinks she's me anyway.[65]

Also, Fielding believes the success of Bridget Jones is due to her belief that "Women are so naturally funny, ironic, and self-deprecating and I think they like books with that sort of tone. I think the book touched a nerve which is something about the gap between how women feel they are expected to be and how they actually are."[66] It is precisely "the gap" that best describes the postmodern, postfeminist woman: stranded in the void between the idealized female of fashion magazines and other media, and the real person who has faults, weaknesses, and real-world responsibilities. Comically, Fielding argues that women's expectations are out of control: "We are bombarded by so many media images of female perfection and conflicting roles—we end up feeling we should be like the girl in the 24-hour mascara ad, rushing from the gym to the board meeting and home to a perfect husband and children to cook dinner for twelve whilst looking like an anorexic teenage model."[67]

Overall, Fielding's strategy is to subvert these expectations through humor and hyberbole. Having said that, however, most of the discussion concerning Bridget's supposed low self-esteem and life careening out of control are over stated. If we look at Bridget's Saturday-22-April entry we find a sensible Bridget whose prose reveals that she is in control of her life, and has a certain ironic balance to the way she represents herself and the way, we have to assume as readers, she conducts her life. Bridget calls her friend Tom to report the "miracle"of finally becoming "thin": "Today is an historic and joyous day. After eighteen years of trying to get down to 8st 7 I have finally achieved it."[68] Tom suggests that perhaps Bridget has tapeworm. Bridget says she will keep this tapeworm because, "Not only am I thin, but I no longer want to smoke or glug wine."[69] This entry comes four days after Bridget sees Mark Darcy at a party and rejects Daniel Cleaver's advances; and so, when Tom asks if she is "in love," she remarks: "I racked my brains, then stopped, shocked by a sudden, stunning realization. I am not in love with Daniel any more. I am free."[70]

In terms of the narrative development, Bridget has been exposed to Darcy's more-positive side, and is willfully turning away from Daniel. But the *character* is not fully conscious of this development. What she is conscious of is her deliberate mastery of herself in relation to Daniel. She refuses his dinner invitation four days earlier, and now she is the slimmest she has ever been. Instead of "longing" for Daniel, she is subconsciously preparing herself for Darcy. And yet, judgment given in regard to her control of her relationships, her body, and her behavior is negative: " 'You just seemed, well, flat tonight. Everyone said you weren't your usual self . . . . I think you looked better before, hon.' "[71] Herein lies the real problem with being "a child of *Cosmopolitan* culture . . . traumatized by supermodels." Bridget cannot win: if she is overweight and seemingly out of control, she is a loser; if she is slim and seemingly in control, she is a loser. It is *this* dilemma that Tooley should focus upon. This idea of a young female's never being "right" is instilled in girls by normalized patriarchal heterosexual society, the media, and consumer culture. Bridget closes the Tuesday-25-April entry with the following lament after she has been told, basically, that she was *better before*:

> Now I feel empty and bewildered—as if a rug has been pulled from under my feet. Eighteen years—wasted. Eighteen years of calorie and fat-unit-based arithmetic. Eighteen years of buying long shirts and jumpers and leaving the room backwards in intimate situations to hide my bottom. Millions of cheesecakes and tiramisus, tens of millions of Emmenthal slices left uneaten. Eighteen years of struggle, sacrifice and endeavour—for what? Eighteen years and the result is "tired and flat." I feel like a scientist who discovers that his life's work has been a total mistake.[72]

For eighteen years, as Bridget repeatedly indicates, she has played this very female game of calorie counting and backing out of the room so that her rear end is not noticed; this means that since Bridget was about fourteen-years old she has been possessed by "*Cosmopolitan* culture . . . traumatized by supermodels." Knowing that she cannot measure up, Bridget and millions like her still try. So, after all the years of strategizing and sacrificing, Bridget's "life's-work-has-been-a-total-mistake" attitude is carried into a woman's thirties so that—as we can see—no matter what choices she makes she is made to feel unhappy. From her body, to her career versus family, to partnership choices a woman is made to feel that she has done the wrong thing, made the wrong decision, cannot measure up (or down). This phenomenon accounts for Tooley's anecdotal numbers concerning the decline, supposedly, of personal happiness in individual women (Tooley fails to mention other factors that might mitigate one's ability to measure "happiness"—age, expectation, life experience, geography, and class). It should not be surprising that women cannot win in the postmodern era; and again, as Fielding stated in an interview, "We are bombarded by so many media images of female perfection . . . rushing from the gym to the board meeting and home to a perfect husband and children to cook dinner for twelve whilst looking like an anorexic teenage model." "Having it is all" is a postmodern phenomenon. Bridget finally rejects it, wishing instead for a premodern world: a Janespotter world. Yet, a postmodern Janespotter world is oxymoronic, so she settles for a "Jonespotter" world positioned in the post feminist "gap."

Irony is produced by Bridget's Americanized "self-improvement" attempts to shape her body and her life. Kelly A. Marsh also argues that Bridget is ironizing the American self-improvement ethos; Bridget "ultimately," according to Marsh, "rejects the American dream of a perfected self in favor of the Blair-era British communitarianism that facilitates both her personal success and the success of her narrative."[73] Marsh further argues that Bridget's disorganized attitude toward aspects of life such as her career and love life make her a poor consumer, which plays into a certain view of New Labor philosophy: "Bridget refuses to play her part in a consumer society and refuses the model of efficient consumer in her personal life."[74] To be an "efficient consumer in her personal life," Bridget would have to latch onto Darcy as a good economic choice, and forego an affair with Daniel, a "v. bad" choice as a prudent consumer. Marsh believes that Bridget is actually subversive to the "profit-maximizing" capitalist machine, "Joel Krieger suggests that for New Labour, community is an alternative to 'the neoliberal reliance on homo economicus, a soulless profit-maximizing individual, inhabiting a society-less world,' and the novel[s] reveal that Bridget chooses the former rather than the latter."[75] This position might be tenable were it not for the fact that Bridget quits her job at the publisher and lands a television job, which, everyone, including herself, views as a step up the capitalist career ladder; additionally, she eventually "quits" Daniel, and ends up with the good consumer choice, Mark Darcy.

In fact, if the 1996 release of the novel *Bridget Jones's Diary* is anything, it is the embodiment of Blair's New Labor support for "creativity and culture" because of this sector's "enormous impact" on the "modern economy of Britain."[76] The character Bridget lives a dream life compared to that of those outside of London, and she is aware that there is pressure to enjoy the internationally famous cultural riches that the city offers. Reflecting on her optimal location, she states that "you think that just because you live in central London you should be out at the RSC/Albert Hall/Tower of London/Royal Academy/Madame Tussauds, instead of hanging around in bars enjoying yourself" (150). From the perspective of those who do not live in London, she represents the single, thirtysomething "Cool Britannia" of seemingly endless possibilities available in 1996 London: "London is happening because London is rich."[77] Similar to the film *Trainspotting*, this London is one in which you can make money, and, for Bridget, find a better job and a marriage partner. In fact, Fielding may have spoofed Irvine Welsh by having Bridget meet Mark Renton (though likely tagged "an emotional fuck-wit" by Bridget's friends) in a London bar; and in justifying his move down from Edinburgh Renton tells her: "After all, this [is] boom town where any fool [can] make cash from chaos and plenty [will]. I quite [enjoy] the sound of it all."

The film *Bridget Jones's Diary* (Sharon Maguire, 2001) utilizes the Austen marriage plot and the postmodern contemporary setting and situation, making it part Janespotter and part Trainspotter. Yet, in the end, the film defies both categories; it realigns itself so that a new contemporary representation of life in the era of New Labor is revealed. The film's Bridget does not, however, opt for the communitarian view of New Labor; rather, she embraces American self-improvement, "Cosmopolitan culture" on her way to "moving on up" to a new job and a new man. The screenplay by Andrew Davies, Richard Curtis, and Helen Fielding is loyal to the Austen marriage plot; but it is Davies and Curtis, the veteran British romantic-comedy screenwriters, who give the film a familiar shape and style. The *New Statesman* review of *Bridget Jones's Diary*, titled "A Bridget Too Far," claims that the film's romantic-comedy formula, overutilized by Working Title Films (*Four Weddings and a Funeral*, *Notting Hill*), "has delighted us long enough":[78]

> In *Bridget Jones's Diary*, all the elements of the previous ebullition are here, warmed up once more and bubbling away, pungently: a gemutlich, Dibleyish script by Richard Curtis (among others); an American leading lady in the swollen shape of Renee (Raging Bull) Zellweger; a cynically chosen soundtrack of cheap but potent music; and some Hallmark Christmas-card scenes to Theme Park England, of the kind designed to please those untravelled Americans (George Bush, for example) who are stupid enough to believe that it snows a lot in central London (just like Oliver), and that anyone with a posh accent must live in a house the size of Castle Howard.[79]

Indeed, Americans loved *Four Weddings and a Funeral*; in fact, the film was released in America *first*. *Notting Hill* traded in Andie Macdowell for Julia Roberts, but kept Hugh Grant. Hugh Grant plays the Brit twit for the first two films, then is billed as the "bad boy" of

Bridget Jones. However formulaic, the Curtis romantic comedy sells—and "untravelled Americans" apparently enjoy the Christmas-card scenes and "the illusion that this kind of comedy is youthful and anarchic, as opposed to dated and conservative."[80] It is exactly this combination of Cool Britannia, youthful and hip in a thirtysomething way, and Janespotter, formulaic and conservative in a heritage sort of way, that adds up to *Bridget Jones* as a Jonespotter film.

Other critics, too, are concerned that these kinds of contemporary British films portray only one segment of British society to the exclusion of the larger heterogeneous representation of the British population. The term heritage has been applied to *Four Weddings*, *Notting Hill*, and *Bridget Jones's Diary* despite the contemporary settings and mainly thirtysomething characters who are, themselves, not primarily nostalgic. Andrew Spicer notes that "*Four Weddings* and *Notting Hill* have been attacked as nostalgic, and disingenuous, avoiding the realities of contemporary Britain in favour of a fey, middle-class never-never land."[81] As Claire Monk also convincingly argues, *Bridget Jones*'s *Diary* embraces a version of Englishness that is "heritage":

> *Notting Hill* (Roger Michell, USA/UK, 1999) and *Bridget Jones's Diary* (Sharon Maguire, US/UK, 2001) project a vision of the nation so uniformly young, white, wealthy, narcissistic and implicitly conservative, within a *mise-en-scene* cleansed of the urban poor, the homeless and ethnic minorities, that by contrast the 1980s heritage film looks like a paragon of socially inclusive, low budget liberal filmmaking. Significantly, in its obligatory rural interlude, *Bridget Jones's Diary* embraces the heritage aesthetic, and the well-heeled country house and National Trust village iconography, with a shamelessness unseen in any period heritage film, and entirely without heritage films' social critique or sense of irony.[82]

In *Notting Hill*, Julia Roberts is an American actress, in London to film a heritage film, and Hugh Grant is a Notting Hill resident. American audiences undoubtedly desire these films' "vision of the nation so uniformly young, white, wealthy, narcissistic and implicitly conservative, within a *mise-en-scene* cleansed of the urban poor, the homeless and ethnic minorities," perhaps as a racist escape from American racial and ethnic heterogeneity. The fact that London and other large British cities, are as multiethnic, multicultural, and multiracial as large U.S. cities is erased. In effect, the values of the heritage film are now being sustained by the white, middle-class thirtysomethings disguised as cool, contemporary Britain.

For *Bridget Jones* to succeed as a romantic comedy in America, the film must play the heritage card and the Cool Britain card at the same time. Instead of a disproportionate beast, the film represents an attractive version of postmodern Britain. The postcard scenes of snow—going home for New Year's Day, going to the Darcy's manor house for their silver wedding anniversary, and the final climatic Bridget-and-Darcy-kissing scene—are examples of the Dickens England Maguire shamelessly utilizes to produce a cozy, traditionally romantic feeling. Yet, at the same time, the heritage film is undermined by such scenes as Bridget's commenting to Daniel, postcoital, "that thing you just did" is "illegal" in many countries; Daniel quips that this is why he is proud to be English. Granted, this is a postmodern and post-feminist film, but there are not any scenes depicting or even containing direct references to anal sex in such homosexual-themed films as *Maurice*. This Jonespotter combination of Austen-meets-Fielding exhibits a cool postmodernism. As Umberto Eco has theorized, we cannot destroy the past, or forget the past, but we can incorporate it—contaminate it:

> [The past] cannot really be destroyed, because its destruction leads to silence, must be revisited: but with irony, not innocently. I think of the postmodern attitude as that of a man who loves a very cultivated woman and knows he cannot say to her "I love you madly," because he knows (and that she know that he knows) that these words have already been written by Barbara Cartland. Still, there is a solution. He can say, "As Barbara Cartland would put it, 'I love you madly'." At this point, having avoided false innocence, he will nonetheless have said what he wanted to say to the woman: that he loves her, but he loves her in an age of lost innocence. If the woman goes along with this, she will have received a declaration of love all the same. Neither of the two speakers will feel innocent, both will have accepted the challenge of the past . . . both will consciously and with pleasure play the game of irony . . . both will have succeeded, once again, in speaking of love.[83]

Indeed, as viewers we know (and we know the filmmakers know that we know) that heritage England is dead, that Jane Austen was a fiction writer, and that Mark Darcy would not read "I hate him!" in Bridget's diary then walk out and buy her a new diary as a gift to "make a new start" (the film's ending). The game of irony at the cinemaplex is quintessentially postmodern—and *Bridget Jones* provides a Cool Britannia version of love in postmodernity.

In addition to the Joneseque postmodern romantic comedy, the American features of the film *Bridget Jones* are important to the success of the "Chick-flick" market that provides an image of the "new woman" as confident, independent, and ultimately a *winner*. Although Zellweger's Bridget is more Lucille Ball than Thelma and Louise, in the end, her own Emersonian "self-reliance" renders her a winner as a career woman and heterosexual. There are two key events in the film that reiterate American-style female-empowerment film citations.

The first event is Bridget's decision to quit smoking and drinking, and start a diet-and-exercise routine. Buoyed by American female musicians throughout (Aretha Franklin, Chrissie Hynd, Chaka Khan), the soundtrack produces nondiegetic music to lift the audience into the correct mood. The two primary diegetic scenes are intentionally mawkish, pathetic, and drunken: Bridget's singing karaoke at the Christmas party; and home alone, Bridget's dramatically miming an emotional performance of the super-bathic "All by Myself" (this new low leads to her decision to clean up). Nondiegetic music, however, accompanies her positive American self-improvement action, which U.S. audiences readily respond to—even men (e.g., the *Rocky* movies). The audience is pumped up by Chaka Khan's "I'm Every Woman," and supports her bid to change her life for the better. During these shots we see Bridget, tossing her cigarettes, wine bottles, and pathetic female self-help manuals into the trash can. In one scene, Bridget, alone on a stationary bicycle at the gym, recalls Barbra Streisand character "cleaning-up" to make herself attractive for her man (Richard Marx's "get pumped" nondiegetic soundtrack) in *The Mirror Has Two Faces* (Barbra Streisand, 1996). In the novel, we know that losing weight leads Bridget's friends to tell her she looks sick and unhealthy. In the film, however, there is no such commentary; in the film Bridget does not have time to complain in her diary: "Eighteen years of struggle, sacrifice and endeavour—for what? . . . . I feel like a scientist who discovers that his life's work has been a total mistake." Quite to the contrary, Bridget's filmic decision to clean up leads her to a new life: a new job and a new man, Mark Darcy. Similar to Striesand's character, when she loses weight and gets fit, Bridget is the "total" woman, able to confidently go on job interviews in a new field, blazing new career trails; and the audience knows she can succeed because she is "fit."

The second citation is from a famous 1980s film, *Nine to Five* (Colin Higgins, 1980), perhaps the first original "Chick-flick," starring the odd trio, Jane Fonda, Lily Tomlin, and Dolly Parton. In this American comedy classic, the "chicks" Judy (Jane Fonda), Violet (Lily Tomlin), and Doralee (Dolly Parton) kidnap Mr. Hart (Dabney Coleman) and take over the business to show that both business and life work better when women are in control. Similarly, Bridget gets her vindication against patriarchy when, having achieved "fitness," Bridget is offered a job with "Sit Up Britain." Ironically her moment of patriarchal triumph occurs when she admits that she must leave her old job because she "shagged her boss." Bridget's victorious *Nine to Five* scene transpires when, in the office as she goes in to tell Cleaver she must quit, he attempts to stop her:

CLEAVER. Bridget—I know it's been awkward as ass, but there's no need to leave.
BRIDGET. But, oh, there is. I've been offered a job in television.
CLEAVER. Television?
BRIDGET, *nods affirmative.* And they want me to start straight away. And I've got to leave in about . . . ohh . . . three minutes . . . so ah——*She gets up to leave.*
CLEAVER. *stammers.* Hold it right there Miss Jones.
Bridget opens door on to the entire office
I am sorry to inform you but I think you'll find that in my contract you are expected to give six weeks notice.
BRIDGET. Yes, well I thought with the company being in such trouble and all, you wouldn't really miss the person who waltzes in in a see-through top and fannies about with the press releases.
She walks out.
CLEAVER. Bridget!
PERPETUA. I want to hear this! Because if she gives one inch, I'm going to fire her bony little bottom for being totally spineless.
BRIDGET, *to Cleaver.* What?
CLEAVER. Well, I just think you should know that—um—you know there's a lot of prospects for talented——
Interrupted by another employee, visibly irritated.
You know lots of prospects for someone who for personal reasons has been slightly overlooked professionally.
BRIDGET. Thank you, Daniel, that's very good to know. But if staying here means working within ten yards of you, frankly, I'd rather wipe Saddam Hussein's ass.
Nondiegetic music, "R E S P E C T find out what it means to me!" *blasts out* ("Respect," Aretha Franklin)

This scene is triumphant because Bridget is more Thelma and Louise than Lucille Ball—and for audiences in the twenty-first century, assertion and retribution are far more attractive than simple whackiness. American audiences love the "thumbing-the-nose-at-the-boss" gesture—so this scene is not only "girl power" (though Perpetua's support of Bridget is sudden), but "workers-unite" power. As Bridget leaves with a smile on her face, all her now former work mates smile and nod with approval.

The film *Bridget Jones* concentrates more precisely on the bare bones of the Austen plot to round out the final action. Instead of Mark Darcy's chasing Julio-the-criminal to Spain, thereby fulfilling the Austen plot of Darcy's chasing Wickham to London, the novel's swindle plot is avoided; and Mrs. Jones simply comes back to her husband at Christmas. Also at Christmas, Bridget finds out that Daniel had lied to her about Darcy's wife, makes another embarrassing public declaration, and goes home alone to London to another wasted year. This low provides some emotional space across which the viewer will have to traverse to get to the happy ending's (after all we know that the film must end happily) London snow scene. Van Morrison's "Someone Like You" has already become Bridget and Mark's signature song, and we hear it as the film ends. Although there is no Austen closure wedding scene, the film ends with the assurance of Bridget and Mark's finally being together. Therefore, *Bridget Jones* does not seem to achieve the postmodern "send-up" ending of *Trainspotting*, especially with the final heritage-scene ending; yet, the viewer has come to understand that there are quotation marks around this film. The viewer knows that, in a different way, this film is also a send up. As Mark Darcy kisses Bridget in the swirling snow we know that the filmmakers know that we know: "At this point, having avoided false innocence, he will nonetheless have said what he wanted to say to the woman: that he loves her, but he loves her in an age of lost innocence. If the woman goes along with this, she will have received a declaration of love all the same. Neither of the two speakers will feel innocent, both will have accepted the challenge of the past . . . both will consciously and with pleasure play the game of irony."

CHAPTER 6

Reterritorializing British Masculinity for American Consumption: *Waterland* and *High Fidelity*

> *"I don't approve of the rubbish you go to watch. I approve of nice well-made films. British films."*
> *"What's on?" my mum asks him.*
> "Howard's *[sic]* End. *It's the follow up to* A Room with a View."
> *. . . my dad says, "You're coming with us. My treat."*
> *"It's not the money, Dad." It's Merchant and fucking Ivory. "It's the time. I'm working tomorrow."*
>
> *Nick Hornby*
> High Fidelity

In this chapter we move from Hollywood citations that deterritorialize Britain's postmodernism images of Cool Britannia from the last chapter to a more wholesale reterritorialization of British literary texts. The texts made into films that we discuss in this chapter deterritorialize literally: the British novel is partially or wholly geographically deterritorialized from Britain and the British cultural context, and reterritorialized in film by changing the geographical and cultural indices in order to appeal to an American viewing audience. The reterritorialization occurs when British places, character types, and even jargon and popular music tastes are brought in line with the American status quo. Despite the exceeding "Britishness" displayed by each of this chapter's novels, the texts selected for inclusion here at first do not seem compatible: Graham Swift's *Waterland* (1983) is set in London 1979, but most of the novel's discourse concerns the fens in history up to 1943; while Nick Hornby's *High Fidelity* (1995) is very contemporary, early 1990s, set in London, with only the narrator's musings on his boyhood in Herefordshire. Perhaps more lucidly than in previous chapters, the novels' contents are not important to the film; the film is driven by a set of Hollywood conventions. The Derridian paradox is alive and well. With *Waterland*, but more so with *High Fidelity*, the British content is simply obliterated: the radical reiteration of the literary text occurs at all levels—narrative, plot, circumstances—into an *Amercian* context, while at the same time repeating familiar *Amercian* citations that reconstitute the film into a *recognizable* and predictable *American cultural* product.

In this chapter appropriation of a British novel for an American film audience asserts that American cultural citations are *universal*, and *male*. The male panic elicited by these texts is the central commonality they share. With *Waterland*, middle-aged Tom Crick's narrative struggles with the memory of his teenage girlfriend, now his middle-aged wife, who after becoming pregnant, aborts the child, which results in her inability to bear children. In seemingly attitudinal and stylistic contrast, *High Fidelity* is another male-centered narrative that deals with an abortion, break-ups, and insecurity of the postfeminist kind. In relation to the pre-feminist specimen and the postfeminist progeny, respectively, both of the male narrators have difficulties with women, both feel insecure and overwhelmed with their gender roles. Each of these novels is also very *British*. Yet, when the novels are picked-up by American screenwriters and film companies, the Britishness is reduced in one, and eliminated in the other. Although quite different in manifestation, each novel deals in its own way with discourse primarily concerned with issues of masculinity, and these are issues that make it attractive to American culture; however, the films reterritorialize and regulate the gendered discourses to fit American expectations and typical formulaic Hollywood motifs.

Waterland: Teenpic and Monster Flick

Graham Swift's novel *Waterland* is narrated by Tom Crick, fifty-two-year-old secondary-school history teacher, who, in 1979, lives in Greenwich (London suburb). The novel has been widely assessed by literary scholars because of its metafictional style and ponderings on historicity and other "grand narratives." Most of *Waterland* is set in the fens and fulfills a Second World War cultural history writer's prophesy, "There is a historical novel, rich in atmosphere, waiting for some writer, but historical novelists seldom tackle agricultural subjects; though, actually, agricultural development was and is every bit as important to a country as Victories in war—and is occasionally just as dramatic."[1] *Waterland* combines myth, history, geography, and fictionalized history in a presentation of the watery fen region, which has been described as the "last England" (due in part to settlement patterns since the Romans, and famously with "Hereward the Wake's" resistance to the Normans in the eleventh century at the Isle of Eels [Ely]). Overtly, the novel is a personal narrative told by Tom Crick, but balloons into a tale about the history of the Fens, including composites of actual historical figures; the Empire; the origins of history with a detailed discourse on the eel—a species without knowable origins; and, finally, Crick puts into question narrative authority (historicity).

There are two epigraphs that begin the text. The second is from Charles Dickens's *Great Expectations*, " 'Ours was the marsh country . . .' " which reminds the reader that Dickens's text begins in the fens. The first epigraph, however, is more paratextually weighty:

> *Historia, -ae*, f. **1.** inquiry, investigation, learning. **2.** (a) a narrative of past events, history. (b) any kind of narrative: account, tale, story.[2]

This definition of history, provided by the author before the reader turns to page one of the novel, sets-up a problem of deciding which form of "history" Crick is telling, and what form of history is this novel, or any novel, generally speaking, capable of telling. As a fictional novel it embodies the latter definition: "any kind of narrative: account, tale, story." But is the novel also parodying "real" history? Or does it show us that there is no such thing as "real" history? These concerns have been explored by various critics. For example, Pamela Cooper's "Imperial Topographies: the Spaces of History in *Waterland*" is an interpretation of Swift's text as a feminized treatment of the fens: "At once spatializing anatomy and anatomizing space, *Waterland* constellates the history/narrative problematic with women's historical agency and with representations of female sexuality within discourse."[3] The emphasis on the woman's body, agency, and history is a kind of text under erasure in Crick's narrative. The novel is all first-person narrative based on middle-aged Crick's memory, which the reader often surmises is faulty or deliberately misleading.

The reason for the emphasis on the feminine is that Crick is in the throes of a crisis because his barren wife, Mary, has created a local scandal by stealing a baby from his pram at the neighborhood grocery store, and then asserting the baby's presence is a gift from God. Crick's narrative sets out to find the point of origin for Mary's crisis: "it must have been always there, lurking, latent, ripening like some dormant, forgotten seed" (41). The forgotten, aborted adolescent seed is indeed the origin of the Cricks's crisis, but the reader is only slowly brought into this awareness. Attempts to find the source of their present trouble takes Tom's narrative back not only to the days of their youth, 1940–1943, or back through generations of Crick and Atkinson family history, but to the formation of the fens in the form of natural history, including a chapter concerning the mating habits of the eel. Mary Metcalf is the only daughter of a wealthy fen farmer, and Tom is the second son of a sluice keeper; Tom's mother died when he was nine years old. The light of Tom and Mary's teenage romance is darkened by Mary's attempts to sexually educate Tom's older brother Dick. Dick, a "potato head" since birth, is mentally handicapped, but works as a dredger, tinkers with his motorbike, and catches eels. Tom never thinks too much about Dick until one summer day the local boys, Freddie Parr, Terry Coe, Peter Baine, and Tom, and girls, Shirley Alford and Mary Metcalf, play games of "tease and dare beside the Hockwell Lode" (182). When the games are taken a bit too far, Shirley departs, and Mary declares a new game for them to prove their manliness through a swimming competition. Although not initially a part of the group, Dick competes and wins the underwater swimming contest. What emerges in this event is not Dick's ability to swim underwater, but the enormity of Dick's penis, "a tubular swelling of massive and assertive proportions," which in his inexperienced potato-head state, Dick: "thrusts this prodigy before him, bracing his pelvis, as if holding sway from himself something he is uncertain whether to acknowledge. 'Me too. M-me swim too.' Mary's eyes—we all notice this—goggle. A flush ignites her cheeks" (186). Young Tom Crick takes note of Mary's reaction; middle-aged Tom retrospectively attributes "curiosity" and "fear" to thirteen-year-old Mary's reaction to seventeen-year-old Dick Crick. While this passage comes more than midway through the novel, it may in fact be the "origin" Tom needs—but never acknowledges—to locate the beginning of Tom and Mary's present-day problems. It may be the origin Tom needs because it is here that Mary becomes fascinated by Dick's "manliness," and Dick, in turn, is capable of sexual arousal manifested in his erection.

This "historiographic metafiction" is told in a nonlinear fashion: the present, the recent past, primordial past, back to the present. Three years later, and one-hundred-and-fifty pages *prior* to this narrating of the Hockwell Lode incident, and near the beginning of the text, Tom's school chum, and (during the war) local black market bandit, Freddie Parr turns up dead at the Crick sluice gate. Freddie Parr's death is officially ruled an accident. Freddie, who was intoxicated, could not swim. The novel's fifty-two chapters, representing the calendar year and perhaps history's circularity, oscillate from Crick's past, fabled past and present without heed to chronology. The narrator has his reasons for not fully confiding in the reader: his own culpability in his failure to act. As events unfold in 1943, "little Tom, whose initiative in this whole affair is so conspicuous by its absence" (263), waits to hear the coroner's report of accidental death, and hesitates to help Mary figure out what to do with the baby; then Tom must wait at Martha Clay's for the abortion procedure to be over.

Young Mary's curiosity, however, is always covertly at fault in this narrative. Tom circles in and around what he cannot know several times. What he cannot know is the "undecibility of the hymen": Did Mary successfully copulate with Dick? Tom recounts for the reader the evening Dick asks their father: " 'Wh-where do ba-babies come from?' " (256), and so we know that subject has come up with Mary. From one perspective, the novel's plot hinges on "did she or didn't she." Middle-aged Tom ruminates on this mystery: "Because how did I know, how could I be a hundred percent sure that when Mary said Dick's was too big, it really was too big? And that Mary hadn't proved to herself that it wasn't Too Big, in fact was just right, at the very beginning of our little educational experiment?" (262). If Dick was not "Too Big," then Mary has not only lied about her activity with Dick, but it is likely that the baby is Dick's.

As Tom Crick persuades the reader that it is possible that Mary has lied about Dick being "Too Big," Tom's narrative to exculpate himself from wrong-doing, or worse, from doing *nothing* in 1943 to help Mary before the botched abortion, is also persuasive. While critics can claim that Crick's narrative is sophisticated and engages in "postmodern histography," Swift's representation of Mary is an old story—as old as Adam and Eve. As Katrine M. Powell asserts in "Mary Metcalf's Attempt at Reclamation: Maternal Representation in Graham Swift's *Waterland*," like Adam, Tom attempts to place the blame of wrong-doing on the woman:

> Both Adam and Crick shirk responsibility for their actions by placing the initiative on the woman. This biblical trope, common in historiographic metafiction (Cooper 394), is used to construct Metcalf as instigator, the subject on whom Crick first inscribes sexual desire. Crick goes to much trouble to describe Metcalf as strong and curious in a sexually aggressive manner. This initial description of Metcalf as initiator serves dual purposes: to show how tragedy can result from a woman enacting control over her body and to show Metcalf's transition

> from a strong woman to a weak woman as a result of her sexual curiosity.[4]

If Powell's argument is correct, then it follows that Mary has several "victims," which include: Tom; Dick for being "led on" by that temptress Mary; Freddie Parr, who was unwittingly caught in web of jealousy he *apparently* knew nothing about; and the unborn child. And yet, even Freddie's involvement in Mary's sexual curiosity is fodder for Tom's narrative suspicions: Why Freddie? Why name Freddie? Mary says she could not think quick enough, and to protect Tom, named Freddie. While the reader might have empathy for sixteen-year-old Tom's emotional and self-centered reaction to these events, the reader has less empathy for fifty-two year-old Tom, who still "shirks responsibility" for both the past and the present.

Because Tom produces hundreds of pages of narrative on the history of his family and the fens, the core of the story which is Mary and/or Mary and Tom's relationship is sometimes buried. Information and history about the fens is wedged in the middle of the narrative describing Mary's attempt to self abort. Having jumped from the windmill platform over and over again, Mary finally states to Tom who merely watches, " 'Something's happened,' she says, looking up with the ghost of a laugh, 'Works after all' " (294). After hours waiting in the windmill for the something to actually happen, Mary begins to have severe cramps, "And Mary says at last, because it's not working, it's not happening: 'We've got to go to Martha Clay's' " (298). As chapter forty-one ends and forty-two begins, Tom introduces Martha Clay as the woman who lives with Bill Clay and may or may not be his wife, a woman "who also got rid of . . . . love-children . . . But first, before I tell you about Martha, let me tell you about our Fen geese . . . . By which I don't mean the feather, beaked and web-footed kind. Not the black-necked Canadas" (298). Certainly, this passage could be read as a narrative by a man unhinged by his role in the past and the terrible outcome of this event on his life and his wife's life; still, there is something so completely self-centered and evasive about Tom's privileging the geese over Mary or even Martha, and his withdrawal from dealing with Mary's life-threatening situation, that the reader loses what empathy she might have had for Tom. This story is not told by young Tom, but by middle-aged Tom, who should be able to sensibly narrate the events: he is, after all, a historian.

Needless to say, a novel that contains not only "flashbacks" to personal history but chapters of history concerning generations of Cricks and Atkinsons and natural history, and orders the events in jumbled and purposefully entangled order, presents a formable challenge to a filmmaker. Screenwriter Peter Prince takes the most obvious route in order to form his "story": pull out the most evident narrative plot cluster from the past on which to build the present narrative of crisis. In the film *Waterland* (1992), Jeremy Irons plays a nervous and nicotine-stained, middle-aged Tom Crick. The Shakespearean stage actress Sinead Cusack (real-life wife of Jeremy Irons) plays the middle-aged Mary. Cusack and Irons bring the British-theater-and-cinema heritage film (Irons played Charles Ryder in the quinessential British heritage miniseries, *Brideshead Revisited*) star power to *Waterland*. Juxtaposed to this British "quality" star power is American Ethan Hawke, who in 1992 qualified as "one of today's hottest young stars" and who had already played the troubled (but brilliant) school boy in *The Dead Poet's Society* (1989); Hawke plays Crick's troubled and troubling history student, Price. The filmmakers also wisely cast younger versions of the middle-aged Cricks: young Tom is played by Grant Warnock and young Mary by Lena Headey.

The film opens in "Pittsburgh 1974" with "one of today's hottest young stars" speaking directly to a mass audience of American teens who "can relate" to Hawke's troubled teen character. Along with Hawke's character are his classmates, who figure much more prominently in the film than in the novel. Two students, other than Price, are created for the film: Stephen is an outspoken African-American with whom Crick often engages verbally; and Judy, an amiable dark-haired teen, who struggles academically to know when to take notes and when not to, and whom Crick, at a particular low-ebb of his mental collapse—and a low-ebb of the film as well—imagines to be sitting in class bare-breasted.

Despite its star cast with Irons, Hawke, and Cusack, and the attempt to be a "teen flick," the film *Waterland* has not received much critical attention beyond the reviews published at the time of its 1992 release. London's leisure guide, *Time Out*, favorably reviewed the film overall, especially in terms of the scenes in the fens, but pronounced that "there are obvious concessions to the US market; and as in his previous film, *Paris Trout*, Gyllenhaal bites off more than he can chew, so that, for example, Cusack's character gets lost somewhere en route."[5] *Sight & Sound* reviewer, Richard Combs, echoes *Time Out*: "The film has taken over the classroom conflict but shifted it, curiously, to Pittsburgh—for US box-office reasons, presumably, but still curious, because although Gyllenhaal quite nicely captures the city, he makes no point of it as an industrial successor (decaying into Nothing) to the primordial fens."[6] Similar to *Time Out* and *Sight & Sound*, Roger Ebert characterized the scenes set in England as the film's strongest because of the "mystery of the fenlands, and the exuberance of the two young actors (Lena Headey and Grant Warnock) who played young Mary and Tom."[7]

With Pittsburgh not fully utilized, and the English scenes clearly the strongest, why did Stephen Gyllenhaal make such a geographic change? In addition to the geographical change, Gyllenhaal changes the time from 1979 to 1974. This temporal change is curious; it appears that the main reason for this change is to make the Cricks younger, thus more appealing to a youth-centered culture, and it also makes it more plausible that Mary Crick *could* have a baby. However, Irons's Crick makes it clear at the beginning of the film, in response to Mary telling him that "God has said" she will have a baby, that it is impossible for her to become impregnated. This solidly informs the audience that Mary is "barren." Therefore, it is my contention that, apart from bringing in the American teenage audience with an American contemporary setting, and Ethan Hawke's box-office appeal, the primary reason Gyllenhaal sets the "contemporary" time frame in "Pittsburgh 1974" is to bring out the American abortion rights debate. This focus in turn forces the audience to enact the moral debate concerning abortion in regard to Mary. As the film-goer participates in the debate as Mary's story unfold, the film-goer chooses a position which mirrors the abortion debate raging in society in 1992.

In the early 1970s, Jane Roe (Norma McCorvey) challenged Texas law, enacted in the mid-nineteenth century, which forbid abortion except under the circumstance of preserving the mother's life. The landmark U.S. Supreme Court ruling on a woman's right to a legal abortion, *Roe v. Wade*, comes in 1973. The issue of privacy and a woman's right to control her body were at the center of the Roe decision. Justice Harry A. Blackmun wrote the court opinion that the right to privacy was "broad enough to encompass a woman's decision whether or not to terminate her pregnancy."[8] By 1974, the new "present" of the film, Crick's students would know about, and perhaps already have had some personal experience with, legalized abortion. Challenged several times in the following years, one case seems pertinent to the release of *Waterland* in 1992. During the 1991–1992 Supreme Court term, the court heard and ruled on *Planned Parenthood of Southeastern Pennsylvania v. Casey*. In American constitutional law the case is significant because it shifts the focus of the individual's right to privacy in the Roe decision to one of gender discrimination in *Planned Parenthood of Southeastern Pennsylvania v. Casey*. Justices O'Connor, Kennedy, and Souter wrote a joint opinion on the case:

> The three justices began, though, by focusing directly on the importance of reproductive choice for women's lives and their liberties. In the process, they seemed to reconceive the right to terminate an unwanted pregnancy as one based more on the prohibition of gender discrimination than on the right to privacy. Women had relied for two decades, the justices said, on the availability of abortion. 'The ability of women to participate equally in the economic and social life of the Nation has been facilitated by their ability to control their reproductive lives,' they continued. The cost of overruling *Roe* for people who have relied on the decision, the justice concluded, cannot be dismissed.[9]

Media focus, and certainly focus on "unwanted" or unplanned teenage pregnancies, makes the abortion issue a hot topic in 1992 for high-school and college students. The fact that Mary's botched abortion is performed illegally in the primitive cottage of fen woman Martha Clay in 1943 seems to work to the advantage of legal abortion rights supporters.

Due to media attention, the viewing audience time-frame, 1992, would have heard about the court case *Planned Parenthood of SE Pennsylvania v. Casey*, and this is further reiterated by the Pittsburgh setting (though Pittsburgh happens to be in Western Pennsylvania). As Combs remarks, the Pittsburgh setting is in no way utilized from a narrative point of view. There has to be another reason, then, and the most plausible is that the resonation with the *Planned Parenthood of SE Pennsylvania v. Casey* will help to centralize the issue of abortion in the narrative. In 1992 many young people would have been aware of or had actually seen, perhaps as an educational experience, the anti-abortion film *The Silent Scream* released in the mid-1980s. In fact, "*The Silent Scream*, which was hailed by President Reagan, sent to every member of Congress, shown in part or *in toto* on television news and other programs across the country, and whose text was read into the *Congressional Record*," would have been difficult to avoid in the mid-to-late 1980s.[10] *The Silent Scream* is considered inaccurate propaganda by abortion rights supporters, and a form of "pornography" by feminists who see the body used in "a system of representation that reinforces the mercenary logic of a market economy. The whole body becomes a visual surface of changeable parts, offered as exchange objects."[11] As Rosi Bradiotti posits, images from *The Silent Scream* of the fetus personified circulate in popular cultural images:

> [T]he theoretical point is that, detached from the mother's body, the fetus has an identity of its own, but it is also reduced to the level of a

> detachable organ. Unrelated to the site of its growth, the fetus gains a separate identity by being disembodied. Even more recently, popular culture, which is always very quick in picking up developments in science and technology, has produced a more lighthearted version of the same principle: a film with John Travolta, called *Look Who's Talking*, starts with the image of a fetus, (clearly a puppet), with a voice of its own; to a feminist eye the resemblance to the text of *The Silent Scream* is striking. The baby boy is then born and continues to dominate the screen by his strong homosocial bond to Travolta.[12]

Thus, Braidotti suggests that if the fetus *could* talk, it would converse with someone other than his/her mother, and it would have something to converse about; it would possess experience, language acquisition, and cognitive development. At the other end of the popular-culture spectrum, we can see that *The Silent Scream* participates in the horror-film genre: the mother who murders her unborn child is a monster.

According to James B. Twitchell in *Dreadful Pleasures: An Anatomy of Modern Horror*, "Modern horror myths prepare the teenager for the anxieties of reproduction . . . they are fables of sexual identity."[13] Audiences can work out the teenpic issues of sexual maturity through young Tom and Mary, and then lay the punishment of her monstrous actions as baby-killer and baby-snatcher at the door of middle-aged Tom and Mary. This enables the sex scenes of young Tom and Mary to retain a pleasurable eroticism for the audience. Still, typical of Hollywood movies the female who enjoys sex must be punished, and so, Mary's character becomes co-extensive with the "monster" or the woman-monster of the clichéd Hollywood citation. The teenpic often has elements of the monstrous female who must be disciplined or punished. Film critic Barbara Creed theorizes the female-becoming-monster through Julia Kristeva's (by way of Georges Bataille) abject in *The Powers of Horror*. Kristeva's formula is that the abject—the very ability to name the abject—requires that one has some position of outsideness, some position of otherness. As Kristeva puts it, "The abject has only one quality of the object—that of being opposed to *I*."[14] In her description, humans abhor those things that threaten the ability to survive, and so they push them away or avoid them—things like defecation, blood, slobber, and other bodily fluids. In horror films we recoil from the otherness of the abject. In this way, Mary is otherness because of her sexuality, lying to Dick, and aborting her child. Yet, Mary is abject before she even acts simply because she is a fertile, adolescent girl:

> Kristeva discusses the way in which the fertile female body is constructed as an "abject" in order to keep the subject separate from the phantasmatic

> power of the mother, a power which threatens to obliterate the subject. An opposition is drawn between the impure fertile (female) body and the pure speech associated with the symbolic (male) body.[15]

Hence, Tom, from a Lacanian perspective, controls language in the novel—he is the father, the law; Mary never communicates with the reader, she is denied the symbolic. In the film we have the same situation, Mary cannot enter the symbolic male sphere in the film—she is objectified, she is abject. With or without the Lacanian analysis, audiences instinctively react to young Mary and Tom as performing the teenpic, and with middle-aged Mary and Tom we get the woman-as-monster film. The film punishes young Mary through her older counterpart, thereby preserving the teenpic experience. Recalling the1950s blob monster movies, the teenpic spawns a terrible outcropping, monstrous Mary Metcalf, who must be and is punished for murdering her child, her future husband's brother, their friend, Freddie Parr, and the Future.

The fact that our first view of Tom Crick in the present "Pittsburgh 1974" is one in which a *baby* is heard crying indicates that Mary's abortion will be the core of the film. The baby is not his baby, but the baby that Mary has abducted from the local Shop 'n' Save. Cusack's wild-eyed portrayal of middle-aged Mary adds credence to the idea that Mary is having a mental breakdown. The audience finds out that the reason for the abduction has to do with something in the Crick's English past. Tom and Mary Crick are English in this backwater American city; childless, they appear slightly odd to Crick's high school teacher social set. The problem that Gyllenhaal will have to resolve is transporting the audience, situated in Pittsburgh 1974, to the fens in the early 1940s. By making the Cricks so mysterious and alien to 1974 Pittsburgh, Gyllenhaal has in fact made it easier to "flashback" to England. The audience, in fact, is eagerly waiting for a scene change because the Pittsburgh in 1974 that Gyllenhaal presents to us in 1992 is so ugly, unfashionable, and uninteresting that the viewer wants to be anywhere other than "Pittsburgh 1974." Gyllenhaal's film technique reveals that the shift in setting is designed to protect the Britishness of the novel as we are first brought into the action through something familiar: Pittsburgh, then slowly, scene-by-scene, weaned away from Americanization. This works because as Doel reminds us, "audience reception is always bound to cultural specificity and contextual contingency" (251). Cinematically speaking, the grainy resolution that accompanies the Pittsburgh scenes is a faux-1970s tonal quality that gives way to a sharper, softer, heritage-style, focus with the fens scenes.

The vehicle for the flashback must have the classroom setting, not so much to be faithful to the novel, but so that the adolescent perspective is constantly with Crick's view of history; the students will function as the film's interior interlocutor, questioning, clarifying, and smoothing out the foreign English material for reterritorialization by American viewers. The vehicle is Crick's own mental distraction and breakdown. Crick begins his own breakdown in front of his history class as he cannot separate the teenagers in his own classroom from teenagers he knew during adolescence. The first example of this is when he calls Stephen, "Freddie." Distracted, thinking of Freddie Parr's death, he cannot conduct his history lesson on the French Revolution. When Crick registers that his students have noticed his strange behavior, he cuts the class short. One student complains that there are still twenty minutes left of class; Crick counters, "So why don't I tell you another story." Stephen exclaims, "Tell us a murder story Mr. Crick." Crick informs him, "Yeah, there'll be murders in it." The scene cuts to the Wash, but Crick's voice-over continues, "Why don't I tell you a story about the fens," then we hear a female voice ask, "What's the fens?" The voice-over describing the fens is taken from the book—which, with the film's visualization of the region, gives the movie-goer a true sense of the flatness, and wateriness of the region.

Our second view of the fens is Tom and Mary's adolescent train-commute to school. As school children gather on the station platform, Mary and Tom contrive not to notice each other; when the train begins to leave the station, they scurry to find an empty carriage. As soon as they are in the carriage and clear of the station, they begin to frantically disrobe to have sexual intercourse. Mary's coaxing and impatient, "Go on," to Tom indicates that she is not only willing, but anxious for sex. This scene sets the tone for Crick's account of his teenage lover, Mary; she's excited about life, and is curious about everything, including sex. After giving the class his account of the ritualistic train-ride sex, Crick's present day American students simply want to know, "Why did you have to do it in the train?" When Crick counters, "We didn't have a car," a series of teasing and suggestive comments are made by various students. This scene works to bring an American audience into the idea that all heterosexual teenagers, of any era, scheme to have sex—in trains, cars, or ruined windmills. But not all the teenagers are comfortable hearing about Crick's adolescent sex life; eventually we learn from Price that some students who do not like Crick's revised lesson plan complain to the administration.

The most difficult aspect from the novel to get across to a contemporary American audience is grandfather Ernest Atkinson's incestuous relationship with Tom's mother, Helen, that results in her first born, Dick. The grandfather's family fortune and sanity are gone by the end of the First World War. Kessling Hall, at one time the great house of the Atkinson's, has become a hospital and convalescent home for physically injured and emotionally disturbed soldiers. Gyllenhaal's device for getting into this crucial part of the narrative is to "transport" literally the entire history class to "see" Crick's family history in the fens. A warped magical mystery tour begins with the class riding in 1920s Beverley Hillbillies–type of vehicle through the muddy roads of Guildsey, England. The ultimate high-school field trip lands them in Guildsey the very night the brewery burns to the ground because the towns people are too intoxicated by Coronation Ale to put out the fire. Despite the mayhem, drunks, and burning buildings, Irons's Crick, in school-teacher-like form, tells the students to "be back in one hour." Troublesome Price stays with Crick, who goes into a pub; this is the first of two bar scenes, in the second of which Crick will assure the bartender of Price's lawful age by declaring that Price is old enough, "I should know. He's my son." While the film must address the tricky incest issue, it does not want to dwell long on the topic or engage the snickers and "gross" comments of the entire class. Gradually then Crick explains one-on-one to Price the delicate issue of his grandfather's coupling with his daughter. These scenes, supposedly portraying the father/daughter coupling, are so evasive that one can easily miss the point. Neither the book nor the film can shed light on the daughter's devotion to her father. Neither can answer the most basic questions: Why does Helen submit sexually to her father? Why is she willing to risk impregnation by her own father?

With the mystery of the source of Dick's genetic defect revealed, the film can stage Tom's confrontation with Dick about the bottle of Coronation Ale he takes from the chest that his grandfather/father left him, and that he used to kill Freddie Parr. In the film this narrative is placed before Mary tries to self abort. The novel, however, ends with Dick's suicidal dive into the Ouse—the final image: "On the bank in the thickening dusk, in the will-o'-the-wisp dusk, abandoned but vigilant, a motor-cycle" (358). This is not only a masculine image, but one which dictates that the narrative center is *male*: Dick, the genetic knot produced by a father and a daughter, who ends the Atkinson line; Dick's action which leads Mary to abort the last of the Crick line. The film needs Dick's suicide scene, but also needs to quickly dispense of this scene, so that it can concentrate the film's climax of Mary's botched abortion. Tom's teenage fear that Dick might not have been "too big" is filmed well so that the viewer, along with Tom, has reason to doubt Mary's veracity. Pushing their bicycles, after Freddie Parr drives by in a car with a blonde girl, Tom and Mary wonder how Freddie has come up in the world. Tom states, "Everybody's doing it"; Mary, "Yeah, but we got caught." After a discussion about "What we gonna do?" Tom dreamily thinks about his future fatherhood:

TOM. A baby. It's my baby.
MARY. Yes, I'm sure it is. I mean, I know it is. It has to be.

Tom looks at Mary with surprise, not to mention doubt, and maybe a little fear—she is the powerful fertile, maternal figure at this point in his life. Her expression is determined, but gives nothing away. That all important implantation of doubt has been established; the undecibility of the hymen (until DNA testing) has driven men mad for thousands of years.

Though this scene produces doubt concerning Mary's faithfulness to Tom, its primary function is to establish the idea that Mary fears having the child because it could be a product of a "potato head." In the very next scene, Tom's father pulls the dead Freddie Parr out of the water. We are supposed to make the connection between Freddie and Dick. The scene again quickly shifts to Tom running after the country bus; upon boarding he sits behind Mary, who has already pieced together the connection, because she is the connection:

MARY. Did anyone say anything?
TOM. About what?
MARY. How he died.
TOM. He drowned.
MARY. How he drowned.
TOM. He fell in the river. He's probably drunk. He couldn't swim could he?
MARY. Somebody made Freddie fall in. Dick made him.
TOM. Why would Dick?
MARY. I told him. I thought he'd have to know and the baby couldn't be his. 'Cause we hadn't really done it. So I told him it was Freddie's.
TOM. Freddie's?
MARY. I don't know why I said it. I couldn't think. And Dick, he scares me. So I said it was Freddie's. Dick killed Freddie Parr because he thought it was him who made the baby. Which means I killed Freddie too.
TOM. You don't know that.

In the next scene, Tom, having punted up a cut to their rendezvous windmill, exclaims the inquest has found that it was death by accident. But Mary is already at work to self-abort the baby. The scene at the windmill shows that her own culpability in Freddie's death and what is potentially the unknown, or uncertain, paternity of the child, have combined to make her repeatedly jump from the windmill steps:

> TOM. That's dangerous for the baby.
> MARY. You are so STUPID.

The knowing look Mary gives Tom when she tells him he is so stupid furthers the idea that it is more than guilt concerning Freddie Parr that is leading her to jump to force an abortion. The quiet "God forgive," does little to change the viewer's interpretation. Amazingly, similar to the text, after Mary has started the process to self abort in the film, we have a scene break to show Tom discovering the Coronation Ale bottle; this scene quickly leads to the next in which the audience is shown the grandfather/father's trunk. A tense scene between Tom and Dick reveals that Dick's father is not Tom's father, but their "grandfather," and then leads to Dick's suicide.

After Dick's suicide, the film comes full circle to the beginning of the film: Tom Crick walks into his Pittsburgh house and hears a baby crying. Mary's recounting of the baby snatching shows she is a mixture of madness and cunning. Although she takes the baby back to the grocery store with Tom, she shows no remorse. In fact, Cusack's Mary looks crushed that she has to give the baby back at all. In the novel there are serious ramifications for her taking the baby. The film does not have the luxury to unfold criminal charges, admittance to an asylum, and Tom's visits to her in her listless state. Rather, the film shifts to Mary and Tom's house; as Mary has a complete melt down, Tom urges her to "talk just talk." "About what?" she asks.

> TOM. You need some help. You stole a baby. What are you going to do next? Kill someone? [pause] I'm sorry. I didn't mean—I'm sorry.
> MARY. No, I've done that, haven't I? [pause] I wouldn't want to repeat myself.

The reason why Mary resolutely decides to abort is not separate from the contemporary issue of keeping abortion safe and legal for those like Mary. Indeed, the trauma at Martha Clay's cottage *is* about *Roe v. Wade* and *Planned Parenthood of SE Pennsylvania v. Casey*. The *Waterland* abortion scene connects the contemporary film audience with its own political world and women's-choice debates. Gyllenhaal urges the audience to connect *Planned Parenthood of SE Pennsylvania v. Casey* to Mary's illegal abortion, but opinions on Mary's culpability will be as varied as the opinions on abortion itself. The lines of interpretation will divide into the all-too-familiar "for" and "against" Mary as a mirror image of the "for" and "against" groups on the issue of abortion. The film proposes these options as well as complicates the issue with Mary's suggested promiscuity. First, if Mary is impregnated by Dick, who is a product himself of an unwanted pregnancy, then the film could be endorsing a pro-abortion perspective. Yet, if Mary is impregnated by Tom (or even Freddie?), then Mary embodies Hollywood's stereotypically negative view; Mary is not only a "whore," but also a monster for killing her own fetus. This view maintains that Mary will not take responsibility for her sexual promiscuity by having the child; therefore, she must be punished for sexual curiosity:

> [I]n many of the films the female is attacked not only because, as has often been claimed, she embodies sexual pleasure, but also because she represents a great many aspects of the specious good—just as the babysitter, for example, quite literally represents familial authority. The point needs to be stressed, since feminism has occasionally made common cause with the adversarial critics on the grounds that we too have been oppressed by the specious good. But this is to overlook the fact that in some profound sense we have also been historically and psychically identified with it. Further, just as Linda Williams has argued that in the horror film woman is usually placed on the side of the monster even when she is its pre-eminent victim, so too in the scenario I outlined at the beginning woman is frequently associated with the monster mass culture.[16]

In *Waterland*, Mary is the "specious good" when she is *young* Mary—and this is the only Mary who "counts" in the film. Despite the fact that the United States, too, has had its share of Martha Clays and "back-street" abortions, Mary seems monstrous in her actions. Not only must she pay her whole life for attempting to abort the baby at sixteen, but Tom, too, must pay with her. Therefore, middle-aged Mary *deserves* her breakdown; she deserves her lot in life by ending, from Tom's point of view, the Crick family-line.

The woman as monster formula addresses a target audience of primarily teens or twenty-somethings; this audience is also familiar and comfortable with the new "teenpic" formula: "Teenpics from the 1950s have focused on issues of maturity and the transition to adulthood. It is not surprising, then, that today because of changing political circumstances regarding the role of women, a major focus had come to include the complex transition from girlhood to womanhood, considering that ideas of womanhood are multiple and changing."[17] In this way, *Waterland* descends into a mixture of "woman-monster must be punished" film and the new teenpic film. What is not "multiple and changing," however, is that the sexually active young female must be punished. Whatever the film's motivation concerning the abortion debate, what becomes most evident in the film is that Mary must endure a lifelong punishment for being "curious" about sex as a teenager.

The final bow to Hollywood is the film's changed ending. In the novel, Mary is institutionalized after she steals the baby. If the film ends as the book, putting aside the fact that book ends with Dick's suicide, then the Cricks are separated and there is no foreseeable reunion or healing of the past in the offing; chapter 47 of the novel begins:

> She doesn't look up as I leave. She allows herself to be kissed and gently embraced, with neither reciprocation nor resistance, so that the touch of my lips on her temple, on the submissive crown of her head, is like a good night kiss to a child. She sits by a strange bed. She doesn't lift an eye or a hand as I give a last look through the wire-strengthened glass of the ward doors . . . . The feeling of permanent departure is all within. The sense that it is not I who am leaving but really she who is receding, into the obscure and irrecoverable distance . . . (328)

This kind of ending for a film targeting teens would simply be a disaster. Because of the irrevocable damage, the screenwriter and director wisely decided to cash in on the best bet: get the middle-aged Cricks out of Pittsburgh and back to the fens. Therefore, given the fact that Mary "killed" three people when she was sixteen-years-old, she was barren her whole adult married life with Tom, she has recently stolen a baby from its pram, and soon thereafter leaves Tom, the film cannot have a true "happy ending." But it can have an upbeat, "redeeming," or even inspirational ending; and that is, at best, how the films ends. It is during Tom's "retirement" speech in front of an assembly of the whole school that we find out that Mary has left him. The cut-away to the fens where we find Tom on the very train he used to ride to school with Mary (young Tom and Mary are there smiling, too, to assist with a "feel-good" ending), and then a taxi out to their old haunts—the open fen country—reveals a car, and across the way, a woman walking. Undoubtedly, this ending is far more "upbeat" and optimistic than the novel's apathetic Mary, who is quite possibly permanently institutionalized. The film ending gives the couple a future, but ironically enough they have to leave Pittsburgh to find it. The film gives the audience the message that they must return and "face" their past collectively in order to be healed. While this might play into an uplifting, feel good, ending, it does not accord well with the abortion rights issue and Mary's "monstrous" past behavior. Those inclined to support abortion rights will probably be very sympathetic to Mary's teenage and middle-aged predicament. Conversely, those inclined to oppose abortion rights can index *The Silent Scream* through Mary's ordeal at Martha Clay's, and catalogue the other evils brought about by Mary's promiscuity. Although Mary is not made to sprout, slither or bleed grotesque alien creatures, she is still monstrous: "The presence of the monstrous-feminine in the popular horror film speaks to us more about male fears than about female desire or feminine subjectivity."[18] In the end, despite the reunion in the fens which suggests Tom's healing, the film has not shown us anything to make us belive that Mary's pain and loss are in any way mitigated. We lack her scene of renewal and healing because the masculine-centered discourse only needs to show Tom's restoration for the story to gain closure.

Complete De/Reterritorialization

Nick Hornby's novel *High Fidelity* (1995) also features a first-person male narrator, Rob Fleming, who lives and works in North London in the early 1990s. Rob begins his narrative with a list of his "all-time, top five most memorable split-ups, in chronological order," whereupon he lists the names of five girls.[19] A used-record store owner, Rob often compiles lists with his two employees, Dick and Barry: " 'Top five Dustin Hoffman films.' Or guitar solos, or records made by blind musicians, or Gerry and Sylvia Anderson Shows" (42). The media and even literary critics have been quick to zero in on the tone of the discourse as masculine, and slightly adolescent. Dubbed "Lad Lit" by the media in Britain, even literary scholars characterize the contemporary novel in this way:

> Literary history enjoins us to appreciate innovation as a gradual process; it also exposes the false claims of literary fashion. A case in point is the rise, in the 1990s, of so-called "Lad Lit" and "Chick Lit" novels that concern themselves with tribulations of urban twenty- and thirty-somethings faced with changing heterosexual mores and the pursuit of a desired lifestyle. This is a prime example of a phenomenon that reveals its significance in an evolving paradigm of novelistic change, but that surrenders its import once refashioned as a new vogue. Nick Hornby might be hailed as the originator of "Lad Lit," whilst its counterpart might be said to originate with Helen Fielding.[20]

From this description it might appear that recent British fiction is binarized—appealing to males or females, but not both. In the previous chapter, I discussed Helen Fielding's *Bridget Jones's Diary* as embodying the 1990s urban career-girl who gets picked up in film as "Cool Britannia." The film of *Bridget Jones's Diary* is set entirely in England whereas the film of Hornby's *High Fidelity* is completely reterritorized into an American cultural context. The fact that *Bridget Jones's Diary* is often noted as the gender completion of *High Fidelity* (or other Hornby novels) in British fiction actually attests to the guiding argument of this book. Two novels—however radically different in content—appear to fulfill a certain niche in a language, culture and society, but when deterritorialized for film, the reterritorized product renders one of the novels as *not even British.* My discussion of *High Fidelity* focuses on some of the elements that cannot be translated into American culture, language, or territory, including the nontransferable "laddish" content, for the film.

In the novel, Rob compiles his top five heartbreaks list to make himself feel better because his live-in girlfriend, Laura, a solicitor, has left him for, we eventually find out, the guy upstairs, Ian, a "new man" kind-of-guy. The narrative's masculine demarcations are very sharp, often startingly funny; yet, the preamble list of girls, and the subsequent looking up each of these women in the present time frame, indicates that Rob is suffering from arrested development. Indeed *High Fidelity* nearly lapses into a *bildungsroman* if we consider the "education" of Rob to be his "education" concerning women and heterosexuality in a normative society.

To illustrate his averageness, Rob tell us about growing up in Hertfordshire: "I might just have well have lived in any suburb in England; it was that sort of suburb, and that sort of park—three minutes away from home, right across the road from a little row of shops (a VG supermarket, a newsagent, an off-license). There was nothing around that could help you get your geographical bearings" (4). This description assures the reader that Rob is a kind of English everyman; and he goes to great lengths throughout the novel to persuade the reader that he is average in everything: looks, intelligence, likes and dislikes, and opinions. Opinions for Rob matter a great deal because opinions guide your record collection, for example, or the films or novels you like. He tells us a quarter of the way through the novel:

> A while back, when Dick and Barry and I agreed that what really mattered is what you like, not what you *are* like, Barry proposed the idea of a questionnaire for prospective partners, a two- or three-page

> multiple-choice document that covered all the music/film/book bases. It was intended a) to dispense with awkward conversation, and b) to prevent a chap from leaping into bed with someone who might, at a later date, turn out to have every Julio Iglesias record ever made . . . . But there was an important and essential truth contained in the idea, and the truth was that these things matter, and it's no good pretending that any relationship has a future if your record collections disagree violently, or if your favorite films wouldn't even speak to each other if they met at a party. (117)

With this quote we can see why the novel has been heralded representative of the 1990s "lad": self-absorbed enough to know that it is not worth the effort to small talk, or gradually find out about a woman; it is much easier to "screen" her first using a dating-service type of questionnaire. There is a certain superficial quality to Rob, Dick and Barry's attitude toward women. It is this superficiality and the idea that the 1990s man cannot waste time on women who do not like the same things as he does which has set off tempers in some factions of British society.

Undoubtedly, those who feel that the reforms and gains that feminism made in the 1970s and 1980s in terms of education, career, eradicating sexual harassment and sexual crimes against women have been been slowly ebbing away with the 1990s backlash against women, are not particularly enamored of the 1990s lad. Yet, Hornby's character strives to rise above polemics on any front (except one's album collection), and stress his "averageness." Though Rob works to persuade the reader of his Everyman qualities, he belies a lad attitude *par excellence*: "I'm average height, not slim, not fat, no unsightly facial hair . . . I vote Labour . . . . I can see what the feminists are on about, most of the time, but not the radical ones" (28). Comments like the latter allow the "lad" to pass under the detection code through humor or irony, but as Imelda Whelehan points out: "Fundamentally sexist comments can be made under the shield of irony; if we complain, it is ample proof that feminists have no sense of humour"; which means, according to Whelehan, that "from a feminist position it is difficult not to interpret the new lad as nostalgic revival of old patriarchy; a direct challenge to feminism's call for social transformation by reaffirming—albeit 'ironically'—the unchanging nature of gender relations and sexual roles."[21] The type of masculinity Rob displays is essentially British. The lad is one who dresses causally, likes football, votes labor, and if he can understand the feminist point of view, well, okay, but he would rather not have to think about it.

The British lad reflects the fact that he is a by-product of the feminist movement in an era when the traditional male employment sector has virtually vanished (heavy industries, manufacturing), and women are earning more college degrees and taking more of the high-level career jobs. This paradigm shift in Britain is discussed by Jonathan Rutherford in his Introduction to *Male Order: Unwrapping Masculinity*; as Rutherford posits, there is a high degree of "uncertainty" for both men and women in the 1990s in terms of gender roles:

> What divides them [men and women] is the differential effect of uncertainty in their lives and their response to it. Whatever the odds, increasing numbers of young women express ambition and a desire to succeed. In contrast, young men appear to be floundering. The old rules and roles have changed and they can no longer expect an allotted place in society.[22]

One interpretation of Rob's laddish character, then, is that Rob is emasculated by Laura's career, her friends from work, and even the way she dresses and makes-up for work; add these things to the fact that Laura had to give him money just to keep his business from going under, and we have a case of a masculinity crisis. The crisis interferes with his relationships to other women in his life, such as his mother, and certainly Liz, who in the following passage is initially supportive of Rob:

> I tell Liz about Ian phoning me up, and she says it's outrageous, and that cheers me up to no end . . . .and Liz says that *she's* just about to go to the States on business, and I'm amusingly satirical at her expense, but she doesn't laugh.
>
> "How come you hate women who have better jobs than you, Rob?" She's like this sometimes, Liz. She's OK, but, you know, she's one of those *paranoid* feminists who see evil in everything you say.
>
> "What are you on about now?"
>
> ". . . And you didn't like Laura wearing clothes that she had no choice about wearing when she changed jobs, and now I'm beneath contempt because I've got to fly to Chicago, talk to some men in a hotel conference room for eight hours, and then fly home again . . ."
>
> "Well, I'm sexist, aren't I? Is that that right answer?"
>
> You just have to smile and take it, otherwise it would drive you mad. (193–194)

This display of Rob's attitude toward women Imelda Whelehan interprets as exemplary of laddishness of the "*Loaded*" male: "The magazine *Loaded* single-mindedly pursues the new lad motif to its extreme—he is almost always white; part soccer thug, part lager lout, part arrant sexist."[23] The *Loaded* male is perhaps the extreme end of the new lad, who is definitely not a new man, but he isn't the old man either. In "Resignifying Masculinity: From 'New Man' to 'New Lad,' " Sean Nixon charts the growth of the men's magazine in Britain as indicative of the status and image of men during the 1980s and 1990s. In Nixon's discussion of Sean O'Hagan's pivotal piece on the new lad in *Arena* in 1991, he quotes O'Hagan: " 'the new lad' was 'a rather schizoid fellow. He aspires to New Man status when he's with women, but reverts to old man type when he's out with the boys.' "[24] In fact, the following quotation could be used to further fill in Rob's fictional profile in *High Fidelity*:

> [H]e tends to be part of the thirtysomething generation—educated, stylish, more often than not well groomed and totally in tune with the shifting codes of contemporary culture . . . [H]e is well versed in the language, and protocol, of post-feminist discourse and he will never ever, even after a few post-prandial brandies, slip into Sid the Sexist mode like a regular (Jack the) lad might.[25]

Even when Rob is at his most angry with Laura or with women, he is never crude. He comes the closest to being crude when he is at the height of his self-righteous self-absorption. And yet, while not exactly crude, Rob knows exactly how to get his way with women. Rob thinks that this is his only genius; while talking up Marie LaSalle, Rob confesses:

> It feels, even to me, like I'm being intimate: I speak quietly, slowly, thoughtfully, I express regret, I say nice things about Laura, I hint at a deep ocean of melancholy just below the surface. But it's all bollocks, really, a cartoon sketch of a decent, sensitive guy which does the trick because I am in a position to invent my own reality . . . (119–120)

The new reality, however fleeting, is that of the sensitive "new man" who can fully appreciate women's views. The new lad can masquerade as a new man. Ian, or "Ray," as he was known when he lived above Rob and Laura, has been made in the image of the "new man" who "of course, never existed—he was a media vision of what pro-feminist men would look like and was usually sent up as dull, ineffectual, emotional and possibly effeminate."[26] Hornby does his best to make Ian/Ray as unattractive, unfashionable, and effeminate as possible—and still—have Laura, of course, move in with him; according to Rob, Ian/Ray can be described in *American* terms, "That Leo Sayer haircut and those dungarees, and the stupid laugh and the wanky right-on politics" (162).

This description connects to the idea that the lad phenomena does not exist as such in the United States. The United States has had the new man, of course, but this is always alongside an enduring masculine figure that has an uneasy relationship with political correctness. Yet, to be sure, the 1990s also had a backlash against feminism and the would-be new man in the United States, and is evidenced in such successful media images as those projected by the film *Fight Club*. Sean Nixon argues that the new lad figure is one that is counter to the "new man" which "took up and gave shape to the ethnic and racial mixing celebrated within certain strands of British popular culture."[27] Perhaps similar to the backlash against feminism, the new lad is a conservative movement away from greater inclusion. Whelehan argues that "the new lads are assuredly the product of identity crises, it is not just that generated by feminism, but also by gay liberation and anti-racist movements, which act as a reminder of what mainstream male culture, such as budget competitive sport, regularly excludes."[28] The popular British men's magazine *Loaded*, Nixon contends, fed this trend:

> . . . [A] recurrent theme—particularly in *Loaded*—concerned the link between these new scripts of masculinity and the ambiguous, reinvogorated [sic] forms of British nationalism condensed in other cultural phenomena such as Britpop and Cool Britannia. Both codings of British ethnicity were important, however, in rooting the shifting codes of masculinity thrown up by the commercial initiatives to expand style and lifestyle consumption amongst British men. They helped to give peculiarly British shape to the resignifying of masculinity within popular cultural forms over the last fifteen years.[29]

While Rob is not particularly nationalistic, he does not have any friends of "color"; and the most exotic person in the novel is the white American folk-rock singer, Marie LaSalle, from Austin, Texas, with whom he has a brief affair. Average Rob lives in his average white-guy world, oblivious to multicultural Britain.

There is a tinge of nationalistic pride in Rob, and this patriotism is evident in the novel as anti-Americanism. Certainly the quotation concerning Liz's business trip to Chicago can be counted as covertly anti-American. Rob has a defensive streak with which he seems to need to protect himself from not only women, but men who are different from him—including not only Ian, the new man, but also T-Bone, an American musician, whom he initially despises (even T-Bone is white). Ironically, of course, most of Rob's popular culture tastes come from America: Junior Wells, Jerry Lee Lewis, Elvis Presley, Otis Redding, Prince, Aretha Franklin. He also prefers American films (his "top five" are: *The Godfather, The Godfather Part II, Taxi Driver, Goodfellas,* and *Reservoir Dogs*), not to mention the hyper-masculine films he rents to watch by himself on his thirty-sixth birthday, which include such Hollywood "action" films as *Naked Gun 2½, Terminator 2,* and *Robocop 2.* The fact that Rob's psyche and his livelihood, to a large extent, are informed by American cultural products does not quite sink into his consciousness.

One particularly scathing interpretation of the United States occurs when Marie LaSalle sings Peter Frampton's "Baby I Love Your Way." Frampton is English, but the popularity of *Frampton Comes Alive* in the mid-to-late 1970s in the United States (US FM radio stations continually played the full fifteen minute live version of "Do You Feel Like I Do?") is 1990s unfashionable; in the 1990s, and for Rob, Frampton's rock pedigree is lacking:

> Imagine standing with Barry, and Dick, in his Lemonheads T-shirt, and listening to a cover of a Peter Frampton song, and blubbering. Peter Frampton! 'Show Me the Way'! That perm! That stupid bag thing he used to blow into, which made his guitar sound like Donald Duck! *Frampton Comes Alive*, top of the American rock charts for something like seven hundred and twenty years, and bought, presumably, by every brain-dead, coke-addled airhead in L.A.! I understand that I was in dire need of symptoms to help me understand that I have been traumatized by recent events, but did they have to be this extreme? Couldn't God have settled for something just mildly awful—an old Diana Ross hit, say, or an Elton John original? (61)

The dig at Americans for keeping Frampton on the charts for "seven hundred and twenty years" is unmistakable. Because Los Angeles becomes the 1970s magnet for British rock stars who "sell out" like Rod Stewart, and is home to "coke-addled" bands such as the Eagles, it is iconic for *bad* rock—or rock music gone wrong. The fact that Americans have no musical taste is evident in keeping Frampton alive on the charts, and for making him a male pop star who was attractive to women. Therefore, "the perm," is an easy target for 1990s shaved or closely cropped footballer heads. Even Marie LaSalle says to the audience after she finishes "Baby I Love Your Way," "I know I'm not supposed to like that song, but I do" (given to us by Rob in parentheticals). As a pop mogul, Rob should know that what is once in vogue will come around again: the popular eventually becomes unfashionable, but if you wait long enough it becomes retro and fashionable once again.

Although Rob is sexually turned on by Marie, much of the novel's derogatory commentary on Americans, generally speaking, occurs when he is with her, though not always. In a conversation with Rob, Liz says, " 'I've seen men like you in Doris Day films, but I never thought they existed in real life.' She puts on a dumb, deep, American voice . . ." (163). Yet, the most telling passage is after Rob and Marie have a would-be one-night stand (Rob surprisingly confesses he didn't "deliver the goods but Marie said she had a nice time anyway, and I believed her" [128]), and they begin to discuss the fact that each of them is just ending a long term relationship. Hornby makes supposedly smart, sensitive, and attractive American Marie say moronic things:

> "But people are allowed to feel horny and fucked-up at the same time. You shouldn't feel embarrassed about it. I don't. Why should we be denied basic human rights just because we've messed up our relationships?"
>
> I'm beginning to feel more embarrassed about the conversation than about anything we've just done. Horny? They really use that word? Jesus. All my life I've wanted to go to bed with an American, and now I have, and I'm beginning to see why people don't do it more often . . . .
>
> "You think sex is a basic human right?"
>
> "You bet. And I'm not going to let that asshole stand between me and a fuck." (130–31)

Marie's discourse is not very believable—especially in the context that Hornby has presented her up to this point. The target is clearly Americans, perhaps not just American females, but also American males who typically appear quintessentially masculine: from the cowboy to the war hero to the action figure. All these images are iconic Hollywood projections, but this *is* the point; all that Rob really knows about America is Hollywood and other media produced representations. Predictably, when Rob not only gets to meet, but also go to bed with, an American, she turns out to be a disappointment, and she is indicative of her nation.

The emphasis on the English male and his American counterpart—though never explicitly represented—in the novel becomes supremely ironic when we turn to the film of *High Fidelity* (2000). The novel has been totally deterritorialized—everything English from opinions on American accents, tastes, personalities, intelligence—is reterritorialized American. The film *High Fidelity* is "all-American": trading in London for Chicago, the geography, cultural index, the language, style, manner, musical taste, and emphasis have been reterritorialized from the novel. The team of screenwriters, D.V. De Vincentis, Steve Pink, and John Cusack are from Chicago and began writing the screenplay with Chicago as Rob's home city, erasing London. Scott Rosenberg's name appears on the film's credits because independently of De Vincentis, Pink, and Cusack, Rosenberg wrote a screenplay of the novel. Due to copyright problems, the Chicago screenwriting trio had to "arbitrate for credit defense of our draft."[30] Pink argues that the drafts were different, "It was very clear that there were no similarities between our drafts in fundamental issues of tone, storytelling, device, and pretty much everything. Obviously we were adapting a novel, so the things in common between our drafts are the things that are common as to the novel itself rather than anything we created separately in screenplays."[31] Despite the differences between screenplays, and Rosenberg's lack of contribution, his name appears on the credits because of the financial factor involved. De Vincentis recounts the situation that led to the inclusion of Rosenberg's credits:

> But the Writers Guild rules say if there are two different drafts on an adaptation of a novel, that the first writer hired gets all of the material that they used from the book to their side of the mathematical credit. It should be said that initially Scott told us that he didn't really feel like he had contributed anything to the script at all, and that he wasn't arbitrating for credit; but then he changed his mind because there's a lot of money involved. He was actually very honest about it and it's cool.[32]

Pink, who evidently is unhappy about Rosenberg's inclusion, adds, "He was very clear that he made no creative contribution to the film, to the making of the film or our screenplay whatsoever."[33] This situation indicates that the film's screenwriters feel decidely protective of their material from a creative perspective, but the issue of the "money involved" and Rosenberg's "mathematical" advantage in terms of what he could claim to be "his" could help to explain changes from the novel to the final film version. What the trio of screenwriters could change could be "theirs" versus the novel's—and "mathematically" Rosenberg's—creative property.

Let us consider momentarily the film from a structuralist perspective; the novel's cardinal points have been readily transferred to the film: the breakup, the top five list of heartbreaks, Rob's eventually finding them one-by-one (and his exoneration), Laura's father's dying, and Rob's reunion with Laura. Film reviewers did not fail to pick-up on the transference process from novel to film. *Sight & Sound's* review at the time of the film's release acknowledges the plot structure from the novel remains in place:

> On the whole, the Americanisation of the story does surprisingly little damage, though Rob's involvement in managing a pair of young skate/grunge musicians strikes a slightly jarring note. It's the only subplot the film adds to the novel, and it feels gestural and tacked-on, too crudely seeking to broaden the audience demographic.

The subplot of Vince and Justin as white teenage skateboarders who make original-sounding rap music was trimmed in the film from the original Chicago trio's published screenplay. Perhaps British film-director Stephen Frears found this particular Americanization to be a bit too much. Frears, most noted for his work with Hanif Kureishi, *My Beautiful Laundrette* (1986) and *Sammy and Rosie Get Laid* (1987), came to *High Fidelity* "late" in the process:

> Frears came to *High Fidelity* late. Nick Hornby's best-selling novel was originally picked up by Disney as a vehicle for Mike Newell. By the time he dropped out, the script, now set in Chicago, had reached John Cusack, and he and his Chicago co-writers were all music fanatics. It was Cusack, acting as co-producer and co-writer, who approached Frears, with whom he worked on *The Grifters* (1990). Frears is famous for only taking on screenplays that are all but finished but on this occasion he worked on the script, bringing it closer to the novel. In particular he insisted on using the interior monologue that is the book's spine.[34]

The screenwriting team had Rob Fleming, now Rob Gordon, speak in "voice-over," but Frears changed it so that Rob, who is played by Cusack, directly speaks to the camera. Rob addresses the audience so frequently through the film that the voice-over is likely to have been a disaster—a disembodied voice hovering over the visualization of scene and characters. Instead, the audience becomes Rob's confidante—beginning with the famous antimony: Am I miserable because I listen to pop music? Or, I am miserable so I listen to pop music?

It would seem that Cambridge-educated Frears is an unlikely person to support the geographic and cultural move to the United States. Yet, he confides in "Conversations with the Director" that the change of geographic setting from London to Chicago made the film more "optimistic" and "romantic":

> The idea of its not being set in England was quite shocking. When the book came out and people said to Nick Hornby what's it about? He'd

> say "it's about England." So in a way you were denying the whole subject matter the author thought he was writing about. But actually it became clear to me when I started reading it that it was rather a good thing taking it out of England—that the human predicament was still there, that it wasn't just about an account of what it was like to be English or to live in London now. People would say to me, if you're going to set this story in an American town, Chicago is the right one—in other words it never made sense in terms of New York or Los Angeles . . . . I like the idea of it being in America—it had a sort of more optimistic way in which Americans live—it seemed to me to add something to it, rather than taking it away—so it lost some of its stoicism; and became slightly more romantic then.[35]

While Frears clearly sees the differences between London and Chicago, the screenwriters advocate the universal quality of the narrative. This universality, of course, is *Americanized* universality. Thus, when the screenwriters were asked, "Did you have a problem with the transition of locations from England, in the book, to Chicago, in the film?" De Vincentis unwaveringly answers, "No. Because the central themes—which are obsession and lack of emotional development—are key in London as well as Chicago."[36]

The film appealed to Cusack and his co-writers because of the musical lore of the novel. And yet, the American scriptwriting team eliminated virtually all of Hornby's English-centered musical preferences. Motown has become clichéd in the States, and certain images of the synchronized dance numbers by trios of female singers or quartets of male singers is unfashionable with the onset of hip hop. The biggest intrusion from the pop music world is of course Bruce Springsteen; this is an American male fantasy realized on film. When the "Boss," Bruce Springsteen, is brought in to give Rob advice on his love life, we know we are in an *all-male, all-American* fantasy world. Moreover, the American centered film chose to feature bands such as Royal Trux, Smog, and The Beta Band.

One can only wonder what a British centered soundtrack might have included: the Clash, Aretha Franklin, Elvis Presley, and maybe the Beatles. The film's promotional posters, soundtrack and home video release feature John Cusack in multiple poses in place of the Beatles on their *A Hard Day's Night* album cover. This image at once recalls a familiar British image to Americans while at the same time acknowledges the American actor's face as a parody. With Cusack's dark, longish hair he does not look so much like a Beatle—even Paul McCartney whose face shape he shares—as he does look like the quintessential American rocker, Elvis Presley. With his front hair looping over, side-burns, and turned-up collar visible in the final square, that Cusack resembles an Elvis imitator is the impression. Yet, the citation, however, is clearly *A Hard Day's Night* which gives *High Fidelity* a slightly more contemporary rock or pop musical index (over 1950s Elvis, or, worse, the bloated Elvis of the 1970s). The promotional shows a record album pulled half out of the sleeve, an image that plays into Rob's own fantasy of being a "rock star." In any case, with the film the music is decidedly not the Britpop of the 1990s. In fact, the film soundtrack is conspicuously contemporary American or British retro (The Kinks, and even Elvis Costello and the Attractions are now retro). After our *Trainspotting* discussion in Chapter Five, one cannot help but wonder if *High Fidelity*, released only a few years after *Trainspotting*, is attempting to cash in on some of the former film's strategies: provide a "one look" marketing campaign; feature an eclectic, but not dated, soundtrack; and appropriate "high concept" "looks" such as the Swinging London 1960s citation, but stamp it firmly in the American mold as the ultimate American rock/pop cultural appropriation.

Apart from Marie Lasalle becoming a black Jamacian singer-song writer and giving credence to her foreign and exotic characterization from the novel as well as a few minor shifts or rearrangments, there are two major additions to the film from the novel which not only give it a more-American feel, but also make Rob's character more sympathetic to an American audience. Rob's novelistic lad characteristics have to be modified so that film-goers are not turned off by his past behavior toward women. The two changes that Americanize and Hollywoodize the film for American reception are the addition of Cusack's sappy "the top five things I miss about Laura," and the skate boarders Vince and Justin subplot. The first endears us to Rob, while the second helps Rob to become a "man" in capitalist America.

The audience has little to go on as to why Rob wants Laura back so badly. In the novel, as Tony Ross also points out, Rob does not really know why he wants Laura back, only that he does not want Laura to be with Ian. When Liz asks Rob why he wants Laura back, Rob's interior voice states, "I'm not going to tell her [Liz] this is a way of regaining control. I don't know if I love Laura or not, but I'm never going to find out while she's living with someone else," and as Ross aptly states, "This is hardly the stuff of traditional Hollywood romance, and would have sucked any wind out of the movie's sails had it been somehow realized on screen."[37] Rob's confessional "top 5 things I miss about Laura" list is not in the original screenplay, and therefore, it must have been added during shooting to soften Rob's rough edges. With the river and the shimmering gold and silver postmodern buildings of Chicago behind him, Rob speaks directly to *us* (not so much the impersonal camera) as if we are now complicit with him. The list is not that of the "lad," nor is it even quite believeable of filmic immature Rob Gordon. The list of the things Rob misses about Laura doesn't include body parts, sounds made while having sex, or how she looks in a certain skirt. Instead, the 5 things he misses about Laura are: one, her "sense of humor" including her laugh; two, her "character" because she is "loyal" and "honest"; three, her "smell" and her "taste" which is a "chemistry" thing; four, the way she "walks around" unaffected which gives her "grace"; five, when Laura cannot get to sleep she "moans" and "rubs her feet together"—this habit of hers, Rob says, "just kills me." Although Laura's role is strengthened in the film from that of the novel, the audience is not given enough of Laura to understand her "character," for instance. Rob's list of "top 5 things I miss about Laura" works in the film to make him look more "grown-up," and is juxtaposed beside the add-on subplot of Justin and Vince.

The primary reason in terms of the plot for the scenes with Vince and Justin is not only to give the film a younger generation perspective, draw in the teenagers as well as the twentysomething and thirtysomething audience, but also to give Rob an important role in musical history: to produce the "musical visionaries," as the scene chapter is titled in the DVD release. Otherwise, the only "growth" that Rob would have by the end of the film would be that he now understands that one needs to make tapes for other people in terms of what *they* like, not what you like. This kind of lesson is one we are supposed to learn as kids: give your friend a gift she will like, not what you would like (or like her to like). Rob's arrested development makes learning this lesson a victory. The fact that Rob might be a DJ once a week is also a personal gain or signifies growth. But for American audiences this is not enough, and De Vincentis, Pink and Cusack knew this fact when they wrote the screenplay. Americans like *improvement* and *success* stories. Sure, Rob and Laura are back together at the end of the film; but if Rob is still a grungey record store owner how will they *progress into the future*? Improvement, progress, success, and growth are all key concepts in the American pysche; and it may be these elements that Frears is actually commenting upon when he states that the film reflects the "more optimistic way in which Americans live." But the success that Rob acquires must come from an unlikely source—street punks ("business-crippling Nazi Youth shoplifters") according to Barry, who routinely try to steal records from Rob's store. Rob also acquires "father" status, a symbol that he is no longer a boy, because, nearly a generation older than Justin and Vince, he talks "down" to the teenagers. Having listened to their rough tape, Rob approaches the pair:

> ROB. You're [*sic*] tape. It's good.
> They mumble thanks.
> ROB. (cont'd) It's rough. But it shows promise. We record a couple of songs right, in a studio. ... I'll put out your record. Any profits we'll split down the middle, between us and you guys.
> VINCE. Wait a minute. You mean a big fat Mercedes.
> ROB. We're not there yet, Justin.
> VINCE. I'm Vince.
> ROB. Whatever. (99–100)

By the end of the film, Vince and Justin's tape is featured at Rob's DJ gig, and the boys themselves now occupy an off-spring position to the older thirtysomethings. Vince and Justin are like Donald Duck's naughty nephews, Huey, Luey, and Duey—cute, but always into something as soon as the adult turns his back. Witnessing Rob's successful future as record producer, DJ, and life partner to Laura, we see that Rob has finally become a "man." Therefore, the two significant add-ons, Rob's "top 5 things I miss about Laura," and the "Justin and Vince" subplot, show that Rob is finally emotionally mature, and financially mature—or on his way to becoming financially mature and successful. Separate from the issue of Rob's maturation and the successful "optimistic" Hollywood ending, the trio of Chicago-based screenwriters can claim more of a stake of the royalties generated by the film, the soundtrack, and home video releases by creating scenes not in the novel.

Lastly, there must be something about Nick Hornby's "lad" adventures that attract Americans to want to adapt, *albeit* American-style, his novels. Hornby's novel about a British soccer fanatic, *Fever Pitch* (1992), and its subsequent film adaptations exemplifies Derrida's point concerning the repetition of the locution exceeding one's ability to control the meaning of the citation. With the first adaptation, British critics complained that Hornby's novel had not been "faithfully" filmed in the British context to portray the Arsenal fanatic (1997, David Evans). In the United States, the British *Fever Pitch* did not "surface here" until summer 2000; and as one reviewer plainly put it, "If you don't operate on the premise that soccer is the most important thing in the universe, you might not go along with everything in 'Fever Pitch.' "[38] While the British adaptation may not be hardcore enough for the rabid English football fan, the Americanized adaptation featuring a Boston Red Sox fanatic will not please the truly devoted baseball fan either. Bobby and Peter Farrelly's adaptation's framing device is the 2004 miracle Red Sox season, but the film itself is no more than an American romantic comedy.

With the American adaptation, Paul—the Hornby lad—is high school math teacher Ben Wrightman (Jimmy Fallon), who is more of a new man than Rob in *High Fidelity* or Paul in the British *Fever Pitch*. Ben spends his first date with Lindsey (Drew Barrymore), a corporate mogul (not a fellow high school teacher), cleaning up Lindsey's vomit in her bathroom. Screenwriters Lowell Ganz and Babaloo Mandel could have easily written an "original" screenplay about a baseball fan who cannot commit to a heterosexual partner because of his obsession to his team—American men have had other obsessions (jobs-making money, adventure-exploration, war-fighting); the British hardly have corner on that market. When Ganz and Mandel were approached by Amanda Posey (a producer of the first *Fever Pitch*) and Alan Greenspan (a producer on *High Fidelity*) to adapt *Fever Pitch*, they were told to "Americanize it."[39] After considering American football, Ganz and Mandel believed that the best equivelant was the Red Sox baseball team "that over the years has instilled in its followers a kind of 'psychosis.' "[40]

Both films, to borrow from a reviewer concerning the Americanized version, are "almost too dull to pan."[41] Yet, the two versions of *Fever Pitch* are useful to conclude our discussion of the film adaptation of the contemporary British novel because they show just how far *incrementally* deterritorialization can be taken. As we have seen throughout *Britain Colonized*, texts always already drift into different contexts, and hence, create different meanings; yet one has to wonder when a text ceases to be a "source" text and simply becomes, at best, "intertextual." My point is that there is nothing left of the British memoir novel *Fever Pitch*—the American film version is actually *beyond* reterritorialization and deterritorialization; all that is left is a "coded" cliched Hollywood romantic comedy, á là Boston Red Sox style:

> Could a performative statement succeed if its formulation did not repeat a "coded" or iterable statement, in other words if the expressions I use to open a meeting, launch a ship or a marriage were not identifiable as *conforming* to an iterable model, and therefore if they were not identifiable in a way as "citation"?

The fact that Nick Hornby is an executive producer, and Greenspan and Posey initiated the American adaptation, indicates that the capitalist enterprise is driving this would-be deterritorialization. Perhaps sports fanaticism is a universal; perhaps British cultural citations are not important; perhaps capitalist Hollywood is now the only global iterable model.

CHAPTER 7

Shakespeare's Counterfeit Signature: *Shakespeare in Love*

WILL, *shouts.* Gentlemen! Thank you! You are welcome.
FENNYMAN. Who is that?
HENSLOWE. Nobody. The author.

Shakespeare in Love

In this final chapter, I am no longer interpreting the contemporary British novel's adaptation into film. With the film *Shakespeare in Love*, there is no "original" text—nothing to adapt. Instead, similar to *Trainspotting* and *Bridget Jones's Diary* in Chapter Five, the overwhelming popularity of the author's discourse is analogous to Foucault's idea of the discourse of the author, in which a false or misleading "mystique" of the author overshadows subsequent interpretations: "It points to the existence of certain groups of discourse and refers to the status of the discourse within a society and culture."[1] This time, *Shakespeare in Love* "defin(es)" the "form" and "characteriz(es)" the "mode of existence" that the discourse on the film is likely to take.[2] The film's text is an assortment of historical detail; fragments of "real" Shakespeare texts, such as *Romeo and Juliet* and the sonnets; period costumes and buildings; "real" characters, such as Ned Alleyn, Queen Elizabeth, and Christopher Marlowe; and fictional characters, such as Viola De Lesseps and the Earl of Wessex. The average American cannot tell what is supposed to be "real" (true to life, factual) and what is fictional. The historically accurate is enmeshed with the purely fictional to form a new textual web, a completely new discourse, the film *Shakespeare in Love*.

There is no "original" text for this film; but also there is no "text" of Shakespeare. "Shakespeare" is the twenty-first century's ultimate floating signifier because the signifier, Shakespeare, never connects to the signified, a material Shakespeare. Of course, hundreds of years and thousands of pages of signifiers have tried to make Shakespeare a transcendent signifier. It is true that Shakespeare's name is like no other in the West, and certainly like no other in the history of British Literature. In "What Is an Author?" Michel Foucault speculates that an author's name is "complex," and Shakespeare's name carries with it an endless series of discursive practices. Shakespeare's name can be added to or subtracted from, but it would take a history-altering discovery to radically change the significance of "Shakespeare." According to Foucault: "The disclosure that Shakespeare was not born in the house that tourists now visit would not modify the functioning of the author's name, but if it were proved that he had not written the sonnets that we attribute to him, this would constitute a significant change and affect the manner in which the author's name functions."[3] In fact, if Shakespeare "was not born in the house that tourists now visit," this new revelation would only add to the Shakespeare mystique (e.g., *Where was* he born?).[4] After four-hundred years, there seems little hope of verifying anything new about the person who might have been called Shakespeare and who might have written plays. From a Foucauldian perspective, all that is left of Shakespeare is the endless discourse produced by texts typically attributed to him. John Drakakis aptly summarizes "our contemporary" Shakespeare: "Shakespeare now *is* primarily a collage of familiar quotations, fragments whose relation to any coherent aesthetic principle is both problematical and irremediably ironical."[5]

In this chapter I discuss how the event of writing in *Shakespeare in Love* is enacted in order to convince the viewer that *this* person bouncing around, running through the dirty streets, slipping around corners, *is* William Shakespeare (Joseph Fiennes). *The* William Shakespeare most American viewers are familiar with is the middle-aged, balding guy with an earring; the Shakespeare most of us know uses archaic words, rambles on about—well we are not sure exactly—and is venerated by high school and college English teachers. To help us connect the "hard body" of Fiennes with the middle-aged, balding guy we thought was Shakespeare, the film presses us with the physical shape of words.[6] Quill-pen-written words flow across the screen; we see them on parchment paper, and we see Fiennes practice "Will Shakespeare." Hence, the act of writing is grafted upon the screen to legitimize and authenticate the film as "really about" Shakespeare before he becomes Shakespeare the middle-aged balding guy.

The words that we see Shakespeare messily scrawl on the page are among the words which create the fragments of the "collage of familiar quotations" that we know to be Shakespeare. It is important that we connect young Shakespeare with the middle-aged guy we already know. We see Shakespeare early in the film repeatedly writing his name—as if to "get it right." As the film proceeds, he becomes the Shakespeare "posterity" knows him to be. *Shakespeare in Love*'s success depends upon the viewer's sustaining the connection between the fictional "Will" and the familiar William Shakespeare of the classroom. The fact that there are few surviving details about Shakespeare's life and the fact that he never actually published his own plays have caused speculation down through the centuries—was there ever such a person as William Shakespeare? The Shakespeare mystique or myth is the black hole that historians and literary textual scholars cannot fill. There is nothing there. As John Madden, the director of *Shakespeare in Love*, states, there are only a few things that we know about Shakespeare (the real person): "The point about Shakespeare's life is that nobody knows anything. All we know is that he paid 50 pounds to join the Chamberlain's Men and that in his will he left his second best bed to his wife—that's about the sum of it."[7] Because of the scarcity of detail concerning Shakespeare's life, thousands of pages have been written to *fill-in* what *could* have happened. The fact that a film concerning a writer who has been dead for nearly four-hundred years could gross over one-hundred-million dollars at the box office (budgeted at twenty-five million dollars) in the United States a few months after its release tells us something either about the Bard's ongoing popularity, or about how the ultimate floating signifier was packaged for the big screen.

A winner of seven Academy Awards, including best picture, *Shakespeare in Love* is jam-packed with "stars" (i.e., Gwyneth Paltrow, Geoffrey Rush, Joseph Fiennes, Ben Affleck, Colin Firth, and Judi Dench). Even a BBC reviewer lauded *Shakespeare in Love* as "a joyous and quite brilliant comedy. It's a career best for Joseph Fiennes as Shakespeare and if Gwyneth Paltrow isn't as good, it's not by much, and the entire cast are [sic] superb," and yet acknowledged that "most of them [cast] are playing actors and there are barbs in here that would sting present-day Hollywood. For once, an all-star cast is a help to the story as well as to the box office."[8] Despite Miramax's attempts to "promote *Shakespeare in Love* (1998) as an independent," the film was clearly beyond the "indie blockbusters" of the scale of Miramax's *sex, lies, and videotape* (1989).[9] Alisa Perren argues that with *sex, lies and videotape*, Miramax "led the way in transforming Hollywood aesthetics, economics, and structure during the 90s," but "the company has now become a crucial part of the system."[10] *Shakespeare in Love*, in fact, is malleable enough to market as an independent, a "Hollywood" blockbuster, a Shakespeare film, a romantic comedy, and most certainly a "heritage" film as well.

The many references and allusions to Hollywood and "show business" are definitely part of American screenwriter Marc Norman's plan to connect sixteenth century England to twenty-first century America. In addition to remaking Shakespeare into an American capitalist in the entertainment business, the film utilizes American and international film-star capital; and significantly, we see these stars enjoying Shakespeare—making Shakespeare fun. Seeing the stars bring to Shakespeare humor coupled with rapid scene cuts and physical action Hollywoodizes the dull Shakespeare we had in high school. Furthermore, the film makes the Bard a new "hard body" ready for heterosexual consumption; the film also "straightens" Shakespeare's sexual preferences by making him completely heterosexual. Finally, *Shakespeare in Love* writes the new world, "America," into the very plot of the film, which portends the great capitalist nation waiting to be born.

Early Modern Cool Britannia

After what amounts to the exposition of the film in which Fennyman (Tom Wilkinson) holds Henslowe's (Geoffrey Rush) feet to the fire, the film frame shows the tip of a quill pen script across the page writing out the title *Shakespeare in Love*. In another early scene we view an ink-stained "Will" Shakespeare practicing his signature. This scene establishes the person of Shakespeare with his signature, which is supposed to identify and verify him as the author. Every act of writing necessitates an addressee. The viewer is the addressee in *Shakespeare in Love*. Writing, the film is secretly telling us, is permanent. This permanence which we see flowing across the screen is demanding that we connect to the permanence of the "real" words of William Shakespeare. In "Signature Event Context" Derrida asserts that "[f]or the written to be the written, it must continue to 'act' and to be legible even if what is called the author of the writing no longer answers for what he has written, for what he seems to have signed . . . absent, or if he is dead . . . the plentitude of his meaning, of that very thing which seems to be written 'in his name.' "[11] The writing in the film literally enacts the event of Shakespeare writing; though we know it is a repetition of this act (it cannot be the dead poet), the writing convinces—at least temporarily—that language is transparent.

If we unfold the layer of writing in *Shakespeare in Love*, a deeper level of reterritorialization of the signature is revealed. The writer signs his name to confirm his *authenticity*; the addressee, the viewer, receives this missive. The film attempts to establish a one-to-one relationship with the viewer. Here in the dark of the movie theater are just you and Shakespeare, your own personal Bard. This act alone Americanizes Shakespeare: a personally designed, individuated Shakespeare for each and every person. Therefore, the film's handwriting frame is there to remind and reassure us that this is the author's hand. The author's hand is a Western fetish; a (whole) sign of presence and authenticity. In an essay primarily about James Joyce's and Ezra Pound's fascination with encrypting "the names and characteristic gestures of past authors, especially Shakespeare," Kathryne V. Lindberg contends that "the signature of Shakespeare, Will, is a special case in point, fluctuating continually between proper name and common property, between the name for English literature and that of an unknown man."[12] Indeed, this is the problem in *Shakespeare in Love*; the signature oscillates between the known and the unknown—who it is we believe to be Shakespeare the author, and the marks on the page by the unknown author. The film is framed in script; the marketing of the film, in the form of a book of Shakespeare's poems, features this script (as well as the internationally famous actors from the film); and a scene in the film is devoted to "Will" writing his signature; but it is all counterfeit since the author of the new play about "Ethel" is not yet *Shakespeare*. The film's writing hand is thus contradictory. It first wants to assure the viewer that this is the authentic Shakespeare; yet, at the same time, it wants to show how a young (hard-bodied) Shakespeare matured into the gifted and famous playwright.

This transparent idea of writing and language (i.e., that *witnessing* the scene of inscription verifies authenticity) brings *Britain Colonized* full-circle with the Searle/Derrida debate concerning the locutionary and illocutionary. The act of writing in the film functions as a performative. Remember that Austin states that fictional utterances are not performative; they are constantive. But what if a fictional frame—*Shakespeare in Love*—performs *real tangible* words that are written, not spoken? The spoken in film (or on the stage) suggests the hollow performative, "an actor on the stage, or if introduced in a poem, or spoken in soliloquy."[13] However, the film's fictional frame presents the *factual* written words of Shakespeare and doubles the impact of writing by showing us the *writing* event: the performative. This double movement of authenticity is reliant on our easy acquiescence to the written word ("logocentrism"), which, generally speaking, Westerners are programmed to perform. According to Derrida, the "written sign, in the usual sense of the word, is therefore a mark which remains, which is not exhausted in the present of its inscription, and which can give rise to an iteration both in the absence of and beyond the presence of the empirically determined subject who, in a given context, has emitted or produced it."[14] Therefore, the film is attempting a double act of authenticity by being "present" at "inscription," thereby performing authenticity. This reiteration, Derrida points out, "carries with it a force of breaking with its context, that is, the set of presences which organize the moment of inscription."[15] Every time a text is read, it forces a break with the scene writing and creates a new context for understanding the text. As Derrida argues, the realization that writing is never stable has always haunted the West; it worried Plato:

> This essential drifting, due to writing as an iterative structure cut off from all absolute responsibility, from *consciousness* as the authority of the last analysis, writing orphaned, and separated at birth from the assistance of its father, is indeed what Plato condemned in the *Phaedrus*. If Plato's gesture is, as I believe, the philosophical movement par excellence, one realizes what is at stake here.[16]

What is at stake is the eternal battle to control the illocutionary. The best way to control the illocutionary is to control the way people think, experience and understand the world. While every chapter in this book so far has discussed the various ways the American film industry has molded how we think, experience and understand the world, the industry has also *paradoxically* enacted the "essential drifting" of the presence of inscription. *Shakespeare in Love* is taking the first part of the equation, controlling the illocutionary, to a new level by attempting to manipulate the iterative potential of the sign by enacting the scene of inscription. The words are doing something: they are authenticating the person Shakespeare. They are performing the *deed* of verification. The double frame of *Shakespeare in Love* is, of course, all "smoke and mirrors." The force of the rupture of presenting the writing out of this "moment of its inscription" allows meaning to wander. Despite the intentional moment of inscription, meaning, in fact, is given license to drift. The ahistorical treatment of Elizabethan history could be construed as one of the troubling facets—or most playful—of the film. Certainly, if the film can create any version of Shakespeare it likes, what is stopping it from creating history for its own ends?

Debunking Shakespeare as the ultimate transcendent signified paves the way to debunking all historical knowledge of the poet and his era. What is fun for the audience is that it is in on the joke of postmodern historicity (an oxymoron). In postmodernity we have lost the subject (e.g., Shakespeare) and forfeited the sign (signifier and signified do not connect), which means that no historical authority is possible. In "*Shakespeare in Love* and the End(s) of History," Elizabeth Klett describes the presentation of the Elizabethan era as "ahistorical" and "full of anachronisms, which include Will's punkish leather doublet, the psychoanalytic stylings of his astrologer."[17] While most of these situations are put into the film for comedy, these seemingly innocuous anachronisms produce, what Derrida terms, a "doubling commentary" which "is not a moment of simple reflexive recording that would transcribe the originary and true layer of a text's intentional meaning"; rather, Derrida argues that every act of "commentary" is always already an interpretation. In the film, anachronisms are an interpretation of what it is we think we know about the Elizabethans, an interpretation of our own era. Yet also at least one interpretation emerges when the Elizabethan era is deliberately presented with anachronistic impossibilities—such as the Shakespeare tourist coffee mug from Stratford-upon-Avon sitting on young Will's desk; or Dr. Moth (Antony Sher), the "apothecary, alchemist, astrologer, seer, Interpreter of Dreams, the Priest of the Psyche" who interprets Will's phallic imagery concerning his broken quill, "organ of imagination" now "dried up," and the "proud tower of [his] genius has collapsed" in Freudian terms.[18] Although these examples are meant to be humorous, they also present the impossibility of interpretation—or the impossibility of a "right" interpretation. Remember that Searle wished to control meaning by limiting the possible ways a citation could be interpreted. *Shakespeare in Love* flies in the face of Searle's philosophy by undermining the very conditions for "one meaning." Like worms in a can, meaning wiggles and squirms about as the film becomes a kind of "paraphrase" of Shakespeare, his life, work and era. As Derrida theorizes, even if one knows a language (French to read Rousseau) one is never able to read the "original":

> I used these words to designate what, in a very classical and very elementary layer of reading, most resembles what traditionally is called "commentary," even paraphrase. This paraphrastic moment, even if it appeals to a minimal competence (which is less common than is generally believed: for example, familiarity with French, with a certain French, in order to read Rousseau in the original text), is already an interpretive

> reading. This moment, this layer already concerns interpretations and semantic decisions which have nothing "natural" or "originary" about them and which impose, subject to conditions that require analysis, conventions that henceforth are dominant . . . [19]

The film is forever paraphrasing its subject matter. Therefore, attempts to appear authentic with the scenes of inscription do not work, and the author's signature is *counterfeit*. It is a fake circulating among all the paraphrases, send-ups, and interpretations that constantly fluctuate and orbit in the film. In this way, the citationality of the text is always multiple because the context is continually changing and deliberately uncertain.

Nevertheless, the American film industry has no problem harnessing the potentially disruptive nature of Shakespeare or his plays. In fact Hollywood with its many 1990s "Shakespeare" films (*Richard III*, Richard Loncraine, 1995; *Looking for Richard*, Al Pacino, 1996; *William Shakespeare's Romeo + Juliet*, Baz Luhrmann, 1996; *Shakespeare in Love*, John Madden, 1998) is continuing a quintessentially American habit: reiterating, often through parody or pastiche, Shakespeare's texts to entertain Americans. While this might sound particularly postmodern, it is actually pre-modern Americana. According to Lawrence W. Levine, in nineteenth-century America Shakespeare was altered in whatever way necessary for the circumstances: "The liberties taken with Shakespeare in nineteenth-century America were often similar to liberties taken with folklore: Shakespeare was frequently seen as common property to be treated as the user saw fit."[20] Although Shakespeare's texts were "Americanized" in the nineteenth-century, his texts were accepted as familiar enough to be parodied by the century's greatest novelist. As Levine points out, the very fact that Twain's "rough" characters in *Huckleberry Finn*, the duke and the king, prepare to sell their version of Shakespeare's *Romeo and Juliet* and *Richard III* to small towns along the Mississippi River tells us that average, small-town America was willing to pay to see Shakespeare's plays performed. Levine argues that Twain's humor succeeds because readers are familiar with Shakespeare's actual texts. Very much like "our contemporary" Drakakis's take on Shakespeare, the nineteenth century "duke" recites " 'king' Hamlet's soliloquy," which turns out to be "a collage of familiar quotations, fragments whose relation to any coherent aesthetic principle is both problematical and irremediably ironical":

> To be, or not to be, that is the bare bodkin
> That makes calamity of so long life;

For who would fardels bear, till Birnam Wood
do come to Dunsinane,
But that the fear of something after death
Murders the innocent sleep,
Great nature's second course,
And makes us rather sling arrows of outrageous fortune
Than fly to others that we know not of . . .[21]

While Levine is partly correct when he argues that the humor is available to those who know Shakespeare's text, there is yet another level of humor available to those who know *Twain's* texts and his unique style of humor. The type of Twain character, in this instance, the duke, carries the humor so that the snatches of Shakespearean language ("To be, or not to be," and "outrageous fortune") juxtaposed with raw American vernacular twisted to sound "Shakespearean" ("bare bodkin" and "fardels bear"). Readers of Twain may be appreciating Shakespeare to some extent, but it is Twain's parody of Americans Americanizing Shakespeare that is so effective. It is this experience that is produced by *Shakespeare in Love.* We enjoy recognizable film citations, *not* Shakespeare. Even the *Romeo and Juliet* passages are already contaminated by film for contemporary viewers. If you are in the movie-theater or at home after renting *Shakespeare in Love*, then it is very likely that you have seen the Baz Luhrmann or Franco Zeffirelli adaptation of *Romeo and Juliet.* It may be that the only previous exposure to *Romeo and Juliet* was through one of these films. Shakespeare is "a movie" for most Americans.[22] Twain's readers who know Shakespeare will also appreciate Twain's parody of Americans who think they know Shakespeare.

Gradually, however, what occurs in American culture is the transition from the Shakespeare texts read and enjoyed by everyone, though often performed in "low brow" contexts, to Shakespeare texts read and performed for the few, the "high brow" cultural elite. Levine argues that the early nineteenth-century theater audience was a "microcosm" of American society—perhaps very much like the Globe's theater audience in Shakespeare's day. But by the end of the century, capitalist axiomatics had, through a sort of pre-modern "market research," created a hierarchical entertainment business; big money went into burlesque, vaudeville, and melodrama because the masses frequented these offerings. The so-called market research is found in class war events such as the Astor Place Riot (1849), in which twenty-two people were killed, dozens hurt, and eighty-six working-class men were arrested. English actor William Charles Macready was pitted against American actor Edwin Forrest as representing the elite culture and the common perspective, respectively. The riots were caused by Macready's performance of *Macbeth* at the Astor Place Opera House; New York theater expert John Kenrick recounts the climactic event that led to the cultural division in the arts:

> A volatile combination of press ballyhoo and widespread anti-British sentiment incited a claque of Forrest's fans to disrupt some of Macready's performances. The actors were bombarded with refuse, rotten eggs—and even seats torn from the gallery flooring. Macready wanted to cut off the engagement, but wealthy patrons publicly petitioned him to carry on. The "haves" seemed to be thumbing their noses at the "have-nots"—which only made Forrest's have-nots angrier. On the night of May 10, 1849, an ugly mob of twenty thousand lower and working class men descended on the Astor Place Opera House. As Macready's performance of *Macbeth* continued before an uneasy (and mostly upper class) audience, those outside broke into a full-scale street riot. As the violence peaked, police fired directly into the crowd, killing at least twenty-two and wounding more than 150. The rioters did not disperse until canon were brought in. The social structure of New York was fractured.[23]

The riot changed the arts in New York City once and for all; as Robert W. Snyder states: "After the Astor Place Riot of 1849 entertainment in New York City was divided along class lines: opera was chiefly for the upper-middle and upper classes, minstrel shows and melodramas for the middle class, variety shows in concert saloons for men of the working class and the slumming middle class."[24] What happened in New York City in terms of the class and entertainment divide occurred all across America. With regard to Shakespeare productions, we can see that the twentieth century inherited these class and cultural divisions; and these divisions perhaps only became more pronounced with the proliferation of new media throughout the twentieth century. Levine concludes that, in the twentieth century, "businessmen" "who managed the new theater chains and huge booking agencies approached their tasks with a hierarchical concept of culture, with the conviction that an unbridgeable gulf separated the tastes and predilections of the various socioeconomic groups," and hence, Shakespeare was rendered "high-brow" culture and "of little interest to the masses."[25]

When the capitalist axiomatic shifts to melodramas, burlesque, and vaudeville, then even "Twainesque" Shakespeare drops from popular sight. In the early twentieth century, the film industry inherited this "low brow versus high brow" situation. Materialist critic Courtney

Lehmann argues that a film like *Shakespeare in Love* transforms what the masses believe to be "high" art into "culture by disguising it":

> The culture industry is a catchall phrase for sites of mass entertainment within late capitalism: television, record companies, Harlequin romance novels, and Hollywood. The culture industry refers to the commercialization of culture and the process whereby "art," masquerading as culture, becomes an industrial product, created not by some solitary genius, but by market trends, mass production, tailorization, reproduction and, of course, consumption. The way that the culture industry disguises this industrial process and seduces consumers into believing that mass entertainment is "high" art or culture is by disguising work in play, business in pleasure, labor in leisure.[26]

Similar to our discussion at the end of Chapter One, American capitalism produces products that are marketed to match trends in consumption. In this way, *Shakespeare in Love* is fun to watch because the audience is privy to the "in" jokes and recognizes the gags as part of the entertainment culture in which they are enveloped. Therefore, "fun" is coded into this leisure product; but it also, as Lehmann points out, masquerades as culture, and with Shakespeare at the center, masquerades as high art. The Bard is reterritorialized, and so is the audience: "American fun, nonetheless, provides its consumers with ritual experiences that are simultaneously attractive and alienating. This double-edged feature characterizes most media-constructed rituals in the U.S.A."[27]

Earlier in the twentieth century, some people actually believed that film could put Shakespeare back in the center of English-speaking culture. But we know that this did not happen. This hierarchy, then, is the cultural legacy of Shakespeare in America; though forced to plough through a few of the plays in high school, the average American fears or dreads Shakespeare. The fear and dread extends beyond the average American to include the professional actor as well. When the actor Al Pacino is asked if as an American he is encouraged to perform Shakespeare, the director of *Looking for Richard* replies that Americans are not given the confidence to perform Shakespeare:

> You're not as encouraged, in America, to do the Shakespeare's plays, simply by the very nature of what's available to us. A certain kind of presentation is expected, because the great English actors who have come across to show us what they have done with it, is so special, and so lauded by us in America, so the tendency is to feel that it's something that belongs in another part of the world . . . I personally learned of it

through the films of Olivier and some of the American films from Orson Welles to *Julius Caesar* with Marlon Brando early on in my life."[28]

Al Pacino's comments should remind us of the nineteenth-century dispute between the American Forrest and the Englishman Macready. Americans cannot really perform Shakespeare; and, besides, most of our knowledge comes from film versions of the plays.

Uninhibited by the English Shakespeare belonging to "another part of the world," American Norman confesses that in order to bring the Bard's early years to life in film he put an " 'American spin on the story.' "[29] The "American spin" is basically showing how the young Shakespeare learned to scheme his way into bettering his situation; and we know from the distribution of property in his will, Shakespeare adapted and thrived in the early days of modern Western capitalism. Norman draws a parallel between Shakespeare's time and contemporary Hollywood: " 'The industry as we know it today was essentially born in Shakespeare's time,' Norman points out. Before that era, playwrights and actors had no home theater and no backers or regular audiences. 'They were itinerants, performing in the streets,' he says."[30] In addition to remaking Shakespeare into an American capitalist in the entertainment business, I would also like to briefly discuss the different ways the film reterritorializes Shakespearean and Elizabethan citations for American consumption. These include utilizing American and international film star capital; also, we see the stars bring to Shakespeare humor coupled with rapid scene cuts and physical action that Hollywoodizes the dull Shakespeare we had in high school; the film, furthermore, makes the Bard a new "hard body" ready for heterosexual consumption; and lastly, completely anachronistically, the film writes in "America," by making Wessex's plantation investments in "Virginia."

First, several incidents in the film showcase the film's "commentary" on the Elizabethan era by inserting anachronistic tidbits from modern entertainment culture. In fact, the film begins with a new capitalist axiomatic in the making. The gag of holding one's feet to the fire is a metaphor few have actually seen enacted but becomes a brilliant opener for the film because it appears to be archaic, all the while playing upon the metaphor. Fennyman, as moneylender to Henslowe, becomes the "producer" of the Rose Theatre's new production when he agrees not to burn his feet, nor cut off his nose or ears, and extend his line of credit to Henslowe. According to Henslowe, he can pay Fennyman what he owes him from the profits of Will Shakespeare's new play:

FENNYMAN. What's the title?
HENSLOWE. "Romeo and Ethel the Pirate's Daughter."
FENNYMAN. Good title.

Despite Fennyman's inability to recognize a good title—and from the contemporary's perspective a Shakespeare classic—he is about to create an early modern capitalist axiomatic:

> FENNYMAN. A play takes time. Find actors . . . rehearsals . . . let's say open in three weeks. That's— what—five hundred groundlings at tuppence each, in addition four hundred backsides at three pence—a penny extra for a cushion, call it two hundred cushions, say two performance [*sic*] for safety—how much is that Mr. Frees?
> FREES. Twenty pounds to the penny, Mr. Fennyman.
> FENNYMAN. Correct!
> HENSLOWE. But I have to pay the actors and the author.
> FENNYMAN. A share of the profits.
> HENSLOWE. There's never any . . .
> FENNYMAN. *Of course not!*
> HENSLOWE, *impressed.* Mr. Fennyman, I think you may have hit on something. (3–3A)

Fennyman establishes the role of the big-money backer of the Rose Theatre, which is, of course, analogous to the big-money backer in the contemporary film industry. Part of the gag is that big business gets the profits while the author and players do not get paid at all; the postmodern audience will not only plug Shakespeare and Ned Alleyn into these slots, but also Marc Norman, Tom Stoppard, Joseph Fiennes, and others into this equation. This is postmodern commentary—the citations run inside and outside the film; the film is pure text, one without boundaries.

The boatman scenes further stage the analogy between the contemporary entertainment industry and the burgeoning early modern entertainment industry. The boatman, whose lines resemble a New York taxi driver (or any big city American taxi driver), is also a street-wise (water-wise) hustler. Chasing Viola/Thomas Kent, Will jumps into a boat-for-hire on the Thames and commands the boatman to "follow that boat"; the reiteration of numerous films and televisions shows ensues:

> BOATMAN. I know your face. Are you an actor?
> WILL. *Oh God, here we go again. Yes.*
> BOATMAN. Yes, I've seen you in something. That one about a King.
> WILL. Really?
> BOATMAN. I had that Christopher Marlowe in my boat once. (32)

The "follow that boat" is familiar to almost anyone in the audience. The conversation that follows is also a film citation that virtually everyone would know. This reiteration of other films—especially American crime drama—provides that ahistorical "commentary" that displaces the historical context. Inside the film, the exchange continues the ongoing belittlement of Will, who at this time is completely eclipsed by the stardom of Marlowe. The conversation with the boatman also establishes the writer-trying-to-get-discovered gag. An aspiring playwright, the boatman tries to interest Will in his script. The next trip, in fact, the boatman (Simon Day) tries to get Will to read his manuscript; Will, however, is confounded because he has just kissed Thomas Kent and is not paying attention to the boatman. The boatman persists, and like the street-smart New York taxi driver, knows more about "what is going on" than Shakespeare:

> BOATMAN. Thank you, my lady!
> WILL, *stunned*. Lady?
> BOATMAN. Viola De Lesseps. Known her since she was this high. Wouldn't deceive a child.
> WILL, *gets out of the boat*.
> BOATMAN, *reaching under his seat*. Strangely, enough, I'm a bit of a writer myself. (57)

These minor exchanges establish the very *contemporary* idea that everyone wants to be a writer—that everyone has a manuscript waiting to be discovered. The citation of the (British) Beatles song "Paperback Writer" lurks just on the edge of this scene. Conflating the values and preoccupations of the Early Modern period with our own contemporary period is done so often in the film, one soon begins to overlook the anachronisms. This radical repositioning of the illocutionary will not allow a "right" interpretation.

Yet, even with the incidental boatman scenes we are forced again to think about the gaping hole of knowledge we have about Shakespeare and his life. Norman researched the Early Modern period enough to know that the theater was just then gaining a professional respectability, and that many a hustler would be "on the make" in a big city like London. However, it is the lack of concrete knowledge about Shakespeare that allows Norman to *invent*—the boatman scenes, for example, or the scenes in the tavern (when the waiter recites the *noveau cuisine de jour*), where we find Norman grafting contemporary society norms onto Elizabethan society and culture. These scenes of everyday life and events showcase Norman's Americanisms and American attitudes:

> There isn't much to read about Shakespeare himself (there's maybe five arguable facts), but there's a fair amount to read about his world, the

> world of Elizabethan theater, and that's where the research hit paydirt. Because what I discovered was our business, the entertainment business, in fact the commercial writing we do, not on some quaint ye-olde English tea shoppe level, but full-bore, cut-throat, the way we know it, with lawyers and goniff producers and blood on the floor, the business we're all still in. And that was the mainspring—Shakespeare in Development Hell, showing promise, writing crap, and not knowing how to get off the merry-go-round, how to get better. Everything else followed from that.[31]

Norman's attitude is very much like that of the early nineteenth-century American readers and performers of Shakespeare. Shakespeare is "entertainment"; he engaged in "commercial entertainment writing." It is at this point that the academic Shakespeare scholar runs screaming from the room: how can the greatest poet of the English language be labeled a "commercial entertainment" writer. Shakespeare is the finest and noblest in the English language, not "entertainment." Norman is not the only outspoken American who has attempted to get to the entertainment level of Shakespeare in the last several years; Pacino thought that if his team could bring out the humor of *Richard III*, of all plays, then they could succeed with American audiences: "We really tried to get the humour. I think there's a kind of innate humour and irony in this play . . . . It sheds a light on it sometimes or makes it more tolerable for an audience when some of those things happen to have humour."[32]

One has to admire Norman's cavalier and comic attitude toward his subject. The lack of English pedigree, however, is the reason why English playwright Tom Stoppard was brought into the project. While the humor remains in the film, the polishing of certain Englishisms is perhaps achieved. One gag that is very English, but American viewers can fully understand, is the continual depiction of Shakespeare as *unoriginal*. When Will races by the preacher who, denounces the two theaters as sinful, exclaims, "A plague on both of your houses," Will stops and makes a mental note of this line; the line of course is one of the most famous in all of Shakespeare. Later, Will meets up with Christopher Marlowe at the pub. The casting of Marlowe and this scene is one of the best examples of the opening up of multiple "commentaries" available in the film. First, the film has already established that "Kit" Marlowe is the most famous playwright in London at this time (1593). When Kit asks him what he is working on, Will replies "Romeo and Ethel the Pirate's Daughter." Both wince at the title—the audience laughs because we know that Shakespeare eventually writes *Romeo and Juliet*. The Elizabethan-theater buff will know that this is a general reference to revenge tragedies popular in that era. However, even if the average American viewer does not register this citation, or know that Shakespeare borrowed most of his plots and characters from pre-existing texts, she will certainly understand that the plagiarizing and plundering onscreen Shakespeare is being characterized in this way for a reason. Kit tries to help Will with his play:

> MARLOWE. What is the story?
> WILL. Well, there's a pirate . . . *confesses* In truth, I have not written a word.
> MARLOWE. Romeo is . . . Italian. Always in and out of love.
> WILL. Yes, that's good. Until he meets . . .
> MARLOWE. Ethel.
> WILL. Do you think?
> MARLOWE. The daughter of his enemy.
> WILL, *thoughtfully*. The daughter of his enemy.
> MARLOWE. His best friend is killed in a dual by Ethel's brother or something. His name is Mercutio.
> WILL. Mercutio . . . good name. (27)

The most uninformed viewer can pick up on the humor of this scene; again, everyone knows there is no "Romeo and Ethel" play by Shakespeare. At another level, the casting of Kit is perfect because the "real life" Marlowe was homosexual, and the actor, Rupert Everett, is a de-closeted homosexual actor. The "real" Marlowe was involved in "espionage" for Queen Elizabeth; he was murdered in Deptford in 1593 under mysterious circumstances. The film's off-stage murder of Marlowe (in 1593), which the audience, and Will, mistakenly believes to have been committed by Wessex, therefore plays into "real" history.

Shakespeare in Love's own plagiarizing and plundering we might characterize as a mirror image of the play itself, and also charitably consider its "lifting" as another manifestation of postmodernity. The fact that the *Shakespeare in Love* screenplay borrows heavily from Caryl Brahms and S. J. Simon's novel *No Bed for Bacon* (1941) has not escaped Shakespeare scholars. Concerning the striking "similarity" between *Shakespeare in Love* and *No Bed for Bacon*, one reviewer notes that:

> not only did the screenwriters imitate the general humorous atmosphere of the novel, but they also lifted several other essential elements . . . the name of the female protagonist—Viola, her taste for plays, her infatuation with young William Shakespeare, her male disguise, her connection with *Twelfth Night*, rehearsals and a performance of *Romeo and Juliet*, the rivalry between two theatre companies,

> the presence of several Elizabethan literary personages, the Bard's suffering from writer's block, and so on. Such specific detail as Shakespeare's hesitation when signing his own name . . . is also found in the novel . . . . A joke about Anne Hathaway's cottage occurs in both works.[33]

In addition to the *No Bed for Bacon* similarities, American writer Faye Kellerman accused the screenwriters of plagiarizing her novel *The Quality of Mercy* (1989) which has been described as a "historical thriller," rather than a romantic-comedy. Co-screenwriter Tom Stoppard is most famous for his play *Rosencrantz and Guildenstern are Dead* (1967) which is a pastiche of *Hamlet*. In *Rosencrantz and Guildenstern are Dead*, Stoppard makes the minor Shakespeare characters Rosencrantz and Guildenstern the central characters of his play, uses the plot of *Hamlet*, and inserts passages of the latter text into his own play. The debt to Shakespeare is obvious, but also overt is Stoppard's debt to Samuel Beckett; Stoppard's Shakespeare characters are unmistakably modeled on Beckett's Vladimir and Estregon in *Waiting for Godot*. One view of *Shakespeare in Love*, then, is that the film simply pushes pastiche and parody onto a new plane of postmodernity. The problem for the screenwriters and the Hollywood studios involved in the film, however, is that Kellerman sued them for her author-function rights, thereby proving that while "intertextuality" might be trendy, capitalism's right to intellectual property is definitely legally binding.

Another way the film Americanized Shakespeare is through its portrayal of sexuality in the Elizabethan era. The fact that Marlowe's homosexuality is never mentioned or even alluded to in the film furthers the film's agenda of "cleaning up" the Elizabethan stage for the contemporary American market. Literary scholar Stephen Greenblatt advised Marc Norman to make the love affair between Shakespeare and Marlowe, not between Shakespeare and Viola. Courtney Lehmann suggests that "*Shakespeare in Love* would have been more interesting but less of a box-office smash under Greenblatt's 'direction.' "[34] To mention the homosexuality associated with the Elizabethan theater, apart from the humor elicited by the boy actor who must play the female lead and Ralph who must play the role of the old nurse, would contaminate the film with unwanted, non-normalized citations. The homosexual body is purged by the film so that, as Lehmann argues, the "hard body" Will can be the center of this heterosexual "romantic comedy." According to Susan Jeffords in *Hard Bodies: Hollywood Masculinity in the Reagan Era*, the contemporary film has staged the body so that the body becomes representative of political values. Jeffords argues that the "soft body" represents all that is wrong in society: "the errant body containing sexually transmitted disease, immorality, illegal chemicals, 'laziness,' and endangered fetuses."[35] The hard body, then, is one that represents the heterosexual normal "body that envelope(s) strength, labor, determination, loyalty and courage."[36] The politicalization of the body occurs as the link between national character and the body. Jeffords argues that the representation of the "indefatigable, muscular, and invincible masculine body became the linchpin of the Reagan imagery; this hardened male form became the emblem not only for the Reagan presidency but for its ideologies and economies as well."[37]

All the characteristics of the hard body are attributed to Will: determination, loyalty and courage. The actor Joseph Fiennes also brings hard-body physical attributes to the film; Lehmann, in particular, remarks upon Fiennes's triceps. Located on the back of the arm, the tricep is only visible in a lean and muscled body. Middle-aged Shakespeare's triceps seem, well, impossible. This Shakespeare is young, dynamic, and sexy; this version bears little resemblance to the middle-aged bald guy we all thought we knew. Yet, again, this is the film's sleight of hand—entertain us with the young, sexy heterosexual Shakespeare, but do not lose the connection between this version and the venerable middle-aged poet. The hard body character and body combination, plus the fact that the film does not allude to Shakespeare's bisexuality (those sonnets were for a young man, remember) further *Americanizes* Shakespeare in the film.

The ahistorical commentary or paraphrase is taken to fantastic heights with the inclusion of America, "the New World," in the life events of William Shakespeare. The fact that the film plays fast and loose with colonial history and the history of Shakespeare's own plays is predictable. However, the fact that the film ends in America—presumably on the shores of Virginia—cannot help but be read as the full scale *colonization of the English playwright* on the part of the film. The audience witnesses Will's heartbreak at Viola's departure; we see him write her into "immortality"; and, inter-laced with scenes of Will's *writing*, we see bodies falling into water, a boat bottom from under the surface of the water. This is the filmic staging of the raison d'etre of Shakespeare's *The Tempest*. Lehmann, too, notes the Hollywood triumph of locating Shakespeare in America at the end of the film:

> And as the film closes with Will's handwriting superimposed on an image of Viola trekking across a sandy coastline, *Shakespeare in Love*

> brilliantly relocates Shakespeare the Author from early Modern England to our own postmodern consumer society, recycling the Bard not as the Marlboro Man of Southern Virginia but as the daydream believer of Southern California: Hollywood.[38]

This sentiment, of course, plays directly into Norman's idea that if Shakespeare—or a guy like Will—were alive in our era, he would be a screenwriter in Hollywood.

As viewers and readers in the twenty-first century, perhaps we should ask ourselves if it matters that the events that inform the film's rendering of this scene take place nearly twenty years after the film's present time frame. Or, is it important for the average American to know that the "real-life" events of the early seventeenth century led Shakespeare to write a play that called into question colonialism? John Wylie in "New and Old Worlds: *The Tempest* and Early Colonial Discourse" discusses the fact that it was not until 1607 that Jamestown was established, and that colonialism, especially the activity of plantation (already well underway in Ireland), was a controversial topic, and Shakespeare's play is a reaction to this and to the wreck of the *Sea Adventure* (1609–1610) that carried planter families:

> The years immediately preceding *The Tempest's* first recorded performance witnessed the setting up by royal charter of the Virginia Company (1606) and the subsequent foundation of the colony of Jamestown in Virginia (1607) . . . This colony was the subject of much contemporary debate. In particular, during 1609–1610, the wreck upon Bermuda of the *Sea Adventure*, a ship carrying colonists to Virginia, became "a focus for debate about the wisdom of plantation" . . . It has been argued that the vicissitudes and controversies surrounding this Virginia colony form *The Tempest's* immediate political and colonial context. Yet more precisely, an account of the Virginia colony by William Strachey, *A True Repertory of the Wracke and Redemption of Sir Thomas Gates* . . . , which includes details of the ship-wreck of the *Sea Adventure*, is one of the very few acknowledged textual sources of *The Tempest*.[39]

The film's romantic-comedy genre has rid all of Shakespeare's era of political intrigue; thus, the idea that *The Tempest* could have been a political response to current events is obviously not broached by *Shakespeare in Love*. The closest the film gets to the political is Queen Elizabeth's upholding of Viola's duty to marry whom her father wishes her to marry. Judi Dench's determined Elizabeth "know[s] something about a woman in a man's profession, yes, by God, I do know about that," but "whom God has joined in marriage, not even I can put asunder."

The last scene of the film features Viola walking on the beach of the new world, and Will writing her into his new play. This final scene of inscription is counterfeited to connect Shakespeare to America. I would argue that another anachronism is the presentation of the "Romantic" poet-prophet foretelling the future: the future lies in America, the future great global capitalist nation. We have seen that the act of writing throughout the film, the scene of inscription, instead of suggesting authenticity, destabilizes the images we see on screen. Fortunately, the depth of connection between the scene of inscription and the radical impossibility that it *is the* scene of inscription is fairly shallow. The film wishes only to maintain a surface connection, and does so by diverting our attention with familiar gags, recognizable film citations, and sexual energy. In the end, Oedipalized, castrated, insipid "Will" Shakespeare deterritorializes nicely from the stiff, unreadable, Elizabethan poet we encountered in school; this "Will" is reterritorialized into a hip, sexy, but, at heart, all-around average film guy.

Conclusion

Each chapter in this book has dealt with the deterritorialization of British cultural and literary identity by filmmakers who reterritorialized it in the image of American cultural products and global capitalist axiomatics. As we progressed through *Britain Colonized*, the level of disregard for the British literary text increased. For instance, the discussion of *High Fidelity* in chapter 6 showed that British novels can be completely reterritorialized so that nothing "British" remains in the film. Chapter 7 depicts the reterritorialization of England's most famous writer into clichéd Hollywood gags and standard stereotypes of the struggling Hollywood screenwriter. Chapter 7 shows that the American film industry is successful when it simply fabricates British literary history, colonial history, and biographical "facts" about historical figures. Marc Norman, John Madden, and company radically reiterated the literary text, which in this case was fragments from Shakespeare's texts put into a mythological framework, at all levels—narrative, plot, circumstances—into a different context of meaning (in order to satisfy a mass-market audience), while at the same time they repeated familiar citations that reconstituted the film into a *recognizable* and predictable product (in order to satisfy a mass-market audience). However much one may object to the "identity theft" of Shakespeare, *Shakespeare in Love* perfectly enacts the paradox of iteration that proves that all texts (fictional and "factual") are capable of continuous iteration and interpretation. This fact should be happy news for the theorist who prides herself on multiplicity and open-ended interpretative models. Indeed, the potential for filmmakers in relation to literary texts is boundless.

Of course, radical reiteration of literary texts into film texts is not done for the sheer joy of play, or for showing-off Derrida's point that the illocutionary fields change the meaning of an utterance. Rather, the films are made to entertain people for money. The tension between allowing theoretically open-ended interpretations and remaining faithful to a text is a problem that seems to have no available solution. Perhaps if one is concerned about the "art of the novel" being turned into Hollywood entertainment, then the best way to approach the reterritorialization by Hollywood of British cultural and literary products is to be critically vigilant. This might be a good way to characterize *Britain Colonized*; the text has not taken the law into its own hands, but it is a critical vigilante: on the alert for capitalist reterritorialization at the expense of literature, culture, and identity. The theoretical paradox, however, remains in all the various forms of our critique, and this book shows for the first time how this works with film adaptations of literary texts.

As we have seen, American culture and film formulae transform and even obliterate the "foreign" quality of British literary texts. From chapter to chapter I have maintained that this reterritorialization occurred in order to make the film marketable. This ongoing assertion is at one level crass; yet, as we have seen, it is the raision d'etre of every adaptation. The film industry is not a nonprofit organization—whatever that means in a global capitalist economy. The bottom line is, as ever, if you do not make a profit, then you do not stay in business. The film industry must make products with surplus-value in order to ensure capitalist investment for more films. The problem with which *Britain Colonized* has been preoccupied is that the redundant formulae filmmakers repeatedly use are applied no matter what the content of the source text might be.

This leads us to the political side of the paradox: Why do audiences continually buy into these formulae? To answer this question is to return to Stuart M. Kaminsky's assertion: "Genre study in film is based on the realization that certain popular narrative forms have both cultural and universal roots—that, for example, the Western of today is related both to folk tales of the past two hundred years in the United States and to the archetypes of myth."[1] We like a familiar story, or, at least, a familiar shape to our story. In terms of thought and generating something "new," we were forced to ask ourselves: Why do American audiences in particular, and, by default, overseas audiences continue to "desire their own oppression?" The film industry has the ability to apply these "tried-and-true" formulae for every human experience. Sometimes all we know about a certain historical event or place is from film. The classic *The Longest Day* (1962), or, more recently, *Saving Private Ryan* (1998), fills in our knowledge of the Second World War. Meanwhile, the Tarzan movies or *Out of Africa* (1985) provide stories and images of Africa. Moreover, we utilize these massive popular film formulae to connect to others or to make a point. Recently, for instance, I heard a sermon attempting to illustrate Moses' initial unwillingness to be God's chosen one by contrasting the familiar image of hyper-masculine Charlton Heston in *The Ten Commandments* (1956): "For those of us who were raised on the epic film starring Charlton Heston, when we see Moses leading the Israelites through the Red Sea and then receiving the stone tablets from God on Mt. Sinai, it is easy to forget that Moses, the liberator, was initially, a very hesitant and reluctant leader."[2] Not only British literature, then, has been colonized and reterritorialized, but virtually every human experience and text—including the *Bible*—have been fodder for Hollywood's movie machine.

In each chapter I have shown how Britain's past has often been a source of interest for Americans, who can enjoy British elitism and racial exclusion without a direct reflection on America's class and racial problems. The heritage-film genre, which promotes images of white British elitism, has become its own capitalist axiomatic, so powerful is its box-office draw. Chapter 2 depicted how Merchant Ivory's film *The Remains of the Day* utilized three key elements from the novel in order to cash in on the heritage boom. First, the film captured the novel's quest to return to a lost England by simply displaying idyllic English landscape; the camera often focused on the grounds of the estate, the rustic country side, and the quaint towns on Stevens's journey. The novel's narrative during Stevens's quest could be interpreted as parodic of the interwar era of the "Little Englander" discourse, which, of course, the film cannot replicate *except* by showing us in a highly effective way this fantasy England. But the second and third formulae involved recognizable and accessible film narratives. These were the "Nazi plot" and the "romance" featuring the May–December supposed romance between Miss Kenton and Stevens. However, as I explicitly showed, the pleasure of *The Remains of the Day* for American audiences was at the level of nostalgia for their great glorious past, not that of Britain's. Thus, despite the English-heritage features of the film, Merchant-Ivory reterritorialized the novel for American viewers, who nostalgically connected to Christopher Reeve's Lewis (Superman) and America's newfound dominance in world politics at the end of the Second World War.

Focusing on a particular American's relationship to Britons in Britain was Neil LaBute's radical reterritorialization of A.S. Byatt's character Roland Mitchell. Labute reterritorializes Byatt's novel into an American favorite: the genre of the classic Western starring the heroic actions of the now-American character Roland Mitchell. Utilizing the classic Western-film genre, the film supposedly led the audience to respond to the conflict that exists in its core American beliefs. As the loner-hero, Roland played the part of the Western "individual" who, in the end, reconciles his willful individual freedom (in a capitalist market economy) with the community and social good. LaBute's deterritorialization of the Englishness of the novel and reterritorialization of Americana, leads to the trivialization of the nineteenth-century characters and the parallel plot of the novel. In fact, there was no parallel plot; rather, LaBute's focused on the Victorians only to dwell, heritage-style, on the Victorian *mise-en-scene.* As the figures in chapter 3 showed, LaBute relied heavily on the "authenticity" of canvases of the Pre-Raphaelite painters and popular portraits of Victorian writers to create easily recognizable Victorian *tableau-vivants.*

While LaBute had difficulty capturing the British narrative of the past, screenwriter and director Anthony Minghella successfully captured colonial Africa of the 1930s. In chapter 4 I explored the imaginative hold that British colonial imperial history of the Empire has had on the American imagination. The global hegemony over knowledge and naming that white European males exerted for hundreds of years over the colonial world was analogous to the postwar capitalist and military dominance the United States has displayed. Hollywood reproduces our fantasy—global American hegemony—through historical and literary figures borrowed from this older European tradition. While the romance between Almasy and Katharine was the narrative centerpiece of *The English Patient*, the colonial desert-adventure story propelled the lovers' fate. The novel exposed colonialist reterritorialization as myopic and exploitive, but the film blindly reterritorialized the Hollywood colonial adventure convention. The film *The English Patient* invited the viewer to share in and enjoy the colonizing discourse; the film became a "blockbuster" because the viewer was allowed to maintain the privileged white eye of the Western camera.

Chapter 5 presented Cool Britannia as the new capitalist axiomatic of the 1990s. "Creative Britain" of New Labor was more than happy to embrace the vast citationality of the packaging of counter-cultural products such as *Trainspotting*. With *Bridget Jones's Diary*, I asserted that the distinction between the 1990s "Janespotter" and "Trainspotter" was deconstructed by the Jonespotter. The film *Bridget Jones's Diary* self-consciously participates not only in contemporary romantic comedy, but also heritage for "untravelled Americans," who apparently enjoy the Christmas-card scenes and "the illusion that this kind of comedy is youthful and anarchic, as opposed to dated and conservative."[3] The combination of postmodern awareness, heritage, and commercial viability made *Bridget Jones* also a part of Cool Britannia: cool, youthful, and hip, in a thirtysomething way, and Janespotter, formulaic and conservative, in a heritage sort of way.

Chapter 6 marked the Atlantic crossing in *Britain Colonized*. With *Waterland*, but more so with *High Fidelity*, the British content was simply obliterated: the radical reiteration of the literary text occurred at all levels—narrative, plot, circumstances—into an *American* context, while at the same time repeated familiar *American* citations that reconstituted the film into a *recognizable* and predictable *American cultural* product. Despite the definite Britishness of the novels, in the hands of American screenwriters the Britishness was reduced in one and eliminated in the other. Although quite different in manifestation, each novel dealt in its own way with the discourse primarily concerned with issues of masculinity; the films reterritorialized and regulated the gendered discourses to fit American expectations and typical formulaic Hollywood motifs.

Hollywood's reterritorialization of British literature was completed with *Shakespeare in Love*. The greatest poet of the English language tradition is reterritorialized to fit the struggling-screenwriter-in-Hollywood mold. In addition to remaking Shakespeare into an American capitalist in the entertainment business, the film utilized American and international film-star capital; and significantly, the stars made Shakespeare *fun*: the ultimate American goal. Furthermore, the film made the Bard a new "hard body" ready for heterosexual consumption, which obliterated Shakespeare's historically factual bisexual preferences. Lastly, *Shakespeare in Love* anachronistically wrote the New World into the story. This final action completed the colonization of British literature; the New World in the final scene signaled that America has reterroritalized Britain by literally remapping the world and rewriting history.

Indeed, it was the literal reterritorialization, the remapping, of the world and rewriting of literary and world history that many in Britain dreaded throughout the twentieth century. For decades, British cultural theorists forecasted and feared the usurpation of British culture by the American media. Additional onslaughts to Britain's power and sovereignty in the postwar era include decolonization by former territories, colonial immigration to Britain, formation of the European Union, and devolution within the United Kingdom. But the damage to British culture by Americanization, film critic Jeffrey Richards acidly argues, began after the First World War: "The Americanisation of the youth culture, underway since World War One, was completed—and the British young now go round in baseball caps, eating Macdonalds, using American slang, watching American films, idolizing macho American stars, and supporting a culture that advocates the virtues of extreme individualism, violent self-assertion and total sexual freedom."[4] This statement indicates that Hollywood and other forms of American media have done their jobs well. All this attests to the power of the media, and, hence, further establishes the need to critique Hollywood's appropriation of British literature and culture.

Reterritorialization has already occurred. Cultural theorist Bill Schwarz asserts that the centuries-long global and geographical domination by Britain in the Atlantic has given way to Asian and Pacific dominance. The shared American and British global dominance centered in the Atlantic is moving away, "[t]he maps have been turned around, or upside down—as least symbolically. The lines of authority, from the centre to the margins, are now less forceful."[5] The axis of power is shifting from the Atlantic to the Pacific Ocean, which means that Britain is replaced by Australia, and the West Coast usurps power, money and prestige from the East Coast of the United States. London and New York are no match for Hollywood, long the quintessential icon of "sunny California": "For a nation which had invested so assiduously in the prerequisites of the culture of the past, the impact of Americanization mass culture did much, as conservatives of all stripes had feared, to dislocate the native culture of the British."[6]

Rather than give in completely to American dominance, Britain fights back with its own reterritorial capitalist initiatives. If Americans, Japanese, and Australians fetishize the old country, then, obviously, the thing to do is *market* the old country as such. The historical authenticity of geographical Britain is a popular tourist attraction; as we saw in chapter 2 in terms of the heritage film, tourists are willing to pay to see, for example, where *The Remains of the Day* was filmed. The British Tourist Authority puts out a series of "movie maps," which feature a map of Britain with the film location starred and numbered. Each map features recent films, or a genre, such as the heritage film, or one film, such as the *Harry Potter and the Philosopher's Stone* (2001). Attempting to attract overseas tourism through the popularity of the film (and books), the *Harry Potter* map's theme is "Magical Britain":

> With such a long and varied history it's no surprise that this country is reputed to have hundreds of ghosts. Here we list just a handful of places with ghostly connections, as well as a selection of the countless myths and legends which make Britain such a magical place to visit![7]

The mapping of Britain as a magical mystery tour of haunted houses and ghostly graveyards is the by-product of the Hollywoodization of

British culture. The decline of Britain, and America's deterritorialization and reterritorialization, echoes Robert Hewison's declaration: "Instead of manufacturing goods, we are manufacturing *heritage*, a commodity which nobody seems able to define, but which everybody is eager to sell." (italics in original)[8]

The fact that Britain reterritorializes *itself* in the image of an American film-set on location in Britain is disconcerting.

The future of British literature, then, seems to be contained in iconic images of Britain produced and circulated primarily for our entertainment. In chapter 7 I used Derrida's idea of the "commentary" to discuss how we now read Shakespeare's texts, but increasingly this "paraphrasing" or "commentary" will inform all texts. Thus, even if one has read the text, one must always confront what "traditionally is called 'commentary,' even paraphrase. [. . .] This moment, this layer already concerns interpretations and semantic decisions which have nothing 'natural' or 'originary' about them and which impose, subject to conditions that require analysis, conventions that henceforth are dominant."[9] Film is forever paraphrasing its literary text. Gradually, as I predicted in the introduction, readers, especially students, will no longer read the text, but rather watch the movie. As I dangerously veer toward the ledge of Conservative Right–reading, I must assert a critical vigilantism by advocating continuous iteration and interpretation.

Notes

Introduction

1. George Bernard Shaw, *The Apple Cart* (London: Constable and Co. Ltd., 1930), 65. My thanks to Ken Radamaker for suggesting Shaw.
2. America is used throughout to refer to the geographical region known as the United States of America. I do not mean the whole of North America, and acknowledge the differences among the peoples of North, South and Central America. Americanization is often interchanged here with Hollywoodization because Hollywood represents "American culture" or "American values," though it should also be acknowledged that this affiliation is completely illusionary. Therefore, the "Americanization of British literature" means the United States's cultural appropriation of texts written by those who identify themselves (and hence their texts) as belonging to Great Britain. Likewise, Britain is typically used to mean the United Kingdom (England, Wales, Scotland, and Northern Ireland), and England is used when the national sentiment is "English" (as many writers will assert they are English not British). The use of the British Empire obviously refers to British colonial territories.
3. William T. Stead, *The Americanisation of the World; or, The Trend of the Twentieth Century*, reprinted by the Garland Library of War and Peace, Sandi E. Cooper, ed. (New York: Garland, 1972), 7.
4. Sir Christopher Furness, *The American Invasion* (London: Simpkin, Marshall, 1902), 7.
5. Ibid., 7.
6. The reprint of Stead's book contains *Punch* cartoons that feature the emasculation of Britain by the United States as well as period advertisements which boast that American made products are welcome in England because it will underscore the superiority of English products; see "Southall's Patent Boots" in the back of the reprint of *The Americanisation of the World*.
7. Stuart M. Kaminsky, *American Film Genres*, 2nd ed (Chicago: Nelson-Hall, 1985), 1.
8. Ibid., 2.
9. John G. Cawelti, "The Concept of Formula in the Study of Popular Literature," reprinted in *Reading Popular Narrative*, Bob Ashley, ed. (London: Leicester Univ. Press, 1989), 73.

10. Justin Wyatt, *High Concept: Movies and Marketing in Hollywood* (Austin: Univ. of Texas Press, 1994), 8.
11. Spencer Golub, "Spies in the House of Quality: The American Reception of *Brideshead Revisited*," in *Novel Images: Literature in Performance*, Peter Reynolds ed. (New York: Routledge, 1993), 140.
12. "Cool Britannia" was the title of a song by the Bonzo Dog Doo Dah Band back in 1967. The phrase refers to a then fashionable London scene with a new generation of pop groups, e.g., the Beatles and the Rolling Stones, who helped to make famous fashion designers, clubs and certain life styles.
13. Andrew Macdonald quoted by Xan Brooks in *Choose Life: Ewan McGregor and the British Film Revival* (Cameleon, 1998), 87.
14. Julianne Pidduck, "*Elizabeth* and *Shakespeare in Love*: Screening the Elizabethans," in *Film/Literature/Heritage* ed. Ginette Vincendeau (London: BFI, 2001), 134.
15. Hobsbawm Eric, and Terence Ranger, Introduction and editors, *The Invention of Tradition* (Cambridge: Cambridge Univ. Press, 1989), 4.

Chapter 1 Context and Desire in the Colonization of British Literature

1. "In relation to American filmmakers, I believe we are all intellectuals—" Truffaut's response to a question concerning American film. Interview with Truffaut, "Francois Truffaut," *Cahiers du cinema* (December 1962), Vol. 138: 55. My translation.
2. Marcus A. Doel, "Occult Hollywood: Unfolding the Americanization of World Cinema," *American Century: Consensus and Coercion in the Projection of American Power*, David Slater and Peter J. Taylor, eds. (Oxford: Blackwell, 1999), 248.
3. Colin Flint, "The 'War on Terrorism' and the 'Hegemonic Dilemma': Extraterritoriality, Reterritorialization, and the Implications for Globalization," *Globalization and Its Outcomes*, John O'Loughlin, Lynn Staeheli, and Edward Greenburg, eds. (New York: Guilford, 2004), 362.
4. Joseph S. Nye, Jr. *Soft Power: The Means to Success in World Politics* (New York: Perseus, 2004), 5.
5. Flint, 370.
6. Paul Willemen, *Looks and Frictions: Essays in Cultural Studies and Film Theory* (Bloomington, IN: Indiana Univ. Press, 1994), 211.
7. Ibid., 210.
8. Eric Hobsbawm, *The Invention of Tradition* (Cambridge: Cambridge Univ. Press, 1989), 4.
9. Michael Ryan and Douglas Kellner, *Camera Politica: The Politics and Ideology of Contemporary Hollywood Film*, (Bloomington, IN: Indiana Univ. Press, 1990), 1.

10. Morris Beja, *Film and Literature* (New York: Longman, 1979), 78.
11. Richard Todd, *Consuming Fictions: The Booker Prize and Fiction in Britain Today* (London: Bloomsbury, 1996), 9–10.
12. Sergei Eisenstein, "Dickens, Griffith and the Film Today," *Film Forum*, trans. Jay Leyda (New York, 1949), 195–255.
13. Joseph Conrad, Preface to *The Nigger of Narcissus* (London: J.M. Dent and Sons, 1945), 5.
14. Virginia Woolf, "The Movies and Reality," *New Republic*, XLVII, (August 4, 1925), 309.
15. Raymond Williams, *Television: Technology and Cultural Form*, (London: Routledge, 2003), 94.
16. Christopher Orr, "The Discourse on Adaptation," *Wide Angle*, 6/2 (1984), 72.
17. William Luhr and Peter Lehman, *Authorship and Narrative in the Cinema*, (New York: Putnam, 1977), 192. The typical tripartite structure of classification for adaptation is found in what is perhaps the most inclusive and influential book devoted to adaptation *The Novel and the Cinema* by Geoffrey Wagner. In this seminal text in the field, Wagner, in discussing Griffith's use of novels, states that "the formulation of life in fiction resulted from the same formal relationships as exist in making a film. In both . . . a point of view is being created." Wagner establishes, admittedly borrowing from the work of Bela Belazs, three perspectives the film takes in regard to the novel or source material which gauge the level of fidelity. The first category is "transposition," "in which a novel is directly given on the screen, with the minimum of apparent interference." Wagner maintains that transposition has been the (most pervasive method used by Hollywood throughout its history," and adds, that the "head-on Hollywood assault on classics of fiction . . . has been typically puerile"; the film exists as "a book illustration." The second level is "commentary" "where an original is taken and either purposely or inadvertently altered in some respect." Wagner's third level is the "analogy" from novel to film in which the "analogy must represent a fairly considerable departure for the purpose of making another work of art . . . an analogy cannot be indicated as a violation of a literary original since the director has not attempted (or has only minimally attempted) to reproduce the original." Wagner admits that these "modes of phrasing fiction in film form may not be exhaustive; but they can help us clarify meaning in each, and appreciate the norms of both" (New Jersey: Associated Univ. Press, 1975), 220–231.
18. Dudley Andrew, *Concepts in Film Theory* (New York: Oxford Univ. Press, 1984), 98.
19. Ibid., 98.
20. Ibid., 99.
21. Ibid., 100.
22. Ibid., 103.

23. Dudley Andrew, *Concepts in Film Theory*, 104.
24. Michael Klein and Gillian Parker, eds, *The English Novel and the Movies* (New York: Ungar, 1981), 9–10.
25. Ibid., 11.
26. Ibid.
27. H. Mark Glancy, *When Hollywood Loved Britain: The Hollywood 'British' Film 1939–1945* (Manchester: Manchester Univ. Press, 1999), 1–2.
28. The films Glancy lists that won an Academy Award, are *Cavalcade* (1932), *Mutiny on the Bounty* (1935), *Rebecca* (1940), *How Green Was My Valley* (1941), *Mrs. Miniver* (1942), and includes as classic films, *David Copperfield* (1934), *A Yank at Oxford* (1938), *The Adventures of Robin Hood* (1938), and *Goodbye Mr. Chips* (1939).
29. Glancy, 2.
30. A few examples should suffice: Gwyneth Paltrow is more famous with an "English" accent than an American one; Cate Blanchett is quintessentially "English" after the release of *Elizabeth*, as she is one of many Australians who are so convincing in their roles as to elide their Aussie identities, this list includes, Russell Crowe, Mel Gibson, Geoffrey Rush.
31. Glancy, 3.
32. Glancy, 4.
33. J. L. Austin, *How to Do Things with Words* (Oxford: Oxford Univ. Press, 1962), 1.
34. Ibid., 9.
35. Ibid., 22.
36. Jacques Derrida, *Margins of Philosophy*, trans. Alan Bass (Chicago: Univ. of Chicago Press, 1982), 326.
37. Ibid., 322.
38. Gilles Deleuze and Felix Guattari, *Anti-Oedipus: Capitalism and Schizophrenia*, trans. Robert Hurley, Mark Seem, and Helen R. Lane (Minneapolis: Univ. of Minnesota Press, 1983), 257.
39. Gilles Deleuze and Felix Guattari, *A Thousand Plateaus: Capitalism and Schizophrenia*, trans. Brian Massumi (Minneapolis: Univ. of Minnesota Press, 1987), 312.
40. Ibid., 312.
41. Ibid., 314.
42. Ibid., 316.
43. Gilles Deleuze, *The Logic of Sense*, trans. Mark Lester (New York: Columbia Univ. Press, 1990), 71.
44. Soren Kierkegaard, *Repetition* (1841), trans. Howard V. Hong and Edna H. Hong (Princeton: Princeton Univ. Press, 1983), 150. I have used this quotation elsewhere because it is unparalleled in terms of its witty accuracy and gift to posterity.
45. Gilles Deleuze and Felix Guattari, *Kafka: Toward a Minor Literature*, trans. Dana Polan (Minnepolis: Univ. of Minnesota Press, 1986), 12–13.

46. Beckett, a suburban, middle-class Protestant, and Joyce, a Catholic whose family was descending the class structure, had radically different childhoods; but both lived in a country that spoke Irish-English.
47. Gilles Deleuze and Felix Guattari, *Kafka*, 19.
48. Ibid., 18.
49. Gilles Deleuze, *Difference and Repetition*, trans. Paul Patton (New York: Columbia Univ. Press, 1994), 134.
50. Ryan and Kellner, 1.
51. Ibid., 1.
52. Ibid.
53. See texts such as *The Mouse that Roared: Disney and the End of Innocence* by Henry Giroux (Rowman and Littlefield, 1999).
54. Deleuze and Guattari, *Anti-Oedipus*, 257.
55. Ibid., 33.
56. Eugene W. Holland, "From Schizophrenia to Social Control," *Deleuze & Guattari: New Mappings in Politics, Philosophy, and Culture*, Eleanor Kaufman and Kevin Jon Heller, eds. (Minneapolis: Univ. of Minnesota Press, 1998), 67.
57. Eugene W. Holland, *Deleuze and Guattari's Anti-Oedipus: Introduction to Schizoanalysis* (New York: Routlege, 1999), 21. I am indebted to Eugene Holland's book, and "From Schizophrenia to Social Control" for providing me a lucid discussion of schizoanalysis, and axiomatics, in particular. Todd May's *Gilles Deleuze: An Introduction* (Cambridge Univ. Press, 2005) and Paul Patton's *Deleuze and the Political* (Routledge, 2000) I also highly recommend as clear and thought-provoking discussions on Deleuze's and Deleuze and Guattari's texts.
58. Willemen, 211.
59. Thomas Schatz, "The New Hollywood," *The Film Cultures Reader*, Graeme Turner, ed. (London: Routledge, 2002), 184.
60. Ibid., 192.
61. Ibid., 193–194.
62. Ibid., 196.
63. Willemen, 211.
64. Holland, *Deleuze and Guattari's Anti-Oedipus: Introduction to Schizoanalysis*, 66.
65. Ibid., 66.
66. Ibid., 81.
67. *Anti-Oedipus*, 346.
68. Gilles Deleuze and Felix Guattari, *A Thousand Plateaux*, 468.
69. T.R. Young and Garth Massey, "The Dramaturgical Society: A Macro-Analytic Approach to Dramaturgical Analysis," *Qualitative Sociology* 1 (September 1978), 78. Quoted in *The American Ritual Tapestry: Social Rules and Cultural Meanings*, Mary Jo Deegan, ed. (Westport, CT: Greenwood, 1998), 4.
70. Ibid., 5.
71. Ibid.

72. Ibid., 6.
73. Deleuze and Guattari, *Anti-Oedipus*, 262.
74. Ibid., 26.

Chapter 2 Heritage and Nostalgia: What Remains of *The Remains of the Day*

1. Martin A. Hipsky, "Anglophil(m)ia: Why Does America Watch Merchant-Ivory Movies?" *Journal of Popular Film & Television*, Vol. 22, No. 3 (Fall 1994), 106.
2. Andrew Higson, *English Heritage, English Cinema: Costume Drama since 1980* (Oxford: Oxford Univ. Press, 2003), 123. Higson also names such films as *The English Patient* in this category.
3. Wendy Wheeler, "Nostalgia Isn't Nasty: The Postmodernising of Parliamentary Democracy," in *Altered States: Postmodernism, Politics, Culture*, Mark Perryman, ed. (London: Lawrence & Wishart, 1994), 98.
4. Ibid., 95.
5. Wheeler lists the typical binaries that modernist thought sets up: "reason/unreason; maturity/childishness; masculinity/feminity; science/art," 96.
6. Ibid., 96.
7. Ibid., 97.
8. Christopher Shaw and Malcolm Chase, "The Dimensions of Nostalgia," *The Imagined Past: History and Nostalgia*, Shaw and Chase, eds. (Manchester: Manchester Univ. Press, 1989), 4.
9. Robert Hewison, *The Heritage Industry: Britain in a Climate of Decline*, (London: Methuen, 1987), 9.
10. Ibid., 10.
11. Fred Davis, *Yearning for Yesterday: A Sociology of Nostalgia* (New York: Free Press, 1979), 258.
12. Eugene W. Holland, *Deleuze and Guattari's Anti-Oedipus: Indroduction to Schizoanalysis*, (New York: Routledge, 1999), 114.
13. Amy Sargeant, "Selling Heritage Culture," *British Cinema, Past and Present*, Justine Ashby and Andrew Higson, eds. (London: Routledge, 2000), 309–310.
14. Alan Parker, quoted in Eckart Voigts-Virchow, ed., *Janespotting and Beyond: British Heritage Retrovisions since the Mid-1990s* (Tubingen: Gunter Narr Verlage, 2004), 14.
15. Claire Monk, "The British Heritage-Film Debate Revisited," *British Historical Cinema: The History, Heritage and Costume Film*, Claire Monk and Amy Sargeant, eds. (London: Routledge, 2002), 187.
16. Ibid., 177.

17. John Hill, *British Cinema in the 1980s: Issues and Themes* (Oxford: Clarendon, 1999), 80.
18. Andrew Higson, "Re-presenting the National Past: Nostalgia and Pastiche in the Heritage Film," in *Fires Were Started: British Cinema and Thatcherism*, Lester Friedman, ed. (Minneapolis: Univ. of Minnesota Press, 1993), 112. See Patrick Wright below.
19. Alison Light, "Englishness," *Sight and Sound*, July, 1991, 63.
20. Colin Flint, "The 'War on Terrorism' and the 'Hegemonic Dilemma': Extraterritoriality, Reterritorialization, and the Implications for Globalization," *Globalization and Its Outcomes*, John O'Loughlin, Lynn Staeheli, and Edward Greenburg, eds. (New York: Guilford, 2004), 367.
21. John Baxendale and Chris Pawling, *Narrating the Thirties A Decade in the Making: 1930 to the Present* (New York: St. Martins, 1996), 167.
22. Susan Aronstein, " 'Not Exactly a Knight': Arthurian Narrative and Recuperative Politics in the *Indiana Jones* Trilogy," *Cinema Journal* 34, No. 4 (Summer 1995), 3.
23. Ibid., 17.
24. Gilles Deleuze, *The Logic of Sense*, trans. Mark Lester (New York: Columbia Univ. Press, 1990), 141.
25. Gilles Deleuze, *Sacher-Masoch*, trans. Jean McNeil (London: Faber and Faber, 1971), 77.
26. Claire Monk, "Sexuality and Heritage," in *Film/Literature/Heritage: A Sight and Sound Reader*, Ginetta Vincendeau, ed. (London: BFI, 2001), 7.
27. David Cannadine, *The Pleasures of the Past* (London: Collins, 1989), 259.
28. Quoted in Patrick Wright, *On Living in an Old Country: The National Past in Contemporary Britain* (London: Verso, 1965), 82.
29. John Pym, *Merchant Ivory's English Landscape: Rooms, Views, and Anglo-Saxon Attitudes* (New York: Harry N. Abrams, 1995), 105.
30. John J. Su, "Refiguring National Character: The Remains of the British Estate Novel."*Modern Fiction Studies* 48.3 (Fall 2002), 555.
31. Kazuo Ishiguro, *The Remains of the Day* (New York: Vintage, 1993), 124. All subsequent quotations from the novel refer to this edition and appear in the text.
32. See Edward Said's *Imperialism* (New York: Vintage, 1994).
33. See "DissemiNation: Time, Narrative, and the Margins of the Modern Nation," in *Nation and Narration*, Homi K. Bhabha, ed. (London: Routledge, 1990), 319.
34. Gikandi argues that Enoch Powell's position was that the land of England could not turn a dark skinned person into an English person. The environment—the land—didn't have that power. A "black" would always be foreign with a British passport.

35. Edward Said, *Orientalism* (New York: Vintage, 1979), 93.
36. Erwin Straus, *The Primary World of the Senses* (Collier-Macmillan Ltd., 1963), 322.
37. Jeremy Black, *Modern British History Since 1900* (London: Macmillan, 2000), 305.
38. Ibid., 305–306.
39. Ibid., 306.
40. In 1993 *Literature Film Quarterly* published Edward T. Jones's interview with Harold Pinter in which the latter discusses his collaboration with James Ivory on *The Remains of the Day*. Pinter asserts, "I expect to work with Merchant Ivory on this one. I wrote the script for Mike Nichols. What happened with *The Remains of the Day* was that I read the book in page proofs. For the first time in my life I took an option on this novel. I've never done that before. And then it became a tremendous best seller. So everyone tried to find out who had the rights . . . .Finally Mike Nichols called—he's a friend of mine—and we worked [*sic*] and discussed it, and he was going to direct it. But now he can't for various complicated reasons." Vol. 21, Issue 1.
41. Edward T. Jones, "On *The Remains of the Day*: Harold Pinter Remaindered," *The Films of Harold Pinter*, Steven H. Gale, ed. (Albany: SUNY Press, 2001), 101.
42. Baxendale and Pawling, 200–201.
43. Harold Pinter, *The Remains of the Day*, Screenplay, (Hollywood: Script City, 1991), 111–112.
44. Ruth Prawer Jhabvala quoted in *The Films of Merchant Ivory*, Robert Emmet Long (New York: Harry N. Abrams, 1991), 20.
45. Ibid., 21.
46. Ibid., 21.
47. The Jhabvala screenplay has not been published. All quotations to the Merchant Ivory film are transcribed from the Columbia release.
48. *Mein Kampf* repeatedly refers to the Jews as a separate *race* from the Germans, with such statements as: "The foremost connoisseurs of this truth regarding the possibilities in the use of falsehood and slander have always been the Jews; for after all, their whole existence is based on one single great lie, to wit, that they are a religious community while actually they are a race—and what a race!" Trans. Ralph Manheim, Boston: Houghton Mifflin Co., 1971, 232. Although toned down from some of Hitler's rhetoric, Jhabvala's "deep cleft" and "fundamentally different natures" suggests she knew Hitler's most powerful and damaging argument. The Nazi racial argument a man like Lord Darlington could willingly embrace.
49. Pinter screenplay, 66–67.
50. Ibid., 163–165.

Chapter 3 American Cowboy in England: *Possession*

1. Michael Ryan and Douglas Kellner, *Camera Politica: The Politics and Ideology of Contemporary Hollywood Film* (Bloomington, IN: Indiana Univ. Press, 1990), 12.
2. Ibid., 12–13.
3. A.S. Byatt, *Possession* (New York: Vintage, 1990), 215. All sequent references to *Possession* refer to this edition.
4. Nathaniel Hawthorne, "Preface to *The House of the Seven Gables*," quoted as frontispiece by Byatt in *Possession*, np.
5. Mira Stout, "What Possessed A.S. Byatt? A British Novelist's Breakthrough Surprises Everyone but the British Novelist," *The New York Times Magazine*, 26 May 1991, 14.
6. Suzanne Keen, *Romances of the Archive in Contemporary British Fiction* (Toronto: Univ. of Toronto Press, 2001), 24.
7. I have discussed the history of the concecpt of desire in *Uncharted Space: The End of Narrative* (New York: Peter Lang, 2001) in terms language. See my discussion of Soren Kierkegaard's stages of desire in *Either/Or* [Part I Edited and Trans. Howard V. Hong and Edna H. Hong, (Princeton: Princeton Univ. Press, 1987)] in chapter three of Uncharted Space. A fuller discussion of Byatt's text, and others, and the concept of desire and narrative can also be found there.
8. Roland Barthes, *The Pleasure of the Text*, Robert Miller, trans. (New York: Hill and Wang, 1975), 64.
9. Michel Foucault, *The History of Sexuality, Vol. 1*, Robert Hurley, trans. (New York: Random, 1978), 20.
10. Will Wright, *Six Guns and Society: A Structural Study of the Western*, (Berkeley: Univ. of Calfornia Press, 1975), 137.
11. Charlotte O'Sullivan, *Sight & Sound* Vol. 12, Issue 11 (November 2002), 53.
12. Quoted from Focus Features *Possession* website: www.possession-movie.com/main.html.
13. Wright, 32.
14. Ibid., 15.
15. John G. Cawelti, from *The Six-Gun Mystique*, in *Reading Popular Narrative*, Bob Ashley, ed. (London: Leicester Univ. Press, 1997), 95.
16. All quotes from Wright, 32–59.
17. All quotes taken from film.
18. Robert Warshow, *The Immediate Experience: Movies, Comics, Theatre & Other Aspects of Popular Culture* (New York: Doubleday, 1962), 137.
19. Ibid., 137.
20. Laura Mulvey's seminal 1975 article, "Visual Pleasure," *Screen* 16.3 (1975), 6–18.
21. Wright, 45.
22. Ibid., 45.

23. O'Sullivan notes in her review that the film makes Roland "a man of action, solving the historical puzzle by stripping off, Mr. Darcy style, and diving in the lake."
24. Ibid., 40.
25. Ibid., 48.
26. Quoted from Focus Features *Possession* website: www.possession-movie.com/main.html.
27. Andrew Higson, "Re-presenting the National Past: Nostalgia and Pastiche in the Heritage Film," in *Fires Were Started: British Cinema and Thatcherism*, Lester Friedman, ed. (Minneapolis: Univ. of Minnesota Press, 1993), 113.
28. Quoted in Tim Barringer, *Reading the Pre-Raphaelites* (New Haven: Yale Univ. Press, 1999), 154.
29. Elizabeth Prettejohn, *The Art of the Pre-Raphaelites* (Princeton: Princeton Univ. Press, 2000), 222–223.
30. Thais E. Morgan, "Perverse Male Bodies: Simeon Solomon and Algernon Charles Swinburne," *Outlooks: Lesbian and Gay Sexualities and Visual Culture*, Peter Horne and Reina Lewis, eds. (New York: Routledge, 1996), 67.
31. Justin Wyatt, *High Concept: Movies and Marketing in Hollywood* (Austin: Univ. of Texas Press, 1994), 8.
32. Sue Sorensen, "Takeing Possession: Neil LaBute Adapts a Postmodern Romance," *Literature Film Quarterly* Vol. 32, Issue 1 (2004), 75.
33. Ibid., 117.

Chapter 4 Cinema's Romance with the Colonial: *The English Patient*'s "AntiConquest" Adventure

1. Mary Louise Pratt, *Imperial Eyes: Travel Writing and Transculturation* (London: Routledge, 1992), 7.
2. Alan Nadel, "Mapping the Other: *The English Patient*, Colonial Rhetoric, and Cinematic Representation," in *The Terministic Screen: Rhetorical Perspectives on Film*, David Blakesley, ed. (Carbondale, IL: SIUniv. Press, 2003), 22.
3. Barbara M. Kennedy, *Deleuze and Cinema: The Aesthetics of Sensation* (Edinburgh: Edinburgh Univ. Press, 2001), 152.
4. Pratt, 38.
5. Ibid., 39.
6. Justin Wyatt, *High Concept: Movies and Marketing in Hollywood* (Austin: Univ. of Texas Press, 1994), 8.
7. Brian Taves, *The Romance of Adventure: The Genre of Historical Adventure Movies* (Jackson, MS: Univ. Press of Mississippi, 1993), 123–124.

8. Maggie M. Morgan, "*The English Patient*: From Fiction to Reel." *Alif*. Vol. 18 (1998), 159.
9. Angela Baldassarre, *The Great Dictators: Interviews with Filmmakers of Italian Descent* (Toronto: Guenica, 1999), 64.
10. David Williams, *Imagined Nations: Reflections on Media in Canadian Fiction* (Montreal: McGill-Queen's Univ. Press, 2003), 209.
11. Ajay Heble, "Michael Ondaatje and the Problem of History." *Clio*. 19.2 (1990), 110.
12. Quoted in Jonathan Coe's review, "From Hull to Hollywood: Anthony Minghella talks about his film, *The English Patient*, and denies that he turning into David Lean," *New Statesman* (7 March 1997), Vol. 126, Issue 4324, 38.
13. Raymond Aaron Younis, "Nationhood and Decolonization in *The English Patient*," *Literature/Film Quarterly* (January 1998), 26:1, 2–9.
14. Michael Ondaatje, *The English Patient* (New York: Vintage International, 1993), 138–139. All subsequent page references appear in the text.
15. Nadel, 22.
16. Quoted in David Hare, *Via Doloros & When Shall We Live?* (London: Faber and Faber, 1998), 33–34.
17. Taves, 13.
18. Ibid., 12.
19. Anthony Minghella, *The English Patient: A Screenplay* (New York: Hyperion/Miramax, 1996), 124–126.
20. Ibid.,135.
21. Taves, 13.
22. Ibid., 13–14.
23. Ibid., 14.
24. Bronwen Thomas, " 'Piecing together a mirage': Adapting *The English Patient* for the Screen," in *The Classic Novel: From Page to Screen*, Robert Giddings and Erica Sheen, eds. (Manchester: Manchester Univ. Press, 2000), 209.
25. Ibid., 203.
26. Martha R. Mahoney, "The Social Construction of Whiteness," *Critical White Studies: Looking Behind the Mirror*, Richard Delgado and Jean Stefancic, eds. (Philadelphia: Temple Univ. Press, 1997), 331.
27. Screenplay, 57–58.
28. Thomas Schatz, *Hollywood Genres* (Austin: Univ. of Texas Press, 1981), 264.
29. John G. Cawelti, *Adventure, Mystery, and Romance: Formula Stories as Art and Popular Culture* (Chicago: Univ. of Chicago Press, 1976), 40.
30. Ibid.
31. Ibid., 41.

32. John G. Cawelti, *Adventure, Mystery, and Romance*, 41.
33. Ibid., 42.
34. *The English Patient*, 85.
35. Taves, 125.
36. Ibid., 130.
37. Alan A. Stone, "Herodotus Goes to Hollywood," *Boston Review* (February/March 1997), quotation taken from http://bostonreview.net/BR22.1/stone.html.
38. Screenplay, 89.
39. Jacqui Sadashige, "Sweeping the Sands: Geographies of desire in *The English Patient*," *Literature Film Quarterly* 26.4 (1998), 248.
40. Ibid., 248.
41. Ibid.
42. John Bierman, *The Secret Life of Laszlo Almasy: The Real English Patient* (London: Viking, 2004), 6, 9.
43. Quoted in Bierman, 7.
44. Ibid., 8.
45. Ibid., 9.
46. Ibid., 28–29.
47. Ibid., 89.
48. Ibid.
49. Screenplay 160–161.
50. Ibid., 162–163.
51. Taves, 42.
52. Ibid., 113–114.
53. Ibid., 166.
54. Taves, 139.

Chapter 5 Cool Britannia for Sale: *Trainspotting* and *Bridget Jones's Diary*

1. Michel Foucault, *Language, Counter-Memory, Practice*, trans. Donald F. Bouchard, (Ithaca, NY: Cornell Univ. Press, 1977), 123.
2. Ibid., 123.
3. While the "Bridget Jones Syndrome" (or "Effect") is used frequently, several books have chapters devoted to the "Bridget Jones Syndrome," including James Tooley's *The Miseducation of Women*, and Imelda Whelehan's *Overloaded*. See below.
4. Stryker McGuire and Michael Elliott, "London Reigns," *Newsweek*, November 4, 1996, 34.
5. Ibid., 35.
6. Ibid., 36.
7. Chris Smith, *Creative Britain* (London: Faber and Faber, 1998), 1.
8. Ibid., 2.
9. Tony Blair, *New Britain: My Vision of a Young Country* (London: Fourth Estate, 1996), 43–44.

10. Chris Smith, 147.
11. Murray Smith, *Trainspotting* (London: BFI, 2002), 19.
12. Wendy Wheeler, "Nostalgia Isn't Nasty: The Postmodernising of Parliamentary Democracy," in *Altered States: Postmodernism, Politics, Culture*, Mark Perryman, ed. (London: Lawrence & Wishart, 1994), 97.
13. Quoted in Derek Paget, "Speaking Out: The Transformations of *Trainspotting*," in *Adaptations: From Text to Screen, Screen to Text*, Deborah Cartmell and Imelda Whelehan, eds. (London: Routledge, 1999), 128.
14. Andrew Macdonald quoted by Xan Brooks in *Choose Life: Ewan McGregor and the British Film Revival* (Chameleon, 1998), 87.
15. Gilles Deleuze and Felix Guattari, *Thousand Plateaux*, trans. Brian Mussumi (Minneapolis, MN: Univ. of Minnesota Press, 1987), 20.
16. Edwin Muir, *Scott and Scotland: The Predicament of the Scottish Writer* (London: George Routledge, 1936), 11–12.
17. Hugh Trevor-Roper, "The Invention of Tradition: The Highland Tradition of Scotland," *The Invention of Tradition*, Eric Hobsbawn and Terence Ranger eds. (Cambridge: Cambridge Univ. Press, 1989), 16.
18. Cairns Craig, *The Modern Scottish Novel: Narrative and the National Imagination* (Edinburgh: Edinburgh Univ. Press, 1999), 14.
19. From MacDiarmid's *Cencrastus*, quoted in *Dooble Tongue: Scots, Burns, Contradiction* by Jeffrey Skoblow (Univ. of Delaware Press, 2001), p. 72.
20. Irvine Welsh, *Trainspotting* (New York: W.W. Norton and Co., 1993), 78. All subsequent references to the novel are to this edition.
21. John W. Books, "Globalization and Alternative Approaches to the Transformation of Nation-States: Scotland as a Test Case," *Globalization and National Identities: Crisis or Opportunity?*, Paul Kennedy and Catherine J. Danks, eds. (London: Palgrave, 2001), 219.
22. Alan Freeman, "Ghosts in Sunny Leith: Irvine Welsh's *Trainspotting*," *Studies in Scottish Fiction: 1945 to the Present*, Susanne Hageman, ed. (New York: Peter Lang, 1996), 256–257.
23. John Skinner, "Contemporary Scottish Novelists and the Stepmother Tongue," *English Literature and the Other Languages*, Ton Hoenselaars and Marius Buning, eds. (Amsterdam: Rodolfi, 1999), 218.
24. Andrew O'Hagan, "The Boys are Back in Town," *Sight & Sound*, Vol. 6, Issue 2 (February 1996), 8.
25. Robert Crawford, *Devolving English Literature* (Oxford: Clarendon, 1992), 6.
26. Muir, 21.
27. The Hiberian football club is located in the northern part of Edinburgh, while the Hearts is in west Edinburgh.

28. Bashir Maan, *The New Scots: The Story of Asians in Scotland* (Edinburgh: John Donald, 1992), 174.
29. Angus Finney, *The State of European Cinema: A New Dose of Reality*, (London: Cassell, 1996), 174–175.
30. Ibid., 181.
31. Ibid.
32. Ibid.
33. Martin Stollery, *Trainspotting: The Ultimate Film Guides* (London: York Press, 2000), 46.
34. Danny Boyle, quoted in Andrew O. Thompson, "Trains, Veins, and Heroin Deals," *American Cinematographer*, vol. 77, no. 8 (August 1996), 80.
35. Ibid., 81.
36. Ibid.
37. Murray Smith, *The Media in Britain: Current Debates and Developments*, Jane Stokes and Anna Reading, eds. (New York: St. Martin's, 1999), 221.
38. Karen Lury, "Here and Then: Space, Place and Nostalgia in British Youth Cinema of the 1990s," in *British Cinema of the 90s*, Robert Murphy, ed. (London: BFI, 2000), 106.
39. Jeff Smith, "Banking on Film Music: Structural Interactions of the Film and Record Industries," *Movie Music: The Film Reader*, Kay Dickinson, ed. (New York: Routledge, 2003), 64.
40. Ibid., 64.
41. Paget, 138–139.
42. Kevin Macdonald, "Afterword—Interview with Irvine Welsh," *Trainspotting: A Screenplay*, John Hodge (New York: Miramax Books, 1996), 120–121.
43. Ibid., 121.
44. Ibid., 46.
45. Ibid.
46. Ibid., 77–78.
47. Ibid., 82.
48. Ibid., 83.
49. Stollery, 73.
50. Hodge, 106.
51. Alison Case, "Authenticity, Convention, and *Bridget Jones's Diary*," *Narrative*, Vol. 9, No. 2 (May 2001), 176.
52. Trevor Field, *Form and Function in the Diary Novel* (London: Macmillan, 1989), 53.
53. H. Porter Abbott, *Diary Fiction: Writing as Action* (Ithaca: Cornell Univ. Press, 1984), 18.
54. Ibid., 18–19.
55. Case, 177.
56. Daphne Merkin, "The Marriage Mystique," *The New Yorker*, Vol. 74, Issue 22, (1998), 71.

57. Cris Mazza and Jeffrey Deskell, eds. *Chick-Lit On the Edge: New Womens Fiction Anthology* (Normal, IL: Illinois State Univ. Press, 1995), np.
58. Cris Mazza, "Chick Lit and the Perversion of a Genre," *Poets & Writers*, Vol. 33, Issue 1 (Jan/Feb 2005), 31.
59. Ibid., 31–32.
60. Helen Fielding, *Bridget Jones's Diary* (London: Picador, 1996), 20. All subsequent references to the novel are to this edition.
61. Imelda Whelehan, *Overloaded: Popular Culture and the Future of Feminism* (London: The Women's Press, 2000), 151.
62. Lisa Habib, " 'Bridget Jones' is today's everywoman, role model or not, and we like her like that," http://www.cnn.com/books/revews/9807/04/review.bridget.jones.diary/, 2.
63. James Tooley, *The Miseducation of Women* (London: Continuum, 2002), 5.
64. Ibid.
65. iVillage.co.uk, Interview with Helen Fielding, 2000–2005.
66. Ibid., np.
67. Ibid., np.
68. Fielding, 105.
69. Ibid.
70. Ibid.
71. Ibid., 107.
72. Ibid.
73. Kelly A. Marsh, "Contextualizing Bridget Jones," *College Literature*, Vol. 31, No. 1, 52.
74. Ibid., 55.
75. Ibid.
76. Chris Smith, *Creative Britain* (London: Faber and Faber, 1998), 1.
77. *Newsweek*, 35.
78. From *Pride and Prejudice*, euphemistically, to halt daughter Mary's singing, Mr. Bennett insists that Mary "has delighted us long enough."
79. Philip Kerr, "A Bridget Too Far," *New Statesman*, Vol. 130, Issue 4534, 23 April 2001, 44.
80. Ibid.
81. Andrew Spicer, "The Reluctance to Commit: Hugh Grant and the New British Romantic Comedy," *The Trouble with Men: Masculinities in European and Hollywood Cinema*, Phil Powrie, Ann Davies, and Bruce Babington, eds. (London: Wallflower Press, 2004), 86.
82. Claire Monk, "The British Heritage-Film Debate Revisited," *British Historical Cinema: The History, Heritage and Costume Film*, Claire Monk and Amy Sargeant, eds. (London: Routledge, 2002), 195.
83. Umberto Eco, "Postmodernism, Irony, the Enjoyable," *Modernism/Postmodernism*, Peter Brooker, ed. (London: Longman, 1992), 227.

Chapter 6 Reterritorializing British Masculinity for American Consumption: *Waterland* and *High Fidelity*

1. Doreen Wallace, *East Anglia: A Survey of England's Eastern Counties* (London: B.T. Batsford Ltd., 1939), 61.
2. Graham Swift, *Waterland* (New York: Vintage, 1992 [1983]), np. All subsequent citations are to the Vintage edition.
3. Pamela Cooper, "Imperial Topographies: the Spaces of History in *Waterland*," *Modern Fiction Studies*, 42.4 (1996), 372. See also Rober K. Irish's " 'Let Me Tell You': About Desire and Narrativity in Graham Swift's *Waterland*," *Modern Fiction Studies*, 44.4 (1998), 917–934.
4. Katrina M. Powell, "Mary Metcalf's Attempt at Reclamation: Maternal Representation in Graham Swift's *Waterland*," *Women's Studies*, Vol. 32, Issue 1 (January 2003), 3.
5. Jonathan Romney, *Time Out Film Guide*, John Pym, ed. (London: Penguin, 2000), 1206.
6. Richard Combs, "Waterland," *Sight & Sound*, Vol. 2, Issue 5 (September 1992), 61.
7. Roger Ebert, "Waterland," *Chicago Sun-Times*, November 6, 1992. Available online, http://rogerebert.suntimes.com.
8. Quoted in *Supreme Court Decisions and Women's Rights*, Clare Cushman, ed. (Washington, DC: *Congressional Quarterly*, 2001), 189.
9. Ibid., 199.
10. See "The Facts Speak Louder" concerning the medical inaccuracies of *The Silent Scream*, Planned Parenthood Federation of American, Inc. http://www.plannedparenthood.org.
11. Rosi Braidotti citing Susan Kappelar's work in *Nomadic Subjects: Embodiment and Sexual Difference in Contemporary Feminist Theory* (New York: Columbia, 1994), 68.
12. Ibid., 69.
13. James B. Twitchell, *Dreadful Pleasures: An Anatomy of Modern Horror* (New York: Oxford Univ. Press, 1985), 7.
14. See Julia Kristeva, *The Powers of Horror: An Essay on Abjection*, trans. Leon S. Roudiez (Columbia Univ. Press, 1982), p. 1.
15. Barbara Creed, *The Monstrous-Feminine: Film, Feminism, Pyschoanalysis* (New York: Routledge, 1993), 25.
16. Tania Modleski, "The Terror of Pleasure: the Contemporary Horror Film and Postmodern Theory," *Studies in Entertainment*, Tania Modleski, ed. (Bloomington: Univ. of Indiana Press, 1986), 163.
17. Sarah Neely, "Cool Intentions: The Literary Classic, the Teenpic and 'Chick Flick,' " *Retrovisions: Reinventing the Past in Film and Fiction*, Deborah Cartmell, I.Q. Hunter, and Imelda Whelehan, eds. (London: Pluto, 2001), 76.
18. Creed, 7.

19. Nick Hornby, *High Fidelity* (New York: Riverhead, 1995), 3. All subsequent quotations from *High Fidelity* refer to this edition.
20. Dominic Head, *The Cambridge Introduction to Modern British Fiction, 1950–2000* (Cambridge: Cambridge Univ. Press, 2002), 248.
21. Imelda Whelehan, *Overloaded: Popular Culture and the Future of Feminism* (London: The Women's Press, 2000), 5–6.
22. Jonathan Rutherford, "Introduction: Avoiding the Bends," *Male Order: Unwrapping Masculinity*, Rowena Chapman and Jonathan Rutherford, eds. (London: Lawrence & Wishart, 1996), 3–4.
23. Whelehan, 58.
24. Sean Nixon, "Resignifying Masculinity: From 'New Man' to 'New Lad,' " *British Cultural Studies*, David Morley and Kevin Robins, eds. (Oxford: Oxford Univ. Press, 2001), 380.
25. Ibid., 380.
26. Whelehan, 61.
27. Ibid., 384.
28. Whelehan, 61.
29. Ibid., 384.
30. George Khoury, "Behind the Music of *High Fidelity*: George Khoury Talks with D.V. De Vincentis, Steve Pink and John Cusack," *Creative Screenwriting*, Vol. 8, Issue 1 (Jan-Feb 2001), 41.
31. Ibid., 41.
32. Ibid., 41.
33. Ibid., 41.
34. Colin MacCabe, "O Lucky Man," *Sight & Sound*, Vol. 10, Issue 6 (June 2000), 20.
35. Stephen Frears, transcribed from the "Special Features" "Conversations with the Director," *High Fidelity* (DVD), *Touchstone Home Video*, nd.
36. Khoury, 41.
37. Tony Ross, "*High Fidelity* Screenplay by D.V. De Vincentis, Scott Pink & John Cusack and Scott Rosenberg," *Creative Screenwriting*, Vol. 8, Issue 1 (Jan-Feb 2001), 46.
38. Desson Howe, "A Moderate 'Fever,' " *Washington Post*, July 28, 2000, www.washingtonpost.com/wp-srv/entertainment/movies/reviews/feverpitchhowe.htm.
39. Charles McGrath, "Translating 'British Obsessive Male' Into American," *New York Times*, April 9, 2005, B1, 13.
40. Ibid., 13.
41. Desson Thomson, "Fallon, Farrellys Strike Out with 'Fever Pitch,' " *Washington Post*, April 8, 2005, WE45.

Chapter 7 Shakespeare's Counterfeit Signature: *Shakespeare in Love*

1. Michel Foucault, "What Is an Author?" *Language, Counter-Memory, Practice: Selected Essays and Interviews*, trans. Donald F.

Bouchard and Sherry Simon (Ithaca, NY: Cornell Univ. Press, 1977), 123.

2. Ibid., 123.
3. Ibid., 122.
4. Foucault refers to John Searle's *Speech Acts: An Essay in the Philosophy of Language* (Cambridge: Cambridge Univ. Press, 1969), 163–174. Perhaps ironically, it is Searle who challenges the long-held view that proper names were not thought to have "connotational" meaning, only "denotational."
5. John Drakakis, quoted in Jim Leach, *British Film* (Cambridge: Cambridge Univ. Press, 2004), 122.
6. Susan Jeffords, *Hard Bodies: Hollywood Masculinity in the Reagan Era* (New Brunswick, NJ: Rutgers Univ. Press, 1993), see discussion below.
7. John Madden, *Shakespeare in Love*, Miramax promotional blurb.
8. William Gallagher, BBC.CO.UK, update 21 May 2001.
9. Alisa Perren, "sex, lies and marketing: Miramax and the Development of the Quality Indie Blockbuster," *Film Quarterly*, Vol. 55, No. 2, (2001), 30.
10. Ibid., 38.
11. Jacques Derrida, *Margins of Philosophy*, trans. Alan Bass (Chicago: Univ. Chicago Press, 1982), 316.
12. Kathryne V. Lindberg, "Re-Signings, Re: Signatures: Joyce and Pound Reading Shakespeare's *Will*," *The Language of Joyce: Selected Papers from the 11 International James Joyce Symposium* (Philadelphia, PA: John Benjamins Publishing Co., 1992), 127, 130,
13. J. L. Austin, *How to Do Things with Words* (Oxford: Oxford Univ. Press, 1962), 22.
14. Derrida, *Margins of Philosophy*, 317.
15. Ibid., 317.
16. Ibid., 316.
17. Elizabeth Klett, "*Shakespeare in Love* and the End(s) of History," *Retrovisions: Reinventing the Past in Film and Fiction*, Deborah Cartmell, I.Q. Hunter, and Imelda Whelehan, eds. (London: Pluto, 2001), 25.
18. Marc Norman and Tom Stoppard, *Shakespeare in Love* (New York: Hyperion Miramax, 1998), 7. All subsequent quotations from the film are from the screenplay and cited in the text.
19. Jacques Derrida, *Limited Inc.*, Samuel Weber, trans. (Evanston, IL : Northwestern Univ. Press, 1988), 144.
20. Lawrence W. Levine, *Highbrow/Lowbrow: The Emergence of Cultural Hierarchy in America* (Cambridge, MA: Harvard Univ. Press, 1988), 42.
21. Ibid., 13.
22. See *Shakespeare, the Movie: Popularizing the Plays on Film, TV, and video*, Richard Burt and Lynda E. Boose, eds. (London: Routledge, 1997), and *Shakespeare, the Movie, II: Popularizing the Plays on Film,*

tv, video, and DVD, Richard Burt and Lynda E. Boose, eds. (London: Routledge, 2003).

23. John Kenrick, "Musicals 101 Theatre in NYC: History Part II," website, 2005.
24. Robert W. Snyder in *The Encyclopedia of New York City*, Kenneth T. Jackson (New Haven: Yale University Press, 1995), 1226. Also quoted on Kenrick's website.
25. Levine, 79.
26. Courtney Lehmann, *Shakespeare Remains: Theater to Film, Early Modern to Postmodern* (Ithaca, NY: Cornell Univ. Press, 2002), 131.
27. *The American Ritual Tapestry: Social Rules and Cultural Meanings*, Mary Jo Deegan, ed. (Westport, CT: Greenwood, 1998), 6.
28. Angela Baldassarre, *The Great Dictators: Interviews with Filmmakers of Italian Descent* (Toronto: Guenica, 1999), 80.
29. Marc Norman quoted in Gloria Goodale, "How they imagined *Shakespeare in Love*," *Christian Science Monitor*, March 5, 1999, Vol. 91, Issue 68, 17.
30. Ibid., 17.
31. See "Interview with Marc Norman," Edited by Robert J. Elisberg, http://www.absolutewrite.com/screenwriting/marc_norman.htm.
32. Ibid., 81.
33. Mercedes Salvador Bello, "Marc Norman and Tom Stoppard 1999: *Shakespeare in Love*," *Atlantis, revista de la Asociacion Espanola de Estudios Anglo-Norteamericanos*, Vol. 21, Issue 2, (June-December 1999), 158.
34. Lehmann, 220.
35. Jeffords, 24.
36. Ibid., 24.
37. Ibid., 25.
38. Lehmann, 231.
39. John Wylie, "New and Old Worlds: *The Tempest* and early colonial discourse," *Social & Cultural Geography*, Vol. 1, No. 1 (2000), 3.

Conclusion

1. Stuart M. Kaminsky, *American Film Genres*, 2nd ed (Chicago: Nelson-Hall, 1985), 1.
2. Charles D. Yoost, "Do You Have Cold Feet?" 28 August 2005, Church of the Savior, Cleveland Heights, Ohio.
3. Ibid., 44.
4. Jeffrey Richards, *Films and British National Identity* (Manchester: Manchester Univ. Press, 1997), 21–22.
5. Bill Schwarz, "Britain, America, and Europe," *British Cultural Studies: Geography, Nationality, and Identity*, David Morley and Kevin Robins, eds. (Oxford: Oxford Univ. Press, 2001), 167.
6. Ibid., 166.

7. British Tourist Authority, "*Harry Potter and the Philosopher's Stone*: Discovering the Magic of Britain," (2001), np.
8. Robert Hewison, *The Heritage Industry: Britain in a Climate of Decline* (London: Methuen, 1987), 9.
9. Jacques Derrida, *Limited Inc.*, trans. Samuel Weber (Evanston, IL: Northwestern Univ. Press, 1988), 144.

Bibliography

Abbott, H. Porter. *Diary Fiction: Writing as Action*. Ithaca: Cornell Univ. Press, 1984.

Ackroyd, Peter. *Notes for a New Culture*. Second ed. London: Alkin Books, 1993.

Altman, Rick. *Film/Genre*. London: BFI, 1999.

Andrew, Dudley. *Concepts in Film Theory*. New York: Oxford Univ. Press, 1984.

Aronstein, Susan. " 'Not Exactly a Knight': Arthurian Narrative and Recuperative Politics in the *Indiana Jones* Trilogy," *Cinema Journal* 34.4 (1995): 3–30.

Ashby, Justine, and Andrew Higson eds. *British Cinema, Past and Present*. London: Routledge, 2000.

Austin, J. L. *How to Do Things with Words*. Oxford: Oxford Univ. Press, 1962.

Baldassarre, Angela. *The Great Dictators: Interviews with Filmmakers of Italian Descent*. Toronto: Guernica, 1999.

Bamford, Kenton. *Distorted Images: British National Identity and Film in the 1920s*. London: I.B. Tauris, 1999.

Barringer, Tim. *Reading the Pre-Raphaelites*. New Haven: Yale Univ. Press, 1999.

Barthes, Roland. *The Pleasure of the Text*. Trans. Robert Miller. New York: Hill and Wang, 1975.

Baxendale, John and Chris Pawling. *Narrating the Thirties A Decade in the Making: 1930 to the Present*. New York: St. Martins, 1996.

Bayley, Stephen. *Labour Camp: The Failure of Style over Substance*. London: BT Batsford, Ltd., 1998.

Beja, Morris. *Film and Literature*. New York: Longman, 1979.

Bello, Mercedes Salvador. "Marc Norman and Tom Stoppard 1999: *Shakespeare in Love*," *Atlantis, revista de la Asociacion Espanola de Estudios Anglo-Norteamericanos* 21.2 (1999): 158–164.

Bhabha, Homi K. "DissemiNation: Time, Narrative, and the Margins of the Modern Nation." *Nation and Narration*. Ed. Bhabha. London: Routledge, 1990.

Bierman, John. *The Secret Life of Laszlo Almasy: The Real English Patient*. London: Viking, 2004.

Black, Jeremy. *Modern British History Since 1900*. London: Macmillan, 2000.

Blair, Tony. *New Britain: My Vision of a Young Country*. London: Fourth Estate, 1996.

Books, John W. "Globalization and Alternative Approaches to the Transformation of Nation-States: Scotland as a Test Case." *Globalization and National Identities: Crisis or Opportunity?* Ed. Paul Kennedy and Catherine J. Danks. London: Palgrave, 2001. 210–223.

Bridget Jones's Diary. Dir. Sharon Maguire. Perf. Renée Zellweger, Hugh Grant, Colin Firth, Gemma Jones, and Celia Imrie. 2001. DVD. Miramax Home Entertainment, 2001.

Braidotti, Rosi. *Nomadic Subjects: Embodiment and Sexual Difference in Contemporary Feminist Theory.* New York: Columbia, 1994.

British Tourist Authority. "*Harry Potter and the Philosopher's Stone*: Discovering the Magic of Britain." Map. 2001.

Brooks, Xan. *Choose Life: Ewan McGregor and the British Film Revival.* London: Chameleon, 1998.

Bruzzi, Stella. *Undressing Cinema: Clothing and Identity in the Movies.* New York: Routledge, 1997.

Burt, Richard and Lynda E. Boose, eds. *Shakespeare, the Movie: Popularizing the Plays on Film, TV, and Video.* London: Routledge, 1997.

———. *Shakespeare, the Movie, II: Popularizing the Plays on Film, TV, Video, and DVD.* London: Routledge, 2003.

Byatt, A. S. *Possession.* New York: Vintage, 1990.

Cannadine, David. *The Pleasures of the Past.* London: Collins, 1989.

Cartmell, Deborah, and Imelda Whelehan, eds. *Adaptations: From Text to Screen, Screen to Text.* New York: Routledge, 1999.

———, I.Q. Hunter, and Imelda Whelehan, eds. *Retrovisions: Reinventing the Past in Film and Fiction.* London: Pluto Press, 2001.

Case, Alison. "Authenticity, Convention, and *Bridget Jones's Diary.*" *Narrative* 9.2 (2001): 176–181.

Cawelti, John G. *Adventure, Mystery, and Romance: Formula Stories as Art and Popular Culture.* Chicago: Univ. of Chicago Press, 1976.

———. "The Concept of Formula in the Study of Popular Literature." *Reading Popular Narrative.* Ed. Bob Ashley. London: Leicester Univ. Press, 1989. 71–75.

———. "The Six-Gun Mystique." *Reading Popular Narrative.* Ed. Bob Ashley. London: Leicester Univ. Press, 1997.

Coe, Jonathan. "From Hull to Hollywood: Anthony Minghella talks about his film, *The English Patient*, and denies that he is turning into David Lean," *New Statesman* 7 (March 1997): 39.

Combs, Richard. "Waterland." *Sight & Sound* 2.5 (1992): 60–61.

Conrad, Joseph. Preface. *The Nigger of Narcissus.* London: J.M. Dent and Sons, 1945.

Cooper, Pamela. "Imperial Topographies: the Spaces of History in *Waterland*," *Modern Fiction Studies* 42.4 (1996): 371–396.

Craig, Cairns. *The Modern Scottish Novel: Narrative and the National Imagination.* Edinburgh: Edinburgh Univ. Press, 1999.

Crawford, Robert. *Devolving English Literature.* Oxford: Clarendon, 1992.

Creed, Barbara. *The Monstrous-Feminine: Film, Feminism, Pyschoanalysis.* New York: Routledge, 1993.

Cushman, Clare, ed. *Supreme Court Decisions and Women's Rights.* Washington, DC: *Congressional Quarterly*, 2001.

Davis, Fred. *Yearning for Yesterday: A Sociology of Nostalgia.* New York: Free Press, 1979.

Deegan, Mary Jo, ed. *The American Ritual Tapestry: Social Rules and Cultural Meanings.* Westport, CT: Greenwood Press, 1998.

Deleuze, Gilles. *Difference and Repetition.* Trans. Paul Patton. New York: Columbia Univ. Press, 1994.

———. *The Logic of Sense.* Trans. Mark Lester. New York: Columbia Univ. Press, 1990.

———. *Sacher-Masoch.* Trans. Jean McNeil. London: Faber and Faber, 1971.

———, and Félix Guattari. *Anti-Oedipus: Capitalism and Schizophrenia.* Trans. Robert Hurley, Mark Seem, and Helen R. Lane. Minneapolis: Univ. of Minnesota Press, 1983.

———. *Kafka: Toward a Minor Literature.* Trans. Dana Polan. Minneapolis: Univ. of Minnesota Press, 1986.

———. *A Thousand Plateaus: Capitalism and Schizophrenia.* Trans. Brian Massumi. Minneapolis: Univ. of Minnesota Press, 1987.

Derrida, Jacques. *Limited Inc.* Trans. Samuel Weber. Evanston, IL: Northwestern Univ. Press, 1988.

———. *Margins of Philosophy.* Trans. Alan Bass. Chicago: Univ. of Chicago Press, 1982.

Doel, Marcus A. "Occult Hollywood: Unfolding the Americanization of World Cinema." *American Century: Consensus and Coercion in the Projection of American Power.* Eds. David Slater and Peter J. Taylor. Oxford: Blackwell, 1999. 243–260.

Ebert, Roger. "Waterland." *Chicago Sun-Times.* 6 November 1992. <http://rogerebert.suntimes.com/apps/pbcs.dll/article?AID=/19921106/REVIEWS/211060304/1023>.

Eco, Umberto. "Postmodernism, Irony, the Enjoyable." *Modernism/Postmodernism.* Ed. Peter Brooker. London: Longman, 1992. 225–234.

The English Patient. Dir. Anthony Minghella. Perf. Ralph Fiennes, Juliette Binoche, Willem Defoe, Kristin Scott Thomas, and Naveen Andrews. 1996. Videocassette. Miramax Home Entertainment, 1997.

Ferrell, William K. *Literature and Film as Modern Mythology.* Westport, CT: Praeger, 2000.

Fever Pitch. Dir. David Evans. Perf. Colin Firth, Luke Aikman, Bea Guard, Neil Pearson, and Ruth Gemmell. 1997. DVD. Vidmark/Trimark, 2000.

———. Dir. Bobby Farrelly and Peter Farrelly. Perf. Drew Barrymore, Jimmy Fallon, Jason Spevack, Jack Kehler, and Scott Severance. 2005. DVD. Fox Home Entertainment, 2005.

Field, Trevor. *Form and Function in the Diary Novel.* London: Macmillan, 1989.

Fielding, Helen. *Bridget Jones's Diary.* London: Picador, 1996.

———. "Helen Fielding: the Woman Behind Bridget." *iVillage.co.uk.* 2001. <http://www.ivillage.co.uk/newspol/readerswriters/authors/articles/0,,532363_533985,00.html>.

Finney, Angus. *The State of European Cinema: A New Dose of Reality.* London: Cassell, 1996.

Flint, Colin. "The 'War on Terrorism' and the 'Hegemonic Dilemma': Extraterritoriality, Reterritorialization, and the Implications for Globalization." *Globalization and Its Outcomes.* Eds. John O'Loughlin, Lynn Staeheli, and Edward Greenburg. New York: Guilford, 2004. 361–386.

Foucault, Michel. *The History of Sexuality, Vol. 1.* Trans. Robert Hurley. New York: Random, 1978.

———. *Language, Counter-Memory, Practice.* Trans. Donald F. Bouchard. Ithaca, NY: Cornell Univ. Press, 1977.

Frears, Stephens. "Conversations with the Director." *High Fidelity.* Perf. John Cusack, Iben Hjejle, Jack Black, and Todd Louiso. 2000. DVD. Walt Disney Video, 2001.

Freeman, Alan. "Ghosts in Sunny Leith: Irvine Welsh's *Trainspotting.*" *Studies in Scottish Fiction: 1945 to the Present.* Ed. Susanne Hageman. New York: Peter Lang, 1996. 251–262.

Friedman, Lester, ed. *Fires Were Started: British Cinema and Thatcherism.* Minneapolis: Univ. of Minnesota Press, 1993.

Furness, Sir Christopher. *The American Invasion.* London: Simpkin, Marshall, 1902.

Gallagher, William. "*Shakespeare in Love* (1998)." *BBC.CO.UK.* 1 May 2001. <http://www.bbc.co.uk/films/2001/05/01/shakespeare_in_love_1998_review.shtml>.

Giroux, Henry A. *The Mouse that Roared: Disney and the End of Innocence.* Lanham, MD: Rowman and Littlefield, 1999.

Glancy, H. Mark. *When Hollywood Loved Britain: The Hollywood "British" Film 1939–1945.* Manchester, UK: Manchester Univ. Press, 1999.

Golub, Spencer. "Spies in the House of Quality: The American Reception of *Brideshead Revisited.*" *Novel Images: Literature in Performance.* Ed. Peter Reynolds. New York: Routledge, 1993. 139–156.

Goodale, Gloria. "How they imagined *Shakespeare in Love,*" *Christian Science Monitor* 5 (March 1999): 17.

Gorbman, Claudia. *Unheard Melodies: Narrative Film Music.* Bloomington: Indiana Univ. Press, 1987.

Habib, Lisa. " 'Bridget Jones' is today's everywoman, role model or not, and we like her like that." *CNN.com.* 4 July 1998. <http://www.cnn.com/books/reviews/9807/04/review.bridget.jones.diary/index.html>.

Hare, David. *Via Doloros & When Shall We Live?* London: Faber and Faber, 1998.

Head, Dominic. *The Cambridge Introduction to Modern British Fiction, 1950–2000.* Cambridge: Cambridge Univ. Press, 2002.

Heble, Ajay. "Michael Ondaatje and the Problem of History." *CLIO: A Journal of Literature, History, and the Philosophy* 19.2 (1990): 97–110.

Hewison, Robert. *The Heritage Industry: Britain in a Climate of Decline.* London: Methuen, 1987.

High Fidelity. Dir. Stephen Frears. Perf. John Cusack, Iben Hjejle, Jack Black, and Todd Louiso. 2000. Videocassette. Walt Disney Video, 2001.

Higson, Andrew. *English Heritage, English Cinema: Costume Drama Since 1980.* Oxford: Oxford Univ. Press, 2003.

———. "Re-presenting the National Past: Nostalgia and Pastiche in the Heritage Film." *Fires Were Started: British Cinema and Thatcherism.* Ed. Lester Friedman. Minneapolis: Univ. of Minnesota Press, 1993. 109–129.

———. *Waving the Flag: Constructing a National Cinema in Britain.* Oxford: Clarendon Press, 1995.

———, ed. *Dissolving Views: Key Writings on British Cinema.* London: Cassell, 1996.

Hill, John. *British Cinema in the 1980s: Issues and Themes.* Oxford: Clarendon, 1999.

———, and Pamela Church Gibson, eds. *Film Studies: Critical Approaches.* Oxford: Oxford Univ. Press, 2000.

Hipsky, Martin A. "Anglophil(m)ia: Why Does America Watch Merchant-Ivory Movies?." *Journal of Popular Film & Television* 22.3 (1994): 98–107.

Hitler, Adolf. *Mein Kampf.* Trans. Ralph Manheim. Boston: Houghton Mifflin Co., 1971.

Hobsbawm, Eric and Terence Ranger, eds. *The Invention of Tradition.* Cambridge: Cambridge Univ. Press, 1989.

Holland, Eugene W. *Deleuze and Guattari's Anti-Oedipus: Introduction to Schizoanalysis.* New York: Routledge, 1999.

———. "From Schizophrenia to Social Control." *Deleuze & Guattari: New Mappings in Politics, Philosophy, and Culture.* Eds. Eleanor Kaufman and Kevin Jon Heller. Minneapolis: Univ. of Minnesota Press, 1998. 65–76.

Hooper, Charlotte. *Manly States: Masculinities, International Relations, and Gender Politics.* New York: Columbia Univ. Press, 2001.

Hornby, Nick. *High Fidelity.* New York: Riverhead, 1995.

Howe, Desson. "A Moderate 'Fever.'" *Washington Post* 28 July 2000. <www.washingtonpost.com/wp-srv/entertainment/movies/reviews/feverpitchhowe.htm>.

Irish, Rober K. " 'Let Me Tell You': About Desire and Narrativity in Graham Swift's *Waterland.*" *Modern Fiction Studies* 44.4 (1998): 917–934.

Ishiguro, Kazuo. *The Remains of the Day.* New York: Vintage, 1993.

Jeffers, Jennifer. *Uncharted Space: The End of Narrative.* New York: Peter Lang, 2001.

Jeffords, Susan. *Hard Bodies: Hollywood Masculinity in the Reagan Era.* New Brunswick, NJ: Rutgers Univ. Press, 1993.

Jones, Edward T. "Harold Pinter: a Conversation." *Literature Film Quarterly* 21.1 (1993): 2–9.

———. "On *The Remains of the Day*: Harold Pinter Remaindered." *The Films of Harold Pinter*. Ed. Steven H. Gale. Albany: SUNY Press, 2001. 99–108.

Kaminsky, Stuart M. *American Film Genres*, Second ed. Chicago: Nelson-Hall, 1985.

Keen, Suzanne. *Romances of the Archive in Contemporary British Fiction.* Toronto: Univ. of Toronto Press, 2001.

Kennedy, Barbara M. *Deleuze and Cinema: The Aesthetics of Sensation.* Edinburgh: Edinburgh Univ. Press, 2001.

Kenrick, John. "Theatre in NYC: History Part II—The Astor Place Riot." *Musicals101.com.* 2005. <http://www.musicals101.com/bwaythhist2.htm#Astor>.

Kerr, Philip. "A Bridget Too Far," *New Statesman* 23 April 2001: 44.

Khoury, George. "Behind the Music of *High Fidelity*: George Khoury Talks with D.V. De Vincentis, Steve Pink and John Cusack." *Creative Screenwriting* 8.1 (2001): 41 + [3p].

Kierkegaard, Søren. *Either/Or Vol. 1.* Trans. Howard V Hong and Edna, Hong, Princeton: Princeton Univ. Press, 1987.

———. *Fear and Trembling/Repetition: Kierkegaard's Writings.* Vol. 6. Trans. Howard V. Hong and Edna H. Hong. Princeton Univ. Press, 1983.

Klein, Michael, and Gillian Parker, eds. *The English Novel and the Movies.* New York: Frederick Ungar, 1981.

Klett, Elizabeth. "*Shakespeare in Love* and the End(s) of History." *Retrovisions: Reinventing the Past in Film and Fiction.* Eds. Deborah Cartmell, I.Q. Hunter, and Imelda Whelehan. London: Pluto, 2001. 25–40.

Kristeva, Julia. *The Powers of Horror: An Essay on Abjection.* Trans. Leon S. Roudiez. Columbia Univ. Press, 1982.

Leach, Jim. *British Film.* Cambridge: Cambridge Univ. Press, 2004.

Lawrence W. Levine, *Highbrow/Lowbrow: The Emergence of Cultural Hierarchy in America.* Cambridge, MA: Harvard Univ. Press, 1988.

Lehmann, Courtney. *Shakespeare Remains: Theater to Film, Early Modern to Postmodern.* Ithaca, NY: Cornell Univ. Press, 2002.

Light, Alison. "Englishness," *Sight & Sound* 1.3 (1991): 63.

Lindberg, Kathryne V. "Re-Signings, Re: Signatures: Joyce and Pound Reading Shakespeare's *Will*," *The Language of Joyce: Selected Papers from the 11th International James Joyce Symposium*, (Philadelphia, PA: John Benjamins Publishing Co., 1992. 127–144.

Long, Robert Emmet. *The Films of Merchant Ivory.* New York: Harry N. Abrams, 1991.

Luhr, William and Peter Lehman. *Authorship and Narrative in the Cinema.* New York: Putnam, 1977.

Lury, Karen. "Here and Then: Space, Place and Nostalgia in British Youth Cinema of the 1990s." *British Cinema of the 90s.* Ed. Robert Murphy. London: BFI, 2000. 100–108.

Maan, Bashir. *The New Scots: The Story of Asians in Scotland*. Edinburgh: John Donald, 1992.

Macdonald, Kevin. "Afterword—Interview with Irvine Welsh," *Trainspotting: A Screenplay*, Ed. John Hodge. New York: Miramax Books, 1996.

Mahoney, Martha R. "The Social Construction of Whiteness," *Critical White Studies: Looking Behind the Mirror*, Eds. Richard Delgado and Jean Stefancic. Philadelphia: Temple Univ. Press, 1997. 330–333.

Marsh, Kelly A. "Contextualizing Bridget Jones." *College Literature* 31.1 (2004): 52–72.

Masters, Brian. *The Swinging Sixties*. London: Constable, 1985.

May, Todd. *Gilles Deleuze: an Introduction*. Cambridge: Cambridge Univ. Press, 2005.

Mazza, Cris. "Chick Lit and the Perversion of a Genre." *Poets & Writers* Jan./Feb.2005: 31–37.

———, and Jeffrey Deshell, eds. *Chick-Lit: On the Edge: New Women's Fiction Anthology*. Normal, IL: Illinois State Univ. Press, 1995.

MacCabe, Colin. "O Lucky Man." *Sight & Sound*. 10.6 (2000): 18–21.

McGrath, Charles. "Translating 'British Obsessive Male' Into American." *New York Times* 9 April 2005: B1, 13.

McGuire, Stryker and Michael Elliott. "London Reigns." *Newsweek* 4 Nov. 1996: 34–36.

Merkin, Daphne. "The Marriage Mystique," *The New Yorker* 74.22 (1998): 70–74.

Metz, Christian. *Film Language: A Semiotics of the Cinema*. Trans. Michael Taylor. New York: Oxford Univ. Press, 1974.

Minghella, Anthony. *The English Patient: A Screenplay*. New York: Hyperion/Miramax, 1996.

Modleski, Tania. "The Terror of Pleasure: the Contemporary Horror Film and Postmodern Theory," *Studies in Entertainment*. Ed. Tania Modleski. Bloomington: Univ. of Indiana Press, 1986. 155–166.

Monk, Claire. "The British Heritage-Film Debate Revisited." *British Historical Cinema: The History, Heritage and Costume Film*. Eds. Claire Monk and Amy Sargeant. London: Routledge, 2002. 176–198.

———. "Sexuality and Heritage." *Film/Literature/Heritage: A Sight & Sound Reader*. Ed. Ginetta Vincendeau. London: BFI, 2001. 6–10.

Morgan, Maggie M. "*The English Patient*: From Fiction to Reel." *Alif* 18 (1998): 159–173.

Morgan, Thais E. "Perverse Male Bodies: Simeon Solomon and Algernon Charles Swinburne." *Outlooks: Lesbian and Gay Sexualities and Visual Cultures*. Eds. Peter Horne and Reina Lewis. New York: Routledge, 1996. 61–85.

Muir, Edwin. *Scott and Scotland: The Predicament of the Scottish Writer*. London: George Routledge, 1936.

Mulvey, Laura. "Visual Pleasure and Narrative Cinema." *Screen* 16.3 (1975): 6–18.

Nadel, Alan. "Mapping the Other: *The English Patient*, Colonial Rhetoric, and Cinematic Representation." *The Terministic Screen: Rhetorical Perspectives on Film*. Carbondale, IL: SIUP, 2003. 21–36.

Neely, Sarah. "Cool Intentions: The Literary Classic, the Teenpic and 'Chick Flick.' " *Retrovisions: Reinventing the Past in Film and Fiction*. Eds. Deborah Cartmell, I.Q. Hunter, and Imelda Whelehan. London: Pluto, 2001. 74–86.

Nixon, Sean. "Resignifying Masculinity: From 'New Man' to 'New Lad,' " *British Cultural Studies*. Eds. David Morley and Kevin Robins. Oxford: Oxford Univ. Press, 2001. 373–386.

Norman, Marc. "Interview with Marc Norman." *Absolute Write*. Ed. Robert J. Elisberg. <http://www.absolutewrite.com/screenwriting/marc_norman.htm>.

———, and Tom Stoppard. *Shakespeare in Love*. New York: Hyperion Miramax, 1998.

Nye, Jr, Joseph S. *Soft Power: The Means to Success in World Politics*. New York: Perseus, 2004.

O'Hagan, Andrew. "The Boys are Back in Town." *Sight & Sound* 6.2 (1996): 6–11.

Ondaatje, Michael. *The English Patient*. New York: Vintage International, 1993.

Orr, Christopher. "The Discourse on Adaptation." *Wide Angle* 6.2 (1984): 72–78.

O'Sullivan, Charlotte. "Possession." *Sight & Sound* 12.11 (2002): 53.

Paget, Derek. "Speaking Out: The Transformations of *Trainspotting*," *Adaptations: From Text to Screen, Screen to Text*. Eds. Deborah Cartmell and Imelda Whelehan. London: Routledge, 1999. 128–138.

Patton, Paul. *Deleuze and the Political*. London: Routledge, 2001.

Perren, Alisa. "sex, lies and marketing: Miramax and the Development of the Quality Indie Blockbuster." *Film Quarterly* 55.2 (2001): 30–39.

Pidduck, Julianne. "*Elizabeth* and *Shakespeare in Love*: Screening the Elizabethans." *Film/Literature/Heritage*. Ed. Ginette Vincendeau. London: BFI, 2001. 130–134.

Pinter, Harold. *The Remains of the Day*. Screenplay. Hollywood: Script City, 1991.

Planned Parenthood Federation of American, Inc. "The Facts Speak Louder Than 'The Silent Scream.' " 1985. <http://www.plannedparenthood.org/pp2/portal/files/portal/medicalinfo/abortion/fact-abortion-silent-scream.xml>.

Possession. Dir. Neil LaBute. Perf. Gwyneth Paltrow, Aaron Eckhart, Jeremy Northam, Jennifer Ehle, and Lena Headey. 2002. Videocassette. Warner Home Video, 2003.

———. Focus Features. < http://www.possession-movie.com/main.html>

Powell, Katrina M. "Mary Metcalf's Attempt at Reclamation: Maternal Representation in Graham Swift's *Waterland*." *Women's Studies* 32.1 (2003): 59–77.

Pratt, Mary Louise. *Imperial Eyes: Travel Writing and Transculturation.* London: Routledge, 1992.

Prettejohn, Elizabeth. *The Art of the Pre-Raphaelites.* Princeton: Princeton Univ. Press, 2000.

Pym, John. *Merchant Ivory's English Landscape: Rooms, Views, and Anglo-Saxon Attitudes.* New York: Harry N. Abrams, 1995.

The Remains of the Day. Dir. James Ivory. Perf. Anthony Hopkins, Emma Thompson, Christopher Reeve, Hugh Grant, Tim Pigott-Smith, James Fox, Peter Vaughan. DVD. Columbia Pictures, 1993.

Richards, Jeffrey. *Films and British National Identity.* Manchester: Manchester Univ. Press, 1997.

Romney, Jonathan. *Time Out Film Guide.* Ed. John Pym. London: Penguin, 2000.

Ross, Tony. "*High Fideltiy* Screenplay by D.V. De Vincentis, Scott Pink & John Cusack and Scott Rosenberg." *Creative Screenwriting* 8.1 (2001):

Rutherford, Jonathan. "Introduction: Avoiding the Bends." *Male Order: Unwrapping Masculinity.* Eds. Rowena Chapman and Jonathan Rutherford. London: Lawrence & Wishart, 1996. 3–20.

Ryan, Michael, and Douglas Kellner. *Camera Politica: The Politics and Ideology of Contemporary Hollywood Film.* Bloomington, IN: Indiana Univ. Press, 1990.

Sadashige, Jacqui. "Sweeping the Sands: Geographies of Desire in *The English Patient.*" *Literature Film Quarterly* 26.4 (1998): 255–262.

Said, Edward. *Culture and Imperialism.* New York: Vintage Books, 1993.

———. *Orientalism.* New York: Vintage, 1979.

Sargeant, Amy. "Selling Heritage Culture," *British Cinema, Past and Present*, eds. Justine Ashby and Andrew Higson, London: Routledge, 2000. 301–315.

Schatz, Thomas. *Hollywood Genres.* Austin: Univ. of Texas Press, 1981.

———. "The New Hollywood." *The Film Cultures Reader.* Ed. Graeme Turner. London: Routledge, 2002. 184–205.

Searle, John. *Speech Acts: An Essay in the Philosophy of Language.* Cambridge: Cambridge Univ. Press, 1969. 163–174.

Shakespeare in Love. Dir. John Madden. Perf. Joseph Fiennes, Gwyneth Paltrow, Geoffrey Rush, Rupert Everett, and Ben Affleck. 1999. DVD. Miramax Home Entertainment, 1999.

Shaw, Christopher and Malcolm Chase, eds. "The Dimensions of Nostalgia." *The Imagined Past: History and Nostalgia.* Manchester: Manchester Univ. Press, 1989. 1–17.

Shaw, George Bernard. *The Apple Cart.* London: Constable and Co. Ltd., 1930.

Schwarz, Bill. "Britain, America, and Europe." *British Cultural Studies: Geography, Nationality, and Identity.* Eds. David Morley and Kevin Robins. Oxford: Oxford Univ. Press, 2001. 157–169.

Skinner, John. "Contemporary Scottish Novelists and the Stepmother Tongue." *English Literature and the Other Languages.* Eds. Ton Hoenselaars and Marius Buning. Amsterdam: Rodolfi, 1999.

Skoblow, Jeffrey. *Dooble Tongue: Scots, Burns, Contradiction.* Univ. of Delaware Press, 2001.

Smith, Chris. *Creative Britain.* London: Faber and Faber, 1998.

Smith, Jeff. "Banking on Film Music: Structural Interactions of the Film and Record Industries." *Movie Music: The Film Reader.* Ed. Kay Dickinson. New York: Routledge, 2003. 63–81.

Smith, Murray. *The Media in Britain: Current Debates and Developments.* Eds. Jane Stokes and Anna Reading. New York: St. Martin's, 1999.

———. *Trainspotting.* London: BFI, 2002.

Snyder, Robert W. *The Encyclopedia of New York City.* Ed. Kenneth T. Jackson. New Haven: Yale Univ. Press, 1995.

Sorensen, Sue. "Taking Possession: Neil LaBute Adapts a Postmodern Romance," *Literature/Film Quarterly* 32.1 (2004): 75.

Spicer, Andrew. "The Reluctance to Commit: Hugh Grant and the New British Romantic Comedy." *The Trouble with Men: Masculinities in European and Hollywood Cinema.* Eds. Phil Powrie, Ann Davies, and Bruce Babington. London: Wallflower Press, 2004. 77–89.

Stead, William T. *The Americanisation of the World; or, The Trend of the Twentieth Century.* Ed. Sandi E. Cooper. New York: Garland, 1972.

Stollery, Martin. *Trainspotting: The Ultimate Film Guides.* London: York Press, 2000.

Stone, Alan A. "Herodotus Goes to Hollywood." *Boston Review.* Feb.–March 1997 <http://bostonreview.net/BR22.1/stone.html>.

Stout, Mira. "What Possessed A.S. Byatt? A British Novelist's Breakthrough Surprises Everyone but the British Novelist." *The New York Times Magazine* 26 (May 1991): 12–15, 24–25.

Straus, Erwin. *The Primary World of the Senses.* New York: Collier-Macmillan Ltd., 1963.

Su, John J. "Refiguring National Character: The Remains of the British Estate Novel." *Modern Fiction Studies* 48.3 (2002): 552–580.

Swift, Graham. *Waterland.* New York: Vintage, 1992.

Taves, Brian. *The Romance of Adventure: The Genre of Historical Adventure Movies.* Jackson: Univ. Press of Mississippi, 1993.

Thomas, Bronwen. " 'Piecing Together a Mirage': Adapting *The English Patient* for the Screen." *The Classic Novel, from Page to Screen.* Ed. Robert Giddings and Erica Sheen. New York: Manchester Univ. Press, 2000. 197–232.

Thompson, Andrew O. "Trains, Veins, and Heroin Deals." *American Cinematographer* 77.8 (1996): 80–86.

Thomson, Desson. "Fallon, Farrellys Strike Out with 'Fever Pitch.' " *Washington Post* 8 April 2005: WE45.

Todd, Richard. *Consuming Fictions: The Booker Prize and Fiction in Britain Today.* London: Bloomsbury, 1996.

Tooley, James. *The Miseducation of Women.* London: Continuum, 2002.

Trainspotting. Dir. Danny Boyle. Perf. Ewan McGregor, Ewen Bremner, Jonny Lee Miller, Kevin McKidd, Robert Carlyle. 1996. Videocassette. Miramax Home Entertainment, 2003.

Trevor-Roper, Hugh, "The Invention of Tradition: The Highland Tradition of Scotland." *The Invention of Tradition.* Eds. Eric Hobsbawn and Terence Ranger. Cambridge: Cambridge Univ. Press, 1989. 15–41.

Troost, Linda, and Sayre Greenfield, eds. *Jane Austen in Hollywood.* Second ed. Lexington, KY: Univ. Press of Kentucky, 2001.

Truffaut, Francois. Interview. *Cahiers du cinéma* Dec. 1962 138:55.

Twitchell, James B. *Dreadful Pleasures: An Anatomy of Modern Horror.* New York: Oxford Univ. Press, 1985.

Voigts-Virchow, ed. *Janespotting and Beyond: British Heritage Retrovisions Since the Mid-1990s.* Tubingen: Gunter Narr Verlage, 2004.

Wagner, Geoffrey. *The Novel and the Cinema.* Cranbury, NJ: Associated Univ. Presses, Inc., 1975.

Wagnleitner, Reinhold. *Coca-Colonization and the Cold War: The Cultural Mission of the United States in Austria after the Second World War.* Trans. Diana M. Wolf. Chapel Hill, NC: Univ. of North Carolina Press, 1994.

Wallace, Doreen. *East Anglia: A Survey of England's Eastern Counties.* London: B.T. Batsford Ltd., 1939.

Warshow, Robert. *The Immediate Experience: Movies, Comics, Theatre & Other Aspects of Popular Culture.* New York: Doubleday, 1962.

Waterland. Dir. Stephen Gyllenhaal. Perf. Jeremy Irons, Sinéad Cusack, Ethan Hawke, Grant Warnock, and Lena Headey. 1992. Videocassette. New Line Home Video, 1996.

Welsh, Irvine. *Trainspotting.* New York: W.W. Norton and Co., 1993.

Wheeler, Wendy. "Nostalgia Isn't Nasty: The Postmodernising of Parliamentary Democracy." *Altered States: Postmodernism, Politics, Culture.* Ed. Mark Perryman. London: Lawrence & Wishart, 1994. 94–107.

Whelehan, Imelda. *Overloaded: Popular Culture and the Future of Feminism.* London: The Women's Press, 2000.

Willemen, Paul. *Looks and Frictions: Essays in Cultural Studies and Film Theory.* Bloomington, IN: Indiana Univ. Press, 1994.

Williams, David. *Imagined Nations: Reflections on Media in Canadian Fiction.* Montreal: McGill-Queen's Univ. Press, 2003.

Williams, Raymond. *Television: Technology and Cultural Form.* London: Routledge, 2003.

Williams, Tony. *Structures of Desire: British Cinema, 1939–1955.* Albany, NY: SUNY, 2000.

Woolf, Virginia. "The Movies and Reality." *New Republic* XLVII.609 (4 August 1926) 308–310.

Worthen, W. B. *Shakespeare and the Authority of Performance.* Cambridge: Cambridge Univ. Press, 1997.

Wright, Patrick. *On Living in an Old Country: The National Past in Contemporary Britain.* London: Verso, 1965.

Wright, Will. *Six Guns and Society: A Structural Study of the Western.* Berkeley: Univ. of California Press, 1975.

Wyatt, Justin. *High Concept: Movies and Marketing in Hollywood.* Austin: Univ. of Texas Press, 1994.

Wylie, John. "New and Old Worlds: *The Tempest* and early colonial discourse." *Social & Cultural Geography* 1.1 (2000): 48–63.

Yoost, Charles D. "Do You Have Cold Feet?" Church of the Savior, Cleveland Heights, Ohio. 28 August 2005.

Young, T.R. and Garth Massey "The Dramaturgical Society: A Macro-Analytic Approach to Dramaturgical Analysis." *Qualitative Sociology* 1 (1978): 78–98.

Younis, Raymond Aaron. "Nationhood and Decolonization in *The English Patient.*" *Literature Film Quarterly* 26.1 (1998): 2–9.

Index